Cambridge International AS & A Level

Thinking Skills

Angus Grogono
Colin Hart

Questions from the Cambridge International AS & A Level Thinking Skills papers are reproduced by permission of Cambridge Assessment International Education.

Cambridge Assessment International Education bears no responsibility for the example answers to questions taken from its past question papers which are contained in this publication.

Some additional Cambridge International material has been adapted and included with the permission of Cambridge. Unless otherwise acknowledged, the questions, example answers and comments that appear in this book were written by the authors.

The Publishers would like to thank the following for permission to reproduce copyright material. Every effort has been made to trace all copyright holders, but if any have been inadvertently overlooked the Publishers will be pleased to make the necessary arrangements at the first opportunity.

Photo credits

p.16 © nattanan726/stock.adobe.com; **p.44** © Sol LeWitt, American, 1928-2007/Location of 6 Geometric Figures: The Location of a Square, 1975/FINE ARTS MUSEUMS OF SAN FRANCISCO/© ARS, NY and DACS, London 2018; **p.69** *l* © Michael Candelori/Shutterstock.com, *r* © AlexOakenman/stock.adobe.com; **p.89** © Everett Collection Inc/Alamy Stock Photo; **p.152** © milkovasa/stock.adobe.com; **p.190** © Sergey Ryzhkov/stock.adobe.com; **p.200** © Photographee.eu/stock.adobe.com; **p.201** © ffotocymru/Alamy Stock Photo; **p.221** © rocketclips/stock.adobe.com; **p.232** © Irina/stock.adobe.com; **p.233** © Tyler Olson/stock.adobe.com; **p.263** RetroColoring.com/Stock.adobe.uk.

Text credits

p.54 'Africa is not a country' as presented by www.gapminder.org; **p.56** Kurt Vonnegut data visualization from The fairytale of Cinderella. Reprinted with permission of Column Five Media; **p.86** Extract from THE COLOSSAL BOOK OF SHORT PUZZLES AND PROBLEMS by Martin Gardner, edited by Dana Richards. Copyright © 2006 by Martin Gardner. Copyright © 2006 by Martin Gardner and Dana Richards. Used by permission of W. W. Norton & Company, Inc; **p.147** map from http://www.natureonthemap.naturalengland.org.uk/MagicMap.aspx which uses Ordnance Survey 'Map of Dartmoor including Dartmoor National Park' – OS Explorer Map OL28; **p.153** 'To mock a mockingbird' by Raymond Smullyan publd by Borzoi Books (1985) and issued by Oxford University Press 1990 and 2000. Reproduced with permission of Knopf Doubleday Publishing Group; **p.154** Extract from 'Problem Solving through Recreational Mathematics' by Averbach and Chein published by Dover 2000. Reprinted with permission of Dover Publications; **p.156** Extract from Sample items from the SDMT copyright © 1973 by Western Psychological Services. Reprinted by K. Ariraman, Hodder Education, by permission of the publisher, WPS. Not to be reprinted in whole or in part for any additional purpose without the expressed, written permission of the publisher (rights@wpspublish.com). All rights reserved.

t = top, *b* = bottom, *c* = centre, *l* = left, *r* = right

Angus Grogono would like to acknowledge the inspiration he has drawn from discourse with Margaret, David, Colin, Mark, Ian and the two Andrews. He would also like to thank Thomasin for solving all his problems. Colin acknowledges the assistance received from Rob.

Every effort has been made to trace and acknowledge ownership of copyright. The publishers will be glad to make suitable arrangements with any copyright holders whom it has not been possible to contact.

Although every effort has been made to ensure that website addresses are correct at time of going to press, Hodder Education cannot be held responsible for the content of any website mentioned in this book. It is sometimes possible to find a relocated web page by typing in the address of the home page for a website in the URL window of your browser.

Hachette UK's policy is to use papers that are natural, renewable and recyclable products and made from wood grown in well-managed forests and other controlled sources. The logging and manufacturing processes are expected to conform to the environmental regulations of the country of origin.

Orders: please contact Hachette UK Distribution, Hely Hutchinson Centre, Milton Road, Didcot, Oxfordshire, OX11 7HH. Telephone: +44 (0)1235 827827. Email education@hachette.co.uk Lines are open from 9 a.m. to 5 p.m., Monday to Friday. You can also order through our website: www.hoddereducation.com

© Angus Grogono and Colin Hart 2018
First published 2018 by
Hodder Education
An Hachette UK Company
Carmelite House
50 Victoria Embankment
London EC4Y 0DZ
www.hoddereducation.com

Impression number   10 9 8 7 6
Year   2023

Cover photo © nikkytok/Shutterstock

Illustration by Peter Lubach

Typeset in ITC Officina Sans Std Book 11.5/13pts by Aptera Inc.

Printed and bound by CPI Group (UK) Ltd, Croydon, CR0 4YY

A catalogue record for this title is available from the British Library.

ISBN: 9781510421899

Contents

INTRODUCTION TO CRITICAL THINKING

Introduction

Thinking Skills

Thinking Skills are transferable mental processes which are vital for success in higher education, employment and private life. They are used for many purposes, including:

» organising information
» solving problems
» evaluating ideas
» planning
» making decisions
» defending opinions, proposals and actions.

Thinking Skills as a discrete subject has a complex relationship with other parts of an educational curriculum. It develops the skills required for success in other subjects, and also makes explicit and validates the skills which are developed by studying other subjects.

Problems and questions set in the exam are intended to resemble those which occur in other settings. So throughout this book, the words 'problem' and 'question' are intended to apply both to the Thinking Skills exam and also to academic assignments and research, work projects and civic and family life. They may be raised by teachers, employers or clients, or they may be problems you set for yourself and questions which you ask yourself.

Cambridge International AS & A Level qualifications in Thinking Skills are for convenience divided into Problem Solving (Units 1 and 3) and Critical Thinking (Units 2 and 4), but this division is not absolute. There is some overlap between these two categories and each of them relies on the other to some extent.

Problem Solving

The Problem Solving half of the syllabus is aimed at the skills and attitudes which allow unfamiliar logical problems to be analysed, investigated and solved. These problems often depend upon numerical relations between their constituent parts, but not always.

There is no general agreement as to what a Problem Solving curriculum involves, and the structure of this textbook reflects the view that the personal development of problem-solving habits and attitudes is as important as familiarity with a toolkit of general problem-solving techniques.

As well as the structured development of a heuristic approach, the course looks at the following tools for analysing the logical structure of a problem:

>> use of manageable numbers
>> diagramming
>> systematic listing
>> trial and error
>> algebra and functions-machines
>> the generation of patterns
>> the use of particular values in solving general problems
>> Venn diagrams.

The heuristic approach which accompanies the use of these tools depends on self-scrutiny, rigour and a creative response to the unfamiliar problems.

Critical Thinking

The Critical Thinking half of the syllabus is based on the Cambridge International definition of Critical Thinking:

Critical Thinking is the analytical thinking which underlies all rational discourse and enquiry. It is characterised by a meticulous and rigorous approach.

As an academic discipline, it is unique in that it explicitly focuses on the processes involved in being rational.

These processes include:

>> *analysing arguments*
>> *judging the relevance and significance of information*
>> *evaluating claims, inferences, arguments and explanations*
>> *constructing clear and coherent arguments*
>> *forming well-reasoned judgements and decisions.*

Being rational requires an open-minded yet critical approach to one's own thinking as well as that of others.

How to use this book

The two halves of a Thinking Skills course are quite different in nature. In the Problem Solving half, the aim is to develop an approach which will enable the classic toolkit of problem-solving strategies to be applied to unfamiliar scenarios and questions. An introduction to the various tools and their application is accompanied by a strand of concepts and activities which develop a heuristic approach, applicable to any problems, and any appropriate tools for solving them. The Critical Thinking half, by contrast, consists of a number of sub-skills to be applied to unfamiliar material. A limited range of questions can arise in relation to Critical Thinking, and they are answered by applying these skills.

For that reason, the halves of this book are different in style. The Problem Solving section focuses on developing an approach, whereas the Critical Thinking half identifies the sub-skills and how to apply them.

There is no extra content for the A Level exam in addition to the AS Level exam. The difference between the levels consists of the difficulty of the assessment. So the book focuses mainly on AS Level, although it fully covers the A Level syllabus content.

Each chapter introduces the skills to be covered in that chapter, with explanations and examples.

To think about

'To think about' questions provide opportunities for class discussion or personal reflection.

ACTIVITY

The Problem Solving half of the book includes a number of Activities. These allow students to practise skills in an artificial environment and develop confidence in using them before facing exam-style questions.

EXTENSION ACTIVITY

The activities in the Critical Thinking half of the book are not so intrinsic to the learning. They are suggested ways of applying Thinking Skills to real-life situations. Depending on how much time is available, they could be done in class, as homework or as optional extras for those who choose to do them.

Key term

The key terms are defined throughout the text.

Sample question

Sample questions with suggested answers are provided. (Note that the answers are shaded.)

Practice question

Practice questions help you to prepare for your examinations. 'Taking it further' questions are beyond what is needed for AS Level.

More information or examples help you to understand the concept are provided.

Cambridge International AS & A Level Thinking Skills (9694) syllabus

The AS Level course comprises Units 1 and 2; the full A Level course comprises Units 1, 2, 3 and 4.

Unit 1

The Unit 1 exam consists of a collection of problem-solving scenarios and questions based upon them.

There are 50 marks available in the paper, and 1 hour 30 minutes are available for this exam.

Unit 2

The Unit 2 exam is divided into two parts, identified as Section A and Section B. Section A consists of several short sets of evidence on a single topic and two questions, while Section B consists of one more extended document, on a different topic, and three questions. Questions 1, 3 and 4 are each divided into several parts.

There are 50 marks available in the paper, and 1 hour 45 minutes are available for this exam.

Unit 3

The Unit 3 exam consists of problems which are similar in style to those in Unit 1, but are likely to involve a more extended stimulus.

There are 50 marks available, spreading over these questions, and 2 hours are available for this exam.

Unit 4

In the Unit 4 exam, you are presented with several documents, offering different approaches to a shared topic. At least one of those documents is likely to present data in a graphic format. The exam includes short questions on evaluating evidence and analysing and evaluating an argument, together with a major integrative question.

There are 50 marks available in the paper, and 1 hour 45 minutes are available for this exam.

Command words

The table below includes command words used in the assessment for this syllabus. The use of the command word will relate to the subject context.

Command word	What it means
Analyse*	Examine in detail to show meaning, identify elements and the relationship between them
Assess	Make an informed judgement
Calculate	Work out from given facts, figures or information
Compare	Identify/comment on similarities and/or differences
Evaluate	Judge or calculate the quality, importance, amount or value of something
Explain	Set out purposes or reasons/make the relationships between things evident/provide why and/or how and support with relevant evidence
Give	Produce an answer from a given source or recall/memory
Identify*	Name/select/recognise
Justify	Support a case with evidence/argument
Predict	Suggest what may happen based on available information
State	Express in clear terms
Suggest*	Apply knowledge and understanding to situations where there is a range of valid responses in order to make proposals

* In Paper 2 and Paper 4, 'analyse' requires you to identify key elements of an argument. 'Identify' means you should find something from within the source itself, whereas 'suggest' means you should come up with an idea of your own.

Angus Grogono and Colin Hart

1 Interpreting the problem

By the end of this chapter you will be able to:

★ take ownership of a problem
★ model a problem
★ pose a problem
★ engage with an exam question.

You may think that problems are like traps. They check whether you, the problem-solving pioneer, are sufficiently skilled and self-aware to locate the 'right answer' amidst the tempting wrong ones. They can appear to be deliberately obscure, designed to confuse the reader by their means of presentation. And, on top of it all, what are they good for, apart from making bright-eyed innocent teenagers, like you, feel stupid?

Real-life problems:

>> rarely have one answer
>> normally allow some scope for interaction (to check that the details mean what they appear to mean)
>> often involve a situation with which you have some familiarity (problems often arise from a context which you have partly created yourself).

Success in posing problems and finding efficient answers will inevitably lead to your success in life. (If you doubt this, then pose yourself the problem: 'How can I achieve success in life?' And then find an efficient solution to it!)

This first chapter will show you how the world of real-life problem solving and the world of the problem-solving exam paper are linked. This is because, in order to successfully solve problems in both situations, you need to:

>> have a feeling for the context of the problem
>> have confidence to interact with and probe the problem
>> be familiar with the difficulties of modelling and articulating the problem.

This will enable you to extract the information from a problem confidently, carefully and efficiently.

You may be tempted to omit some of the sections, since they seem too distant from the reality of problem solving. But beware: you don't become a performance musician by studying what a performance musician looks like. You need to cultivate the underlying disciplines and attitudes as well as the surface-level skills. The foundational work on how a problem is created and presented will ensure you are genuinely prepared for new problems, both in your everyday life and when tackling an exam paper.

1.1 Owning the problem

Every problem-solving course should begin with the creation of problems so, first, let us look at what we mean by 'a problem'.

At its heart, every problem is a question that needs to be answered, so we must begin by considering anything (and everything) about which you could pose a question.

> ### ▶ ACTIVITY
>
> Here are 14 questions relating to food as they might occur to a day-dreaming, inquisitive human like you.
>
> What different types of questions are there? Read through them all, and then choose a way of sorting them into groups. (Make sure that every question is included in a group.)
>
> There is not meant to be one correct way of grouping the questions. Once you have chosen your own method of grouping, discuss it with your classmates. Did they choose to group their questions differently? How? Why?
>
> 1 How much food can I fit in my stomach?
>
> 2 How long has anyone ever lasted without food?
>
> 3 Is a perfect pineapple more delicious than a perfect plum?
>
> 4 Don't you just love eating raw carrots?
>
> 5 Does the number of times food is chewed affect the amount of energy extracted from it?
>
> 6 How much of this cake should I give to my sister?
>
> 7 What is the shortest route that allows me to buy bread (B), cheese (C) and jam (J) in a supermarket with this floorplan?

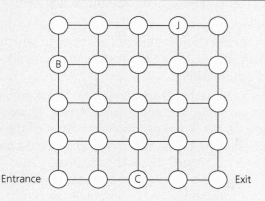

Entrance ⟶ ... ⟵ Exit

8 Can I get to the shop before it closes?

9 What is the best way to cook this food?

10 Can a meal be a work of art?

11 Is paper edible?

12 If the chutney I have bought lists the following ingredients – onions, peppers, sugar (10%), oil, vinegar and spices – and I know that they are in quantity order (with onions being the largest ingredient), what percentage of the chutney could be oil?

13 Should I eat animals?

14 What carnivores do humans eat?

How have you grouped the questions?

You may have divided them by:

» whether they are subjective questions (involving the tastes and values of the questioner) or objective (independent of the tastes and values of the questioner); for example, Questions 3 and 9 are typically subjective, and Questions 5 and 7 are typically objective.

» whether they are closed questions (which can be answered with a brief factual answer, sometimes just yes/no) or open (which invite discussion, justification, analysis); for example, Questions 1 and 9 are typically closed questions, and Questions 10 and 13 are typically open.

» whether they are personal, **indexical** questions (where the answer differs depending on who asks the question, and when they ask it), or whether the answer is independent of who asks; for example, Questions 1 and 8 are typically indexical, and Questions 2 and 7 are not.

» whether they are normative (about what *should* be the case) or descriptive (about what **is** the case); for example, Questions 6 and 13 are typically normative, and Questions 12 and 14 are typically descriptive.

» whether they can be answered by Google™, or not: this will change over time, but Google™ offered answers to Questions 11 and 13 at the time of writing, but not Questions 4 or 8.

Key term

Indexical (adjective) – Where the meaning or truth of a statement depends on who says it.

The questions relevant to this course will be ones which are:

» seeking an answer, rather than just being 'rhetorical'. Question 4 is an example of a rhetorical question, in which the primary aim of the question is to *state* that carrots are wonderful things, rather than to *find out* anything.

» descriptive rather than normative. These are not essentially about what we value, but about what is true. Some questions have normative elements which are not the main focus of the question, for example, 'How should I divide this irregularly shaped piece of cheese between me and my sister?' where it is necessary to clarify the evaluative element before progressing. Once it is determined what value structure we are conforming to (for example, equal distribution might be the primary value structure), the problem becomes descriptive: 'How can I divide the object up into equal sections?' (by trial and error, and using a pair of balancing scales, for example).

» not just a fact-checking exercise. For example, Question 2 essentially requires a list of how long anyone has ever lasted without food – once we have found and sorted this information, the answer is self-evident. Such questions may be challenging to answer because the information is hard to find, but the difficulty of the task lies in the effort in locating and accessing the right source of information, rather than in analysing the (available) parts to achieve the goal.

In reality, most problems require a combination of two processes – information search and analysis. Problem solving, as an independent skill, focuses on analysing how different parts of a problem can be combined to achieve a particular goal (where the relevant information is given).

In the list of questions from the activity, the following questions would immediately qualify for this course:

» 7 and 12 – the relevant information is given. The question can be answered by analysing the options.

The questions below would be good vehicles for problem solving if sufficient additional information was given:

» 1 – possibly, given information about the dietary habits of the person asking the question

» 6 – if some criterion for dividing up cake were given

» 8 – (given information about where the shop is, how fast the question poser can move, when the shop closes.

While these questions would be a test of information finding rather than analysis:

» 2 – as suggested, this requires a historical look at who ate what, when, and who survived

» 5 – a classic vehicle for scientific enquiry

» 14 – like 2, this essentially requires a list of people's eating habits.

The remaining questions require either an examination of tastes, values and meaning, or are not primarily seeking an answer:

▸▸ 3 (taste); 4 (rhetorical); 6 (values); 9 (taste); 10 (values); 11 (meaning); 13 (values).

> ### ACTIVITY
> ....
>
> **Generating problems**
>
> Create 14 questions of your own relating to transport (rather than food).
>
> Try to make them as diverse as possible, and ensure that some of each of the four question types above are included.

The power of inference and Fermi estimation problems

As we have seen, real-life problems naturally involve a combination of seeking out relevant information and making inferences from that information. The second part of problem solving involves choosing how to combine information.

What exactly constitutes 'choosing how to combine information'? You might begin by considering the range of possible ways information can be combined. Some problems clearly lay out the different pieces of information and, in doing so, allow you to see the range of possible combinations. For problems like this, all you need to do is exhaustively check them (see Section 2.3 on systematic listing).

The example below shows how it can be easy to choose how to combine the information – and easy to identify the right answer once it is done – but still be a challenging problem.

Sample question

The Footietown soccer squad is playing in a tournament in Sportsville. There are 30 people in the squad. In order to travel to Sportsville, the squad decide to hire transport from a particular company. The vehicles that are available, the total number of people that a particular vehicle can carry and the hire costs are given in the following table:

Type of vehicle	Number of people	Hire cost
Car	4	$11
People-carrier	7	$16
Minibus	13	$34

Try this problem yourself, before reading the analysis!

To improve its carbon footprint, the company offers a discount of $3 if fewer than 6 vehicles are used to transport 30 people. Large numbers of each type of vehicle are available.

What is the minimum cost of vehicle hire for this journey?

(Adapted from Cambridge AS & A Level Thinking Skills 9694, Paper 11 Q6, November 2016)

➤

Hopefully you can see what kind of activity is necessary to answer this question: with no time limit, you would simply add up the numbers of people that can be carried in combinations of the three different vehicles, to see which one costs the least. In this instance the answer would be: $72.

But even this manageable quantity of data tempts us to seek shortcuts: when tackling the question, you cannot avoid the little voice in your head which protests that we do not need to list *all* the options. 'Can we not just find the number of dollars per person for each means of transport and then focus on the one with the cheapest rate?'

Even without this, there is a difficulty inherent in optimisation problems (finding minima, maxima, the slowest, the highest, the smallest, the dumbest) which is: how can you ever be sure that you have listed all the answers, and so be sure that what you think is the best is actually the best?

If you want to be sure that you have reached an optimal answer, you need to be obsessed about ensuring nothing is left out. For the sample question, you might end up producing something looking like this:

M	P	C	# of vehicles	Cost	Cost with discount
3	0	0	3	102	99
2	1	0	3	84	81
2	0	1	3	79	76
1	3	0	4	82	79
1	2	1	4	77	74
1	1	3	5	83	80
1	0	5	6	89	89
0	5	0	5	80	77
0	4	1	5	75	72 ←
0	3	3	6	81	81
0	2	4	6	76	76
0	1	6	7	82	82
0	0	8	8	88	88

Here you can see all the different ways you can transport 30 people using three minibuses, then two minibuses, then one, and then none, arranged in order so that none is missed out. This gives us our answer, that the cheapest transportation costs $72.

In order to decide how to combine the information given to reach a stated goal, you must be willing to tap into your first-hand knowledge of the world and be willing to experiment. One of the best vehicles for honing this skill (that of extrapolating from your own experience into new realms of thought) are **Fermi estimation problems**. These problems are boundless in their scope – the crazier the better – and are explicitly casual with the hard facts, focusing instead on creative use of our experience, and on process rather than outcome.

> Try this problem yourself, before reading the analysis!

A classic example is: 'Estimate what length of hair you will grow in your lifetime.'

Fermi estimation problems are named after Enrico Fermi, the Italian physicist who was famously adept at making good estimates with very little data. Success at these problems depends on three elements:

1   The ability to choose *relevant information* to enable a solution.
2   The ability to make *reasonable estimates* of size and quantity.
3   The ability to *combine your estimates and rates appropriately*.

The second element is a useful life skill to have, but this textbook focuses on the first and third elements as, together, they offer a perfect opportunity for problem solving both in the real world and for this course. Note that at the end of this section, a Fermi helpsheet has been included which you can refer to when making estimates. Or there are internet search engines which, one must remember, are as fallible as the person who entered the data.

Practising Fermi estimation problems enables you to develop two important attitudes to problem solving:

» Confidence in selecting what needs to be done. There are many different ways to tackle a Fermi estimation problem. The first step is always to 'inhabit' the problem, visualise what kind of solution is needed and then try to find a way to break it down into manageable parts. You have to begin with what you know.

» Aptitude in combining bits of information, and in particular the use of rates, to reach the goal.

Answering Fermi estimation questions is dependent on linking simple bits of familiar information (the size of a human, the amount of loose change in your pocket, the number of students in a school, the speed you can run) with appropriate rates (multipliers) to answer perilous-looking problems.

The machinery of problem solving which many students find most difficult relates to the use of rates and compound measures: it is found in questions about speed, ratio, proportion, cost per unit, price per person, people per square mile, anything per anything.

There is a more in-depth look at the particular mathematical skills associated with rates and compound measures in Section 5.2; however, experience with Fermi estimation problems will certainly give you a better feel for this.

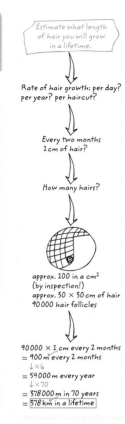

Estimate what length of hair you will grow in a lifetime.

Rate of hair growth: per day? per year? per haircut?

Every two months 1 cm of hair?

How many hairs?

approx. 100 in a cm^2 (by inspection!)
approx. 30 × 30 cm of hair
90 000 hair follicles

$90\,000 \times 1$ cm every 2 months
$= 900$ m every 2 months
$\downarrow \times 6$
$= 54\,000$ m every year
$\downarrow \times 70$
$= 378\,000$ m in 70 years
$= \boxed{378\,\text{km in a lifetime}}$

▲ **Estimates and rates used in solving a Fermi estimation problem**

By beginning this book (and this course) with Fermi estimation questions, the hope is not that you spend a fortnight practising estimation skills and then move on. Rather, it is that estimation questions exemplify one important aspect of problem solving, and should accompany your studies throughout the course.

On the left is a worked example of how Fermi estimation questions might be solved. It is not meant to be the only way to tackle the question, or even the best, rather it exemplifies a way of tackling daunting problems by cultivating the 'inner voice' which stabilises you when the data is disorientating. The question to be answered is the example we looked at previously: *estimate what length of hair you will grow in your lifetime*.

> ## ACTIVITY
> ....
>
> ### Fermi estimation problems
>
> Try to answer the following Fermi estimation problems. To get the most out of these, you should ensure that you:
>
> **a** Approximate an answer to every question – based upon some combination of your estimates. Don't worry if you feel your estimates are 'plucked from thin air'.
>
> **b** After trying the question on your own, discuss it with fellow students. Decide on whose answer is the most convincing.
>
> **c** Use the internet to check your estimates and to see if your answer was any good: if not, try to establish what aspect was mistaken.
>
> **1** Estimate how many miles you will walk in a lifetime.
>
> **2** Estimate how much cash there is in the world.
>
> **3** Estimate the number of playing cards needed to completely cover the area of Manhattan.
>
> **4** Estimate how much each person would get if the land on the planet was divided up equally between them.
>
> **5** Estimate how much your time is worth if you decide to wash up rather than buy a dishwasher.
>
> **6** Estimate what percentage of the planet's surface you could see from the top of Mount Kilimanjaro on a clear day.
>
> **7** Estimate how much you should charge to wash all the windows in Karachi.
>
> **8** Estimate how many petrol stations there are in the USA.
>
> **9** Estimate how long it would take to move Mount Fuji by wheelbarrow.
>
> **10** Estimate the number of primary school teachers in Buenos Aires.
>
> **11** Estimate how many people have ever lived.

This helpsheet is intended to help you answer the Fermi estimation problems on page 8.

FERMI HELPSHEET

Some useful estimates that can help you solve estimation problems (either given to 1 significant figure, or identified with *) are as follows:

- The number of people on the planet is roughly 7 billion (7 000 000 000).
- Just over half of those people live in cities.
- The global median household income per year is roughly $10 000.
- The global average life expectancy at birth is just over 70.
- The average height of an adult male is roughly 175 cm*.
- The average height of an adult female is roughly 165 cm*.
- People walk at roughly 4 km/hour (or 1 m/s).
- The top speed of a commercially sold car is roughly 120 km/h* (or 30 m/s).
- The speed of a jet aircraft is roughly 800 km/h (or 200 m/s).
- The speed of sound through air is roughly 1200 km/h* (or 300 m/s).
- The radius of planet Earth is roughly 6000 km.
- The top of Mount Everest is roughly 8 km above sea level.
- 70 per cent of the Earth's surface is covered in water.
- The distance to the Moon is roughly 380 000km*.
- The distance to the Sun is roughly 150 000 000 km*.

There are a number of great websites with problems and advice on how to tackle Fermi estimation problems. For more see:

https://goo.gl/S0XG6x

https://goo.gl/74a7kL

How to interrogate the question

Hopefully you have a sense of what types of problems we are addressing, and hopefully you have begun to feel the freedom that can accompany solving such things.

Next you need to look at how you can apply this to problems with a precise, preconceived answer, where both the detail and the intentions of the problem setter are important.

In this section you will look at how a good problem solver views a problem and how this attitude can be developed.

When sitting and reading through a problem-solving question, it can sometimes seem as though the question is just sitting there and staring back at you, silently and unhelpfully.

When faced with such a question, it is important to interact with it, asking it questions and listening out for its answers. Unfortunately you will have to supply these answers on behalf of the problem – but the answering is the easy bit. Asking the right questions is the bit you need to practise.

Animal, vegetable or mineral?

Asking questions is the basis of the game known as 'Animal, vegetable or mineral?'. In this game, a person (known as the 'Riddler') is chosen to think of an object. The rest of the group must then race to discover it by asking questions to which the Riddler can answer only 'Yes' or 'No'. In the example below, the object the Riddler is thinking of is a telescope.

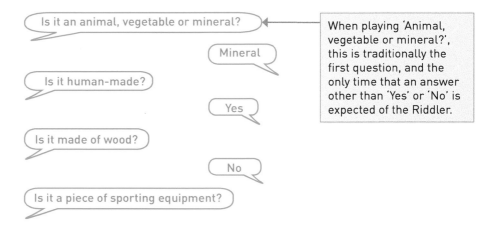

Is it an animal, vegetable or mineral?

Mineral

Is it human-made?

Yes

Is it made of wood?

No

Is it a piece of sporting equipment?

When playing 'Animal, vegetable or mineral?', this is traditionally the first question, and the only time that an answer other than 'Yes' or 'No' is expected of the Riddler.

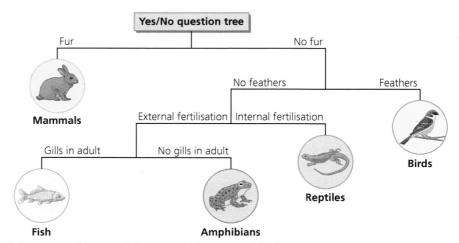

Yes/No question tree

Fur — No fur

Mammals

No feathers — Feathers

External fertilisation | Internal fertilisation

Birds

Gills in adult — No gills in adult

Reptiles

Fish

Amphibians

▲ How a machine would approach the game of 'Animal, vegetable or mineral?'

> **▶ ACTIVITY**
>
> ....
>
> Applying the 'Animal, vegetable or mineral?' method
>
> The following puzzle should be solved as a group activity.
>
> If 9669 = 4, 8998 = 6, 1816 = 3, 1513 = 0, then 1689 = ?
>
> In your group, use the animal, vegetable or mineral method to tackle the above puzzle. You should first decide who will be the Riddler and allow them to read ahead to see the explanation for this activity's puzzle. The explanation for this puzzle is on page 305.

Here is a list of questions which may have been asked during your interrogation of the Riddler:

» Is it to do with prime numbers?

» Is it to do with factors?

» Could you get an 'output' bigger than 10?

» Could the input number have fewer than four digits?

» Does it involve adding the digits together?

» Would a calculator help?

» Could my little brother do it?

» Does the answer involve all four digits?

» Does an input of '0' give an output of '0'?

» Do the output numbers have their everyday meaning?

» Does it matter what order the digits are in?

» Would it give the same answer if I wrote the numbers in binary?

» If the input was a word (like the word 'number'), would you get an answer?

Still in your activity group, discuss which of these questions would have been most useful to ask for this puzzle. Which would you say were good questions generally?

How to generate good questions is not something you can learn mechanically. You must try to come at the problem from as many angles as possible, and also consider what the limits are to the information you have been given. Much of our 'natural' problem-solving ability comes from making intuitive assumptions about what is going on. This is very useful when you are faced with problems from the natural world.

For example, imagine you receive a series of calls on your mobile phone, spaced only a minute or two apart, where you hear nothing on the end of the line.

This is a problem for you – both a nuisance and a puzzle – and you might consider how to work out the cause of the calls. Consider this on your own for a minute.

Realistically you would probably factor in a number of assumptions and clues – about whether your phone has been working normally, about whether the number was displayed, about whether the silence you hear sounds like a bad connection or a lack of any connection, about whether this has ever happened before, about whether anyone you know is likely to be responsible for the calls. From this collection of intuitions, assumptions, hypotheses and fragmentary evidence you would normally come to some kind of conclusion in a matter of seconds.

Unfortunately, these natural assumptions are more likely to hinder rather than help you in the artificial world of problem-solving exam papers. This is because exam questions are designed to separate the rational problem solver from the instinctive problem solver. In the 9669 puzzle on page 11, your instinct was likely to treat the four-digit numerals as counting numbers (nine thousand, six hundred and sixty-nine) and to analyse the possible characteristics of that number.

As a problem solver you must train yourself to expose these intuitive assumptions and think outside of the box.

The ability to come up with good questions is part of what will make you a flexible problem solver.

Outside the exam hall it enables you to interrogate the question, eliminate unfruitful lines of enquiry, and stalk the solution. It also makes you alert to possible tricks in the question, possible shortcuts to the solution, and possible ways of checking your answer.

The skill of creating fruitful questions is at the heart of developing a personal heuristic.

It must be experienced, reflected upon, and integrated into your world view. Regular practice and discussion with experienced problem solvers is the key to this.

What follows is a series of stepped activities that will move you from simple cases to the tough cases that require more advanced problem-solving skills.

▶ INTRODUCTION ACTIVITY

Animal, vegetable or mineral?

In a small group, decide who will play the Riddler. The Riddler should think of an object, and the rest of the group should race to discover it by asking questions to which the Riddler can answer only 'Yes' or 'No'.

Refer back to the 'Animal, vegetable or mineral?' example on page 10 if needed.

If there is time, take turns playing the Riddler within your group.

▶ DEEPENING ACTIVITY

WhyDunnit

'WhyDunnit' is a similar game to 'Animal, vegetable or mineral?' but here the focus is on unpicking an event and uncovering its explanation. When playing 'WhyDunnit', the Riddler begins by offering one, carefully phrased clue about the event in question. The team then ask questions, to which the Riddler can answer only 'Yes' or 'No' (in the same manner as 'Animal, vegetable or mineral?').

A collection of famous 'WhyDunnit' clues is given below. The explanations – to be read by the Riddler only – are at the end of the book on page 305.

1 A man enters a field with a bag; and he dies.

2 A man and his wife race through the streets in their car. They stop, and the husband gets out and runs away from the car. When he gets back, his wife is dead, and there is a stranger in the car.

3 A man is lying dead, face down in the desert. There's a match near his outstretched hand.

4 Romeo and Juliet lie dead on the floor surrounded by broken glass. There is an open window nearby.

5 A man walks down a corridor, carrying a letter, when the ceiling lights go dim. He stops, turns round and leaves the building.

6 A man enters a room through a window. The furniture is gold-painted. There is a chandelier hanging from the ceiling, but none of the lights work. There are four dead men dressed in black tie.

7 A man goes into a restaurant, orders albatross, eats one bite, and kills himself.

For further examples of 'WhyDunnit' puzzles, see:

http://www.folj.com/lateral/

http://www.rinkworks.com/brainfood/p/latreal1.shtml

> ### ACTIVITY

Interrogating questions

The skill and attitude that led you to success in the game of 'Animal, vegetable or mineral?' and in the 'WhyDunnit' puzzles are what you need to cultivate when faced with tricky problem-solving puzzles.

You must always consider what different ways there might be of tackling the problem you are struggling with.

When training for a specific problem you might interrogate someone who knows their way through the problem already. Asking questions is a far more effective way of understanding a problem as, through questioning, you become aware of the different ways the problem might be resolved. If you had asked just for an explanation, you would become aware of only one method of solving the problem – and it might not be the best method!

Interrogate the Riddler now to try to answer the puzzle below. The Riddler can look to the end of the book to get the explanation.

Riddler: You have a drawer which has 20 socks in, all of which are identical in shape – you know that 8 are red and 12 are black. If you reach in and grab a number of socks without looking at their colour, how many do you need to take to be sure that you have at least one matching pair? Explain your answer.

Practice questions

Try to solve the following problems by interrogating the Riddler.

1 If $6 = 3$, $18 = 8$, $30 = 6$ and $31 = 9$, then $4 = ?$

2 Imagine you are in the basement of a building faced with three switches, one of which controls the light bulb in the attic. How can you manipulate the switches in a way that will allow you to work out which one controls the light bulb after only **one** journey to the attic?

3 What comes next in this sequence? 1, 11, 21, 1112, 3112 …

4 Some languages use letters which are not in the 26 letters of the **a–z** of the American alphabet. There is no consistency in how words containing such letters are considered when sorting into alphabetical order. For example, an **ä** could be placed in four positions according to different national styles. It could be found:
   - as just '**a**' without the dots (American style)
   - as two characters **ae** (German style)
   - as a separate character between '**a**' and '**b**' (Austrian style)
   - as a character after '**z**' with extra letters in the order **åäö** (Swedish style).

   A particular computer program has sorted a list of words using one of the above styles, but we do not know which one.

   In how many places might we have to look to find the word **överträda**?

(Adapted from Cambridge AS & A Level Thinking Skills 9694, Paper 11 Q19, November 2016)

5 A school is deciding who to choose to send to a national spelling competition. It decides to give all 80 pupils at the school two spelling tests and rank the pupils from 1 to 80 (with no joint places) in each test. There are 10 places available on the team: they decide to take anyone who is in the top 10 in both tests. This produced less than 10 pupils, so they looked at anyone in the top 11 in both tests. This also produced less than 10 pupils. They continued to raise the threshold (top 12, top 13, top 14, ...) until they had 10 pupils. Mateusz thinks he did really badly in one test. What is the lowest ranking that he could have achieved on that test and still been selected for the team?

6 Zipf's law states that if you examine the populations of cities in a country you will find that the second-largest city will have about half the population of the largest, the third largest will have one-third the population of the largest, the fourth largest will have one quarter of the population of the largest, and so on. In Zipfonia, where Zipf's law operates exactly, the 10 largest cities make up 30 per cent of the country's total population. Zipfonia has a border with Hedania, which has only half of Zipfonia's population. However, Hedania's largest city has a population that is 50 per cent higher than the population of Zipfonia's largest city. Assuming Zipf's law works in Hedania, what percentage of Hedania's total population lives in its 10 largest cities?

(Adapted from Cambridge AS & A Level Thinking Skills 9694, Paper 11 Q21, November 2016)

1.2 Modelling the problem

So far in this chapter you have gained a flavour of the creative process at the heart of problem solving and are in the process of developing the art of interrogating the problem.

You now need to consider how problems from the real world can be pinned down on the written page.

In this section we will consider the process of modelling a real-world problem: what choices have to be made, and what aspects of a problem might make this difficult.

Modelling means 'grabbing hold' of the problem and taming it by expressing it in a form that is manageable. Any prediction about the world requires a model and any problem that you have seen (or will see) in an exam paper has already been modelled to some extent – but almost any serious engagement with a problem like this involves further modelling.

Models can be **physical**, **symbolic** or **computational**.

For example, imagine you are playing in a snooker tournament this weekend. To help you win, you want to maximise your success at the opening shot (the break). You could choose to use a physical, symbolic or computational model to help prepare for this.

1 Physical

You make (or buy) a model of the balls and table on which you will be playing; this need not be exactly the same as the 'tournament equipment' but it needs to be similar in the relevant ways. In particular, the relative physical dimensions of the balls and table need to be correct. If the force with which you strike the balls is important, the weight also needs to be appropriate. This physical model will allow you to simplify the event (the break), perhaps beginning with a triangle of three balls, then considering a triangle of six, or to control certain aspects (you could strike the cue ball right in front of the triangle of balls, so that you have more control over the angle and force). You could use the model to train your fine motor skills to strike the cue ball with just the right force and angle to maximise the impact of that first shot.

2 Symbolic

You could study the logic behind that initial strike. In particular, the geometry that underlies the contact between the balls, and the laws of physics which apply in these cases.

This kind of analysis would start with diagramming the relevant aspects of the initial collision of two balls and writing the relationship symbolically (or algebraically). Any basic relations can then be established and expanded to more complex cases.

3 Computational

A computer simulator could be used to investigate alternative options at the break. This might involve an interactive 2D picture of the table, which captured some of the aspects of the game: I may be able to control the angle and force of the cue ball, but may not be able to control the spin. The use of such a 'game' would depend on whether the model satisfies basic 'representational fidelity criteria' (requirements regarding how close key aspects of the simulation were to 'real life').

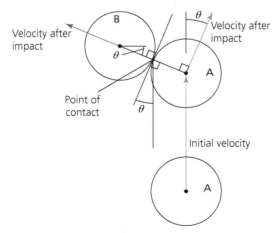

▲ The geometry behind two balls striking

These three types of model reveal some of the choices that need to be made when simplifying a situation in order to experiment with it and achieve some goal. In this case the model may be deemed unnecessary – you could decide to just go out and play in the competition at the weekend, see how you do, learn from any mistakes, and play again next year. This is like treating the actual event as a model for future events.

Here is a list of some features of the situation which might be relevant when creating a symbolic model for an opening snooker break.

>> The angle at which the ball is hit.

>> The force with which the ball is hit.

>> The speed and angle at which the ball is spinning.

>> The geometry of a set of 15 snooker balls packed together (the angles and distances between the individual balls).

>> The geometry of the table (the angles and distances between the pockets).

>> The 'bounce' of the snooker balls (with each other: their coefficient of restitution, in the terminology of physics).

>> The 'bounce' of the cushions at the sides and ends of the table.

>> Any tilt in the surface of the table.

>> The wind.

>> The Earth's gravity.

>> Any asymmetries in the make-up of the balls themselves.

>> The effect of the 'chalk' transferring from cue to cue ball to other balls on contact.

>> The temperature in the room.

>> The number of people in the room who might interfere with play.

>> The health of your competitor.

This list could go on.

Whenever we make a model we choose to focus on the key **variables**: those that we think will allow us to determine the answer to our question, to a sufficient degree of accuracy. When we have chosen the wrong variables, or measured them with insufficient accuracy, we find the model is inadequate.

Key terms

Constants and variables (noun) – In any problem, one can expect certain values to remain constant (such as the force of gravity on Earth, or the number of people in a family) and certain values to vary (such as the speed of a stone, or the number of people who vote for a candidate). The former are called constants; the latter are called variables. Whether a value is a constant or a variable will depend upon the particular model being analysed.

> ## ACTIVITY

Classifying the variables in a model

Take the list of features that might be used in a snooker model and classify each variable as one of the following:

→ Axiomatic: vital for understanding this problem, and almost all similar problems.

→ Essential: necessary for understanding this problem.

→ Peripheral: having some influence on the outcome of this problem.

→ Irrelevant: could have no influence on the outcome of this problem.

Some of the variables fit clearly into one of the categories, while others are 'up for discussion'. Classic examples of each are given below:

→ Axiomatic: the Earth's gravity.

→ Essential: the angle and the force at which the ball is hit.

→ Peripheral: tilt in the table and asymmetries in the balls themselves (if small).

→ Irrelevant: the temperature of the room.

> ## ACTIVITY

Modelling a situation

A company is selling toffee apples at a school charity fair; they want to make as much profit as they can for their charity and so are going to model the sales (and profit) ahead of the event.

Working in pairs, consider the different factors which could be relevant to this model. List as many variables as possible that might affect their final profit total. Make sure to include a couple of aspects which you consider to be of each type (Axiomatic, Essential, Peripheral, Irrelevant).

When you have generated a list, compare it with that of another pair in your class. Can you identify which variables they intended to be Axiomatic, Essential, Peripheral and Irrelevant?

In the next six sections we will consider aspects of the modelling process that require particularly precise articulation. Each aspect stimulates an attitude of 'special care' in the modeller and should provoke a level of heightened awareness in the problem solver.

» Discrete and continuous variables
» Rounding
» Time and speed
» Relative measures
» Representing 3D
» Units and bases

Key terms

Discrete variables are things you can count, rather than things you can measure.

Continuous variables are things you can measure, rather than things you can count.

Discrete and continuous variables

You may already know the distinction made between a discrete and a continuous variable from your study of statistics.

Discrete variables represent quantities that can be counted, rather than measured. Significantly, discrete variables can come only from a finite set of values. For example, you can have one child, or two or three or more children sitting on a sofa. You cannot have 1.5 children sitting on a sofa. Discrete variables avoid the gaps between the numbers that can lead to nonsensical answers.

The number of balls on a pool table (0, 1, 2, 3 ...) is a discrete variable, as is the century in which someone was born (nineteenth century, twentieth century, twenty-first century ...), or what shoe size you are (7, 7.5, 8, 8.5 ...).

This last example reveals a split personality to discrete measures: they may either reflect the fact that part-objects are not possible (a pool ball that has been cut in half is not a pool ball), or reflect the way we measure objects (it is common for shoes to be measured in half sizes).

We do not tend to define what a unit is for a discrete variable – although sometimes it is necessary to. For example, we may want to measure how big a city is in number of households, rather than number of individual people. Households and individuals are both plausible discrete units, and therefore we need to state which we are using. Normally, when dealing with discrete variables, the unit ('one thing') is the smallest object you can have one of.

Although discrete variables often feel nicer than continuous variables, because the numbers are easier, one must be more careful when dealing with them: if you are not careful you could accidentally 'fall into one of the gaps' when you give your answer, or in your working.

Diophantine problems – named after a mathematician from ancient Greece, called Diophantus – are puzzles which relate a number of discrete variables.

Sample question

Try this problem yourself, before reading the analysis!

→

A Diophantine problem:

I have three piles of marbles, each of a different colour.

If you gave me a marble, exactly half of them would be one colour.

Right now exactly one third of them are one colour.

If you took away one marble, then one quarter of them would be one colour.

How many marbles do I have?

➤

This problem shows how a simply stated problem can be difficult to get a grip on.

One way to a solution is to realise that if one third are one colour right now, then that number must be a multiple of 3. Remove one, and the number must be a multiple of 4. Add one and the number must be a multiple of 2.

A quick search reveals 9 as a likely candidate.

The number of individual colours needs to be checked: and indeed 3 of one colour, 2 of another and 4 of the third will satisfy the restrictions.

Continuous variables represent quantities you can measure, rather than things you can count. These can take any value on a section of the number line, meaning there are no unfilled gaps between numbers. Examples include the distance between your finger and thumb (measured in millimetres), the weight of a feather (measured in grams), the length of time you have been alive (measured in seconds).

As you can see, unlike discrete variables, continuous variables are defined by their units (what counts as 'one'). Continuous variables may seem harder to deal with (since they are likely to produce fractions and decimals), but most of the mathematical tools you have learned are geared towards them – equation-solving techniques, as well as basic arithmetic operations, assume that any number on the number line is feasible.

Sample question

Try this problem yourself, before reading the analysis!

The median puzzle

If you want to find the balancing point of a (uniform) plank 12 metres long, you naturally choose the point 6 metres from the end.

If you have 12 people who are lined up in height order (with regular spaces between their heights), why is it not appropriate to choose the sixth person as the person with the middle height?

Is this question 'too obvious to answer'?

The question can make a difference to what is the right answer – and is something you will be familiar with from school if you have ever been told that the median can be found using the 'formula' $(n + 1) \div 2$.

When you are finding the halfway person, you are essentially treating the first person as the beginning (as 'zero') and finding half the 'distance' back to them. This is most easily seen with five people:

1st 2nd 3rd 4th 5th

$$1 + \frac{5-1}{2}$$

$$1 + \frac{n-1}{2}$$

$$= \frac{2+n-1}{2}$$

$$= \frac{n+1}{2}$$

Rounding

Rounding is the inevitable outcome of considering continuous measures. If you tried to give an absolutely precise answer in terms of continuous measures, you would be listing an infinite decimal: 'I am 1.824 657 918 374 928 734 982 7394 ... m tall.'

The relationship between rounding and measurement is peculiar – the diagram below shows a series of attempts to measure the length of the coastline of Great Britain, using different scales. As the unit of measurement becomes smaller (200 mile units, 100 mile units, 50 mile units ...), the perimeter increases: this is because, when you reduce the size of the unit, you always replace one straight line with some smaller zig-zagging sections of line, which will always increase the length. This paradox leads to the study of fractal geometry – which is not necessary for problem solving.

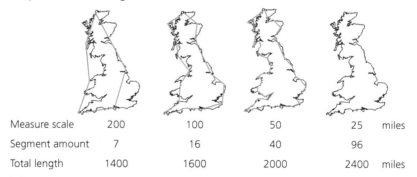

Measure scale	200	100	50	25	miles
Segment amount	7	16	40	96	
Total length	1400	1600	2000	2400	miles

▲ The paradoxical relationship between distance and rounding – the finer the detail, the longer the perimeter

The practical use of continuous variables does not produce such paradoxes and involves treating any measurement as an interval. For example, when I say I am 1.65 m tall, I mean that I am between 1.645 and 1.655 m tall (there is a reminder of how to find these limits and round to varying degrees of accuracy in Section 5.5).

It is important to remember, however, that rounding interferes with modelling at two different points in the process: when you start and when you finish.

When you start modelling

As has just been explained, whenever you offer a measurement you – for practical purposes – round the number up or down. This process can produce strange results; consider the following puzzle:

Sample question

Try this problem yourself, before reading the analysis!

In the 100 m space between two roads there are a number of adjacent plots of land. Their measurements are as follows:

4 m   4.34 m   836 cm   12.4 m   70.9 m

These lengths add up to 100 m; however, when they are rounded up to the nearest metre (and added together), 1 metre is 'lost':

4 + 4 + 8 + 12 + 71 = 99 m

You have five different lengths which, when added together, equal 100 m. If you round each of these five lengths to the nearest metre, what is the greatest amount that can be lost? Give an example of lengths that would produce the result.

In the given example you can see where the missing metre has gone. 0.34 m, 0.36 m and 0.4 m are discarded when those lengths are rounded down, and 0.1 m is gained when that length is rounded up.

To solve the question 'What is the greatest amount that can be lost?', you can maximise the process by beginning with four numbers that round down 'maximally' and one length that does not.

For example:

0.49 m   0.49 m   0.49 m   0.49 m   98.04 m

will round to:

0 + 0 + 0 + 0 + 98 = 98 m

This seems very unrealistic – because the small lengths have been reduced to zero, and because the plots are very small – but it shows the extreme case well.

When you finish modelling

When you offer an answer to the problem, having modelled it, you re-integrate with the world and offer a rounded answer. It is at this moment that you should always consider what unit you are using. This is both to check that they are appropriate for the question asked (if the question asks for the maximum number of eggs that can be carried in one basket, and your answer is 3 baskets, then something has gone wrong!) and to check they are sensible if it is a discrete unit (2.71 eggs?).

Sample question

Try this problem yourself, before reading the analysis!

A staff survey showed that 92 per cent of respondents did not think the library should be converted into a meditation centre. Assuming that the figure is quoted to the nearest whole number, what is the smallest possible number of staff who responded?

The following working shows a 'trial and error' approach (see Section 2.4) revealing the critical idea for solving the sample question: that you are looking for the smallest number for which a fraction gives 8 per cent. The answer is that the percentages could have been generated by as few as 12 people.

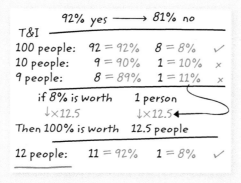

Rounding is normally done 'to the nearest unit', but there are some cases where we naturally round up or round down. The most pervasive case is when we discuss someone's age. It is normal to say that someone is 17 years old until the day of their 18th birthday. Children and elderly people who claim they are 'nearly 9' or 'nearly 90' are quietly resisting this rounding mechanism.

As a problem solver you must be aware of this unusual rounding mechanism.

Sample question

Try this problem yourself, before reading the analysis!

Today my three closest friends are 23, 24 and 25 years old.

What is the smallest number of days that there could be between when the oldest and when the youngest was born?

The answer is a year and a day: 366 days.

You can see this by considering three people born 1 January 2000, 1 January 2001 and 2 January 2001. Their ages on 1 January 2002 would be 2, 1 and 0 respectively. This age separation would obviously continually occur on that day through the years.

1   A farmer is planning to create a temporary 'pen' for livestock, by cutting
    a large section of plastic netting into strips, joining the strips together and
    then fixing the combined length to posts. He decides the fence must be 2 m
    high, and must form a shape that is nearly square: either a precise square or a
    rectangle whose length and width do not differ by more than 5 m.

    If the length and width are both whole numbers of metres, what is the
    greatest area than can be created from 156 m² of netting?

2   Mateusz and Carla decide to poll their fellow students to find out how many
    wish to pay for an end-of-year celebration. They turn their fractions into
    percentages, and round them to the nearest whole number: Mateusz finds
    that 14% are in favour; Carla finds that 17% are in favour; and when they
    combine their results they find that 15% are in favour in total.

    What is the smallest number of people that they could have asked, in total?

3   Quickfence Ltd has the following method for calculating the price it will
    charge to put up a new fence:
    • Labour is charged at $25 per hour, or part of an hour. It takes
      45 minutes of labour per metre to put up a new fence.
    • Fence panels are 2 m long and cost $20 each. If they have to be cut, the
      price of a full panel is charged.
    • Fence posts cost $5 each. A post is needed between fence panels and at
      both ends.

    What will be the price for a fence 13 m long?

    (Adapted from Cambridge AS & A Level Thinking Skills 8436, Paper 1 Q38, June 2005)

4   Dale visited the graves of his two friends, Troy and Barin, on his 61st
    birthday, in November 2004. The gravestones showed the years that his
    two friends died: 'Troy 1942 – 2003' and 'Barin 1942 – 2004'.

    Which of the following statements must be true?

    A   Troy lived longer than Barin.

    B   Dale was born after both Troy and Barin.

    C   Troy and Barin died within 12 months of each other.

    D   Dale, Troy and Barin all died at the same age.

    (Adapted from Cambridge AS & A Level Thinking Skills 9694,
    Paper 13 Q5, November 2015)

Taking it further

5   Large blocks of stone can be moved by 'rolling' them. The diagram here
    shows how a single stone can be moved in this way.

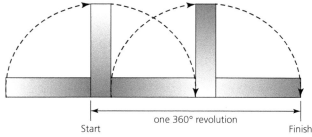

one 360° revolution

Start   Finish

When
tackling this
problem you
should round
appropriately
when giving
an answer to
each of the
questions,
but keep the
numbers used
in any working
as precise as
possible. One
way to do this is
to use fractions
where possible.
Another is to
use the memory
capabilities of
your calculator.

It is quicker to lower a tall stone than to raise it. From experience, a stonemason knows that he can turn a stone through 90° in (b/h) minutes, where b is the length of the face that is flat on the ground, and h is the vertical height of the stone as he is about to turn it.

For example, a block that has two of its dimensions as 5 metres and 2 metres can be turned 180° in $\frac{5}{2}$ minutes + $\frac{2}{5}$ minutes = 2 minutes 54 seconds.

The stonemason wishes to move large blocks of stone in order to then cut them into manageable pieces for tombstones. He is considering how to move them most quickly.

In order to move a block, he chooses the initial orientation, and then rolls it in the same direction for the whole journey.

He will only consider blocks that are cuboid in shape and have dimensions that are whole numbers of metres.

a   Consider a block with dimensions 2 m × 2 m × 6 m. Calculate the minimum possible **time** that it would take to roll the block through 360°.

b   Consider a block with dimensions 1 m × 4 m × 6 m. Calculate all the different possible **distances** that the block could travel in one 360° revolution, according to the different initial orientations.

c   If a 24 m³ block is to travel at least 610 m, what is the smallest possible number of 90° turns that will be needed?

610m

d   What dimensions for a 24 m³ block will allow for the smallest possible time to move it 610 m? State the time it will take, to the nearest minute.

(Cambridge AS & A Level Thinking Skills 9694, Paper 31 Q3, June 2011)

Time and speed

The passage of time is inescapable. And it can be difficult to deal with in problems.

With time comes change – and getting a grip on the rate of change (or the rate of rate of change) can be both critical and tricky. The problem-solving tool that is best suited to managing and tracking changes in a problem over time is that of taking 'snapshots'. In this way you can control time, by pausing it.

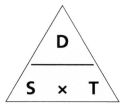

▲ Relationship between distance, speed and time

The relationship between distance, speed and time is frequently presented as a triangle of variables, as shown in the diagram.

The triangle is not wrong: it certainly helps if you are trying to remember the formulae that link the three variables (you need to remember what order they are in, obviously!).

But the balanced symmetry of the triangle hides a deeper relationship:

» Speed is a compound unit.

» It measures the rate of distance covered over time.

» It is proportional to the distance covered, but inversely proportional to the time.

» It is the gradient of the timeline.

» It tells you how many metres are covered in one second (and a billion other little facts about other distances).

It is particularly useful to remember that the unit (metres per second, or miles per hour, or whatever) tells you a specific, intuitively accessible fact about how long it takes to cover a certain distance. This allows speeds to be converted into snapshots, and enables you, the problem solver, to gain control of a slippery situation.

Sample question

Try this problem yourself, before reading the analysis!

The diagrams below show the vertical cross-sections of some barrels.

Water flows into each barrel at a constant rate until it is full. Record the heights of the water in each barrel at regular intervals and draw a graph of the results. Sketch what the graphs of water height (on the vertical axis) against time (on the horizontal axis) would look like, making it clear when the line is straight and when it is curved.

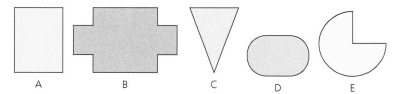

A   B   C   D   E

There is nothing deep about this problem – apart from the difficulties inherent in modelling time. There are sophisticated mathematical tools for dealing with something like this but, when faced with problems such as this, it is helpful to imagine you have a magical 'remote control' which you can use to pause time. Pausing time at various points gives you a clear snapshot of the puzzle, and allows you to observe what is happening (and how things have changed) over the course of the problem.

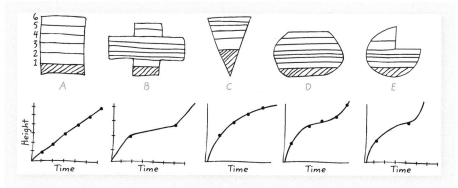

In each of these graphs, the shaded area aims to represent a standard unit of water (which is added at a constant rate). Using your remote control, you pause time after each unit has been added and record the height of the water. As the width of the barrel varies, the height of these units changes. This yields a dependable relationship between the width and the gradient of the line (the wider the barrel, the shallower the gradient).

Sample question

Try this problem yourself, before reading the analysis!

Gepeto and Goliath are two keen swimmers. Every Sunday they always complete the same number of lengths as each other. Gepeto swims faster than Goliath, but each swimmer always swims at the same speed, week in, week out. This week Gepeto noticed that Goliath finished 3.5 minutes after him. The previous week, they had swum 10 lengths fewer and when Gepeto finished, Goliath was exactly one length behind. Goliath swims at two lengths a minute.

How many lengths does Gepeto swim in a minute?

This fairly challenging problem offers a disorderly collection of pieces of information about Goliath and Gepeto. It is worth considering what information we can derive, and which snapshots we have been given, before diagramming the problem. The speed that Goliath swims (two lengths per minute) can be used to derive a number of related pieces of information:

➤ Goliath swims one length in $\frac{1}{2}$ a minute.

➤ Goliath can swim seven lengths in 3.5 minutes.

➤ Goliath can swim ten lengths in five minutes (and four lengths in two minutes, six lengths in three minutes, and so on).

The possible snapshots (when we are given some information about their relative positions) are:

➤ when Gepeto finished last week (and Goliath was one length behind)

➤ when Goliath finished last week ($\frac{1}{2}$ a minute after Gepeto)

➤ when Gepeto finished this week (10 lengths 'further on' than the previous week, and seven lengths ahead of Goliath)

➤ when Goliath finished this week (3.5 minutes after Gepeto).

There are a number of options. One is to consider the two times at which Gepeto finished, and how far both swimmers had gone between these times. Gepeto had travelled ten lengths further, during which time Goliath travelled four lengths further. The diagram below shows this:

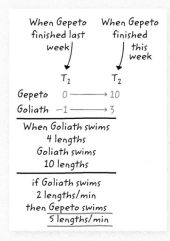

Practice questions

1   The Sisyphus monastery is on a hill, and every day donkeys climb the hill carrying water from the well in the valley. There are many donkeys, and they leave the well (at the bottom of the hill) every 15 minutes. They take one hour to climb the hill, 10 minutes to unload their water, and then half an hour to return to the well.

When a donkey goes uphill carrying water, in the middle of the day, how many does it pass coming down?

2   Zachariah and Ednei are playing with their toy cars on a two-lane circular track. They decide to release their cars from positions which are at opposite ends of a diameter, with the two cars travelling towards each other. The two cars both travel at constant speeds, but Ednei's car is faster than Zachariah's. If they pass each other for the third time at exactly the position where Zachariah released his car, what is the ratio of their speeds?

3   A container ship is overtaking a stationary oil tanker on the way out of Harwich Harbour, and the first mate notices that if he starts walking from the front of the container ship when the two ships start overlapping, he reaches the back as the two ship separate. He walks at 3 km/hour.

If the container ship is 100 m long, and travelling at 12 km/hour, how long is the oil tanker?

4 There is an escalator in the underground station which I use on my way to work. I normally climb the escalator at one step per second, and at one pace per second. This takes me 15 paces to reach the top. Sometimes (if I am in a hurry) I still take one pace per second, but climb two steps with each pace. This takes 12 paces to reach the top. One day the escalator has broken down, and I walk up one step at a time. How many steps are there?

(Adapted from Cambridge AS & A Level Thinking Skills 9694, Paper 13 Q29, November 2015)

Taking it further

5 A cartwheel in a film often appears to be turning backwards or standing still even though the cart is moving forwards.

Consider a simple cartwheel with 4 spokes, turning one full revolution (clockwise) per second. This will appear not to be moving if the camera takes 1 frame every second (or $\frac{1}{4}$ frames per second), or 1 frame every $\frac{1}{2}$ second (2 frames per second), or 1 frame every second, since each spoke will land precisely where one of the other spokes was in the previous frame.

In the example below, the wheel will appear to turn backwards because, after 1 frame, a spoke is just behind (i.e. anticlockwise from) where a spoke was previously.

| Frame 1 | Frame 2 | Frame 3 | Frame 4 |

In this series of 4 frames, the cartwheel has turned just less than 90° clockwise each time, and yet would appear to be turning anticlockwise. A similar effect is created if the wheel turns just less than 180°, or just less than any multiple of 90°.

For the purposes of the whole of this question, you should assume that:

- a 4-spoke cartwheel will appear to be turning **forwards** whenever the next frame shows the spokes up to 45° beyond (i.e. clockwise from) where the spokes were last
- a 4-spoke cartwheel will appear to be turning **backwards** whenever the next frame shows the spokes up to 45° behind (i.e. anticlockwise from) where the spokes were last
- at 45° the cartwheel's direction of motion will be ambiguous
- cameras can take only whole numbers of frames per second.

For parts (a) to (d), the cartwheel is turning at 1 revolution per second.

a Will the cartwheel appear to be going backwards or forwards if the camera takes 36 frames per second? Justify your answer.

b At what number of frames per second will a 4-spoke cartwheel's direction of motion be ambiguous?

c What is the minimum number of frames per second to make the cartwheel's motion appear backwards? Justify your answer.

The method of determining when a cartwheel's motion appears to be forwards or backwards described above involves *halving the angle between the spokes*. This halving method can be applied however many spokes a cartwheel has.

d A particular cartwheel has 12 spokes. My camera takes 25 frames per second.

   What is the slowest that this cartwheel can be turning (measured in revolutions per second) for its direction of motion to be ambiguous when filmed by my camera?

e Two differently-sized cartwheels, both with 12 spokes, appeared to be turning in different directions when filmed by my camera (25 frames per second).

   Suggest a possible speed of rotation (measured in revolutions per second) for each of the two wheels. Justify your answer.

f A cartwheel was filmed with an old camera which took 14 frames per second. The cartwheel appeared to go backwards when revolving at 1 revolution per second.

   How many spokes could the cartwheel have? List all the possibilities. (You may assume that no cartwheel has more than 25 spokes.)

(Cambridge AS & A Level Thinking Skills 9694, Paper 32 Q3, November 2013)

Units and bases

A second aspect of time which affects how we model it and how we solve problems is the unusual units we use. We work in sexagesimal:

a.k.a. base 60 – a.k.a. minutes and seconds.

We are so used to working in base 10 that we have trouble seeing the choices that have been made in the way we represent numbers and the restrictions that these choices might place on us. Working in 'base 10' means that we use just ten different numerals (the digits 0 to 9) before leaping 'up a level' and introducing a new column (the tens column), and referring to the next number as 1 ten and 0 ones. This introduction of a new column is like the introduction of a new unit of time after 59 seconds – we refer to the next unit as 1 minute and 0 seconds. Another unit is introduced when we reach 60 minutes (we refer to elapsed times, for example, as '1 hour and 12 minutes and 30 seconds later …').

This use of base 60, rather than base 10, is also favoured by global navigators: degrees of latitude are divided up into minutes of latitude, which are further divided into seconds, which are normally known as nautical miles (roughly equal to a regular, statute mile).

Hopefully, by the time you complete this course, working in sexagesimal should come naturally to you, even if you don't think of it as a change of base. As problem solvers you should be aware that the use of standard time notation in a problem (be it the 24-hour clock, or a.m. and p.m.) requires an attitude of 'heightened alertness'.

It is easy to read 'add 1.5 hours to 1:50 p.m.' and write down the answer 15:00, if you are not paying attention.

(What should the time be here, instead of 15:00?)

Sample question

> Try this problem yourself, before reading the analysis!

I have a grandfather clock. It runs slightly fast, gaining one second every four hours. It needs winding once a week, which I do just before noon every Saturday. The clock has to be stopped to carry out this process, and after it has been restarted it is always 15 seconds slow at precisely 12 o'clock.

Today is Thursday, and the correct time now is 8 p.m.

How many seconds past 8 o'clock does the clock show?

(Adapted from Cambridge AS & A Level Thinking Skills 8436, Paper 1 Q36, June 2004)

This question can be answered by skipping carefully ahead through the week, with an eye on the number of seconds in an hour, and the number of hours in a day:

Time difference	Correct time/day
−15	12 pm Sat
−14	4 pm Sat
−13	8 pm Sat
↓ 6 seconds	↓ 24 hours = 6 × 4 hours
−7	8 pm Sun
−1	8 pm Mon
+5	8 pm Tues
+11	8 pm Wed
+17	8 pm Thurs

▲ Timings for the grandfather clock, with shortcuts

There are other cases where our instinctive use of base 10 can lead to misjudgements, but these are less common in problem-solving papers:

» Binary: the use of only two symbols (1 and 0 or on and off) to represent information lies beneath all computer coding. In this case, the column headings become powers of 2, rather than powers of 10. Students are not expected to be fluent in converting numbers between bases. (See Section 5.8.)

>> Dates: the numbers of days in the different months are not bases, but they can produce similar problems, and require care. You do need to know how many days there are in each month!

>> Using non-metric units: you will not be expected to remember any of the subdivisions that make up the Imperial unit system (how many inches there are in a foot, feet in a yard, yards in a mile, and so on). However, you do need to be able to apply the logic of units to systems where you are given the conversions (such as the fictitious measuring system used in *Nondecima* in Question 3, on the next page).

You should be particularly sensitive to 'converting the wrong way': for example, concluding that 35 dm = 350 m (given that 1 decimetre is $\frac{1}{10}$ of a metre). The correct conversion is 35 dm = 3.5 m.

The following puzzle depends on the conversion between units:

Sample question

Try this problem yourself, before reading the analysis!

When I visited *Cryptos*, I discovered that the Cryptic currency consists of four different coins known as *trulls*, *yimps*, *klooks* and *dwoins*.

I had no idea, at first, of the relative value of each coin. However, shortly after my arrival I was asked if I could exchange a *klook* and a *yimp* for two *trulls*, and a short time later a similar request involved the exchange of a *klook* and a *dwoin* for three *trulls*.

Based on my encounters, I could conclude that one of the coins must be worth more than one of the others.

Which coin was worth more than which other one?

(Adapted from Cambridge AS & A Level Thinking Skills 8436, Paper 1 Q8, June 2004)

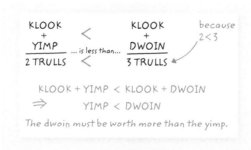

Practice questions

1 A large international company is experimenting with a system called New Decimal Time (NDT). All its offices are being fitted with clocks which divide a 24-hour day into 10 'D-hours'. Each D-hour is divided in turn into 100 D-minutes. So, for example, 12 o'clock midday becomes 05:00 NDT.

One morning, the new clock on the wall correctly shows:

What time is it according to the 24-hour clock?

(Adapted from Cambridge AS & A Level Thinking Skills 9694, Paper 11 Q12, June 2016)

2   Rides at the Prudosian Funfair are designed to accept up to three tokens. The values of the tokens are designed by the fairground to cater for all prices. There are tokens worth 1¢, 2¢, 4¢, 8¢ and 15¢, as well higher denominations.

   a   What is the lowest price that cannot be paid for with up to three of the low denomination tokens listed?

   b   If a new token is introduced at every value that cannot be paid for (with three tokens or less), how many different-valued tokens are needed to pay for every price below 50¢?

3   The unit of currency on Nondecima is the *awk*. There is a whole number of *beks* in an *awk*, and a whole number of *cets* in a *bek*. A visitor has forgotten both how many *beks* there are in an *awk* and how many *cets* there are in a *bek*. At the first shop he buys two cakes costing 3 *awks*, 12 *beks* and 4 *cets* **each** and he pays exactly 7 *awks* for these.

State how many *beks* there are in an *awk* and how many *cets* there are in a *bek* which could explain this.

(Adapted from Cambridge AS & A Level Thinking Skills 9694, Paper 13 Q19, November 2013)

Taking it further

4   An archaeologist has found some coins from a Bronze Age village, and is trying to establish what values they could have had. There are three sizes of coin: Small (S), Medium (M) and Large (L). He has also found some records of the prices of goods sold, given as numbers of these coins. He makes the following assumptions:
   - The larger the coin, the more it is worth.
   - The three coin sizes he had found were the smallest three types used.
   - When writing a price, the bigger coins are always used where possible. So an item with a price of 5 Smalls (for example) would be evidence that a Medium could not be worth 5 Smalls or less.

- No price ever requires more than 9 of any type of coin.
- The Small coin has a value of 1.

a If the Medium coin had a value of 5 and the Large coin had a value of 19, how would the price of an item with a value of 30 be written, in terms of L, M and S?

b If a price of 2L, 0M and 1S can be paid for precisely with 1 Large, 3 Medium and 4 Small coins, give one example of possible values for the Medium and Large coins.

c The first price found was for a jug priced 3M, 6S. What are the only four possible values for this jug?

d Some time later, a necklace priced 1L, 6M, 7S was found.

   i) What is the largest possible value for this necklace?

   ii) What is the smallest possible value for this necklace?

   iii) Initially, the archaeologist believes the necklace has a value of 118. Deduce what the values of the Medium and Large coins would be if this were the case.

   iv) What is the smallest possible value for the necklace which would **not** allow the values of the Medium and Large coins to be deduced?

   v) What value for the necklace could still be explained by three different values of the Large coin?

(Cambridge AS & A Level Thinking Skills 9694, Paper 32 Q3, June 2016)

Representing 3D situations

There are three classic mechanisms for representing three-dimensional objects on the two-dimensional page: isometric drawing, nets and plans/elevations. Each of these has its strengths and drawbacks, and each requires familiarity in order to be used competently.

Competence and confidence in dealing with problems which arise only in three dimensions can be achieved by manipulating the three mechanisms mentioned above, and by developing visualisation skills. The latter process has the graphic powers of interactive three-dimensional Computer Generated Imagery as its goal, and some people find this easier than others.

ACTIVITY

Visualising 3D shapes

1 Imagine you have a cube of cheese, which has a white crust on the outside and is yellow inside. What different two-dimensional yellow shapes could you make with one straight slice of a knife?

2 Imagine cutting a cube with one slice, the knife entering exactly along the diagonal of one face and leaving at the opposite corner. How many edges and faces would this shape have?

3 If you had a pile of these shapes, how many would you need to assemble into a cube?

Confidence in the use of isometric drawing, nets and plans/elevations requires technical mathematical skill. The best way to do this is to take an actual three-dimensional object (made from interlocking cubes) and represent it using the three mechanisms.

To think about

Three spiders are considering how to complete certain journeys on the surface of a cube, which is suspended in space.

One decides she wishes to go from the middle of the face numbered '5' to the middle of the face numbered '2'.

One decides she wishes to go between two corners that are furthest apart.

One decides she wishes to traverse every face of the cube.

```
      ┌───┐
      │ 1 │
  ┌───┼───┼───┐
  │ 2 │ 3 │ 4 │
  └───┼───┼───┘
      │ 5 │
      ├───┤
      │ 6 │
      └───┘
```

Net   Isometric   Plan, front and side elevations

   [3] [5] [2]

- Which path is shortest for each spider?
- Which means of presentation is best for analysing each situation?

1 The diagram shows a solid cube and its reflection in a mirror.

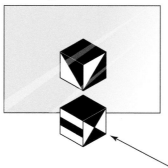

The bottom face of the cube is completely white.

Draw what can be seen from the direction of the arrow (looking up towards the bottom corner, on the right-hand side of the picture).

(Adapted from Cambridge AS & A Level Thinking Skills 9694,
Paper 13 Q28, June 2011)

➤

2 A plan view of the buildings at a college campus is shown below, along with the heights of each of the buildings 1–6.

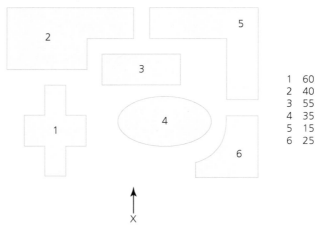

1	60
2	40
3	55
4	35
5	15
6	25

Draw an outline sketch of the skyline view from 'X'.

(Adapted from Cambridge AS & A Level Thinking Skills 9694, Paper 11 Q18, June 2015)

3 A decoration is made from a cardboard net, folded into a prism, with the letter 'A' written on it. It is to be hung from one corner, where a hole is made for the string, which is marked with an arrow in this diagram:

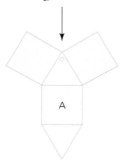

Where should the hole be made on the following net if it is to be folded into a decoration which will look exactly the same?

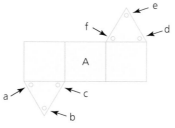

Taking it further

4 The ruins of old Illyrian temples in the featureless plains of Bolandia have been used as a source of stone blocks for building houses over the years,

so the various photographs that have been taken over time show columns of different heights. As it's usually cloudy, there are no shadows to help to determine from which direction any particular picture has been taken. All temples originally had columns that were made from six blocks, and all the blocks were identical cylinders, one cubit in height. No blocks have been added to the temples since they were originally built.

One temple has four columns, and this is a plan view showing the heights (in cubits) of the columns now:

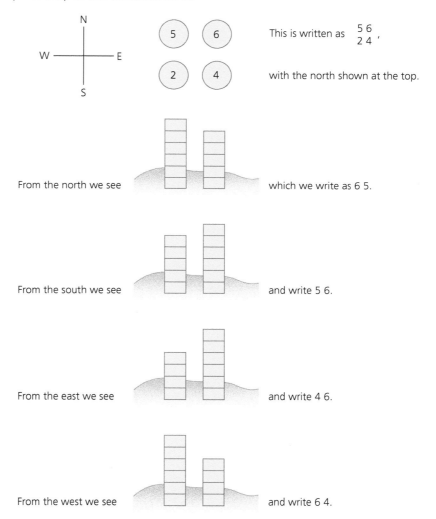

a   A different temple of four columns also has the heights 5 6 as seen from one side and 4 6 from another.

i)   What is the greatest possible total number of blocks in this ruin?

ii) What is the smallest possible total number of blocks in this ruin?

b Two pictures of another four-column ruin have been found.

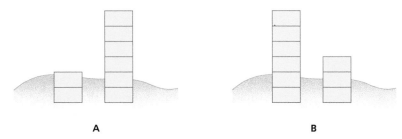

A   B

 i) Draw a possible plan view of the ruin to show that these pictures could have been taken at the same time.

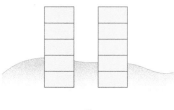

C

A further picture of the same ruin was found.

From this it is now certain that the three pictures A, B and C were all taken at different times.

 ii) Give the order in which they were taken, and draw a possible sequence of plan views showing the ruin at the three times.

(Cambridge AS & A Level Thinking Skills 9694,
Paper 31 Q1 (a) & (b), June 2011)

Relative measures

When measures are significant in relation to their group, or when values change over time, there are a number of ways of expressing the change.

These are barely part of the modelling of the problem, in that most of the alternatives are logically equivalent (in fact, they relate to the model descriptions rather than the model). But as a developing problem solver you must be well aware of in the different ways of referring to absolute and relative changes, and be able to choose the most appropriate.

For example, if the number of one cent coins in my pocket goes from three (out of twelve coins) on Monday to four (out of twenty coins) on Tuesday, this could be presented in any of the following ways:

How the change is described	How the figure is achieved
A The number of one cent coins increased by 1	$4 - 3 = 1$
B The total number of coins increased by 8	$20 - 12 = 8$
C The increase in the total number of coins was 8 times the increase in one cent coins	$8 \div 1 = 8$
D The number of one cent coins increased by $\frac{1}{3}$ (or roughly 33%)	$\dfrac{\text{Change in number of one cent coins}}{\text{Initial number of one cent coins}} = \dfrac{1}{3}$
E The total number of coins increased by $\frac{2}{3}$ (or roughly 67%)	$\dfrac{\text{Change in total number of coins}}{\text{Initial total number of coins}} = \dfrac{8}{12} = \dfrac{2}{3}$
F The proportional increase in total coins was double the proportional increase in one cent coins	$\frac{2}{3}$ [from E] $\div \frac{1}{3}$ [from D] $= 2$
G On Monday 25% of the coins were one cent coins	$\dfrac{3 \text{ [one cent coins]}}{12 \text{ [coins in total]}} = 0.25$
H On Tuesday 20% of the coins were one cent coins	$\dfrac{4 \text{ [one cent coins]}}{20 \text{ [coins in total]}} = 0.2$
I The proportion of one cent coins decreased by 5% from Monday to Tuesday	$\frac{3}{12}$ [from G] $- \frac{4}{20}$ [from H] $=$ $\dfrac{25}{100} - \dfrac{20}{100} = \dfrac{5}{100}$
J The proportion of one cent coins decreased by $\frac{1}{5}$	$\dfrac{\text{Change in proportion}}{\text{Initial proportion}} = \dfrac{5\% \text{ [from I]}}{25\% \text{ [from G]}} = \dfrac{1}{5}$
K The proportion of coins that were not one cent coins increased by $\frac{1}{15}$	$\dfrac{\text{Change in proportion}}{\text{Initial proportion}} = \dfrac{80\% - 75\%}{75\%} = \dfrac{1}{15}$

This is not an exhaustive list, but it shows how the combination of proportion and change can be presented in diverse ways. As a problem solver, one is often trying to make inferences about the original data from the summaries given.

> ### ACTIVITY
>
> **Describing change**
>
> *Find as many ways as possible of describing the following change.*
>
> At the beginning of last year, four out of the ten students in my form were girls.
>
> At the end of the year, one girl joined the class and two boys left.

1

> Try this problem yourself, before reading the analysis!

Imagine you calculate that you have $300 and 99 per cent of it is in cash (the rest is in the bank). You then go shopping and spend some of your cash, and when you return you calculate that 98 per cent of your wealth is in cash. How much did you spend?

The key to this question is to focus on the amount of money that is in the bank. This remains $3 throughout the shopping expedition, but changes from being 1 per cent of the total money available to 2 per cent. This allows the total to be calculated:

$3 is 2 per cent of $150, and therefore this is what must have been left after the shopping trip. This implies that $150 was spent.

1 In a local soccer league where a win counts for three points and a draw one point, the leaders at the end of March were Yoxall, with 40 points. They had lost one-third of their games, drawn half as many as they lost and won three times as many as they had drawn. At the end of the season, the number of games they had lost had doubled, and their final total was 42 points.

How many games did they play between the end of March and the end of the season?

(Adapted from Cambridge AS & A Level Thinking Skills 9694, Paper 11 Q13, November 2014)

2 The hardware superstore is selling the paint I want at '3 tins for the price of 2'. This weekend I can get a further 10% off with my loyalty card. What will be the overall reduction from the full price if I buy three tins of paint this weekend?

(Adapted from Cambridge AS & A Level Thinking Skills 9694, Paper 12 Q1, June 2013)

3 Monsurat and Nafisa empty their loose change onto the table. Monsurat calculates that she has 10% more money than Nafisa. But Nafisa points out that Monsurat owes her $10 from lunch. After Monsurat gives this to her, Nafisa calculates that she has 10% more than Monsurat.

a If their calculations are correct, how much must Monsurat have had to start with?

Nafisa then realises that she has not got 10% more than Monsurat, but only 1% more.

b How much did Monsurat start with?

Taking it further

4 Juseph is trying to recreate the breakfast that his grandmother used to make for him – it involved adding some ingredients to 'pre-mixed' muesli. He can remember a few facts about it.

The pre-mixed muesli contained raisins, oats and wheat in the ratio 4:3:2 (by volume).

His grandmother used to then double the amount of oats, and add in an extra handful of wheat.

At this point, the mix contained equal amounts of oats and wheat.

a What fraction of the mix was muesli at this point?

Juseph's grandmother would then add a 'load of dried fruit' from her jar. He remembers that the jar contained dried figs, dried cherries and berries in the ratio 1:2:3

After the fruit had been added, the amount of fruit (including the raisins) equalled the amount of cereal (including oats and wheat).

b What fraction of the mix was cherries at this point?

Finally she would add 'two dollops of yoghurt and a dollop of honey'. The dollops were delivered using one of her imperial table spoons – Juseph has one of these, and calculates that it contains 100 ml.

This mixture would exactly fill one of the '1000 ml' bowls that breakfast was eaten out of.

➤

c   What is the smallest quantity of any of the ingredients (in ml)?

Juseph realises that he has not got any extra wheat, and so will have to reduce the quantities of everything in order to achieve the right mix.

d   What quantity of oats will he need to remove from the pre-mixed muesli?

e   How much honey will he need?

1.3 Presentation of information

You have looked at the sources of problems.

You have interacted with them.

You have looked at how a problem can be tamed, by modelling it, and the difficulties that accompany this.

We must now look at how a problem is presented on the written page.

The point at which a problem is presented is the moment at which a real-world situation begins to transition into a real-world solution. Some of the modelling will have been completed, and there will be some left to do. The following flowchart offers a schematic structure of this process, followed by an example:

Phase 1: The raw problem, as it occurs in the world

A problem in the real world is, by its nature, the problem in its 'raw' state. It cannot occur on the page without losing its 'rawness' and any attempt to describe it here will inevitably shift it into Phase 2.

Phase 2: Articulation of the problem verbally

A spoken description of the problem, for example:

> *Last summer we ran a summer training camp for our football team – the first we've ever done – and it does look like we were scoring more goals this year as a result. In previous years most internal games (between our own teams) involved three goals or fewer being scored, whereas this year there were more goals ...*

Phase 3: A formal presentation of the problem

All elements of the problem, and data related to the problem, are presented clearly on the page.

The table below records the scores of 100 games in a football league. The entries show the number of games in which the teams have scored the number of goals shown in the headings (for example, there were ten games in which the home team scored two goals and the away teams scored one goal).

		Goals scored by the home team				
		0	1	2	3	4 or more
Goals scored by the away team	0	12	8	8	4	4
	1	3	7	10	3	2
	2	5	7	8	3	2
	3	5	3	2	0	0
	4 or more	3	1	0	0	0

In how many games were three or more goals scored?

*(Adapted from Cambridge AS & A Level Thinking Skills 8436,
Paper 1 Q20, June 2005)*

Phase 4: Representation of the problem by the problem solver

As a problem solver you take the information presented on the page and represent it in a way that makes the solution self-evident.

▲ The table of goals, with relevant information highlighted

Phase 5: Presentation of a solution

As a result of your analysis, you are able to clearly present the solution to the problem.

> *Last season there were 57 games (100 – 43) in which three or more goals were scored.*

> *This was significantly better than previous years, and on balance the training camp seems to have been effective. Let's organise another one this year.*

This five-phase process is an excellent way of breaking any problem into manageable segments. The problems you face may vary in level of difficulty; for example, within this course you will encounter some questions that are closer to Phase 2 and others that are closer to Phase 4, but, regardless of how difficult they are, you need to develop a refined, directed alertness when engaging with presented information.

Information can be presented in a number of different formats, and each comes with its own peculiarities. These are discussed below.

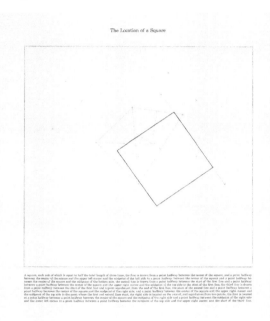

The Location of a Square

▲ This work by Sol Lewitt shows how the choice of the way in which information is presented dramatically affects how accessible it is

Text

Text is capable of supporting, and communicating, the most diverse range of information, and all problems will require some text.

All problems, as presented in exam questions, may contain some surplus information which is not vital for the solution of the problem. This is even more the case in real-life problem solving! Take, for example, the case of a doctor trying to diagnose the cause of a patient's illness. The doctor will begin by questioning the patient about their troubles and, from the information the patient gives, will identify and select the details which are relevant – these are the aspects requiring further investigation.

The first job is to separate the information which is needed to solve the problem from that which is not needed.

Example	

In the first phase of the annual Kolfeit Ice Hockey Tournament, the 32 participating teams are divided into 8 groups of 4. In each group all the teams play each other once.

The group winners progress to the knockout phase, which consists of quarter-finals, semi-finals and the final. This means that all the teams play at least 3 matches, while the two teams that contest the final play 6 matches.

As well as the winners' trophy, there is an award made to the team with the highest average number of goals scored per game during the tournament. This year's 'highest average' award was won by the Blizzards, with an average of 4.75 goals per match.

How far did the Blizzards progress in this year's tournament?

(Adapted from Cambridge AS & A Level Thinking Skills 9694, Paper 11 Q7, June 2015)

A version in which details not needed to solve the problem were redacted would look like this:

> *In the first phase of the annual Kolfeit Ice Hockey Tournament the 32 participating teams are divided into 8 groups of 4. In each group all the teams play each other once.*
>
> *The group winners progress to the knockout phase, which consists of quarter-finals, semi-finals and the final. This means that all the teams play at least 3 matches, while the two teams that contest the final play 6 matches.*
>
> *As well as the winners' trophy, there is an award made to the team with the highest average number of goals scored per game during the tournament. This year's 'highest average' award was won by the Blizzards, with an average of 4.75 goals per match.*
>
> *How far did the Blizzards progress in this year's tournament?*

A redacted version with the key elements highlighted might look like this:

> *In the first phase of the annual Kolfeit Ice Hockey Tournament the 32 participating teams are divided into 8 groups of 4. In each group all the teams play each other once.*
>
> *The group winners progress to the knockout phase, which consists of quarter-finals, semi-finals and the final. This means that all the teams play at least 3 matches, while the two teams that contest the final play 6 matches.*
>
> *As well as the winners' trophy, there is an award made to the team with the highest average number of goals scored per game during the tournament. This year's 'highest average' award was won by the Blizzards, with an average of 4.75 goals per match.*
>
> *How far did the Blizzards progress in this year's tournament?*

The key information extracted and bulleted:

» 8 teams of 4

» knockout phase of 3 rounds

» average number of goals per match is 4.75.

This is clear enough to prompt a breakdown of the average into a possible fraction – see Section 5.3 for a reminder of how averages work.

$$4.75 = 4\tfrac{3}{4} \text{ or } \boxed{\tfrac{19}{4}} \text{ or } \tfrac{38}{8} \text{ or.....}$$

A brief consideration of the alternatives shows that the only candidate is $\frac{19}{4}$ and that the Blizzards must have competed in four games. As a result they must have reached the quarter-finals. The process of redacting, then highlighting, then writing bullet points formalises what you should do when faced with complex pieces of text, where selecting and arranging the relevant data is challenging. You do not need to do it every time, but you should try it with some complex cases since it is a useful part of your toolkit for interacting with tough questions with time limitations.

Practice questions

Apply the 'redact – highlight – bullet' approach to each of these questions.

1 One of the most important parts of a railway track are the sleepers (also known as ties) to which the metal rails are attached. These sleepers make sure that the rails do not move and the distance between the rails remains the same.

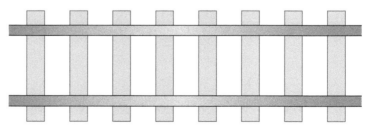

Originally, sleepers were made from wood like oak, but in modern times they are made from concrete. As wood rots, the oak sleepers are replaced with concrete ones. Each 10 km section is replaced over a period of three months. There are 2400 sleepers per km of track.

In the first month, one third of the sleepers were replaced. In the second month, two fifths of the remaining sleepers were replaced.

How many sleepers had to be replaced in the final month to complete the task?

(Adapted from Cambridge AS & A Level Thinking Skills 9694, Paper 11 Q9, June 2015)

2   The cost of a mortgage (loan) for buying a house used to be very simple:
a fixed cost for paperwork, cost of a survey depending on the house value,
and then a specified interest rate for an agreed number of years. There is
now a bewildering range of mortgages. The variety is supposedly to cater
for different markets, but it makes it hard to compare the offerings of
different providers.

One type provided by many companies is a discounted rate, where there
is a fixed 'arrangement' fee, and then an interest rate which remains lower
than the company's regular rate for a given time, but with an early-
repayment charge if the loan is repaid before the end of the discount
period. At the end of the discount period, the rate switches to the regular
rate, and there is then no repayment charge.

The Best Prudosian Bank's one-year regular (simple) rate is 3.0%, but it
offers discounted rates:

Arrangement fee	Discounted (simple) rate	Early-repayment charge
$1000	2.6%	1.00%
$2000	2.5%	1.50%

If not repaying early, what is the minimum loan for which the total cost to
have the discounted rate with the higher fee is less than either the other
discount or the regular rate?

(Adapted from Cambridge AS & A Level Thinking Skills 9694,
Paper 12 Q23, June 2012)

Taking it further

3   Three sisters have devised a method to share a cake between them.
Although none of the three is very good at cutting 120° slices, they are
all good at identifying a fair portion. Assume that all portions are a whole
number of degrees.

Their method involves allowing one of them to propose a cut by marking
lines on the icing on the top of the cake. The cake is then passed to the
next sister who will improve upon the proposed division, if she can, by
smoothing out one of the lines and re-marking it herself. The third sister
then does the same.

Their method for improving upon a division involves moving the line between the largest and smallest portions so as to even out those portions. Where the largest and smallest portions add up to an odd number of degrees, one of the resulting portions is 1° bigger than the other. For example, portions of 110° and 136° would be adjusted to become two portions of 123° each, and portions of 110° and 137° would become portions of 123° and 124°.

The first sister's division never includes portions bigger than 165° or smaller than 75°. The sisters never attempt to improve a division where the difference between the largest and smallest portions is 10° or less.

The first sister marked a cake into portions of 102°, 128° and 130°, and each of the other two sisters made an improvement upon the division.

a   What sizes were the portions after each sister had made her improvement?

The first sister marked a second cake into portions, which was then improved by the second sister, giving portions of 104°, 128° and 128°.

b   Give an example of what the first division might have been.

(Cambridge AS & A Level Thinking Skills 9694, Paper 32 Q2 (a) & (b), June 2015)

While a mantra such as 'redact – highlight – bullet' can be useful, it is worth remembering that this is just a gimmick.

Written text often obscures logical relationships, and particular care must be taken when extracting them. The logical relations of sufficiency and necessity are particularly tricky and need great care (see page 67).

The grammar of a sentence in English does not always reflect the logic. Try to ensure that you interrogate all sentences written in English if their grammar is unclear, especially if English is not your mother tongue. The more varied the sentence structures you encounter, and interrogate, the more alert you will be to subtleties in grammar.

A famous example of how ambiguous statements can be is:

> *Let's eat Grandma!*

Consider why this is ambiguous. It is normally accompanied by the advice: 'Punctuation saves lives.'

Tables

Tables are the classic way of showing how two variables relate to each other. What is true of all such tables is *the meaning of any number in a cell can be inferred by linking the row heading and the column heading.*

Whenever faced with an unfamiliar table or graph, you should check that you are able to articulate its basic relationship first (**unpack it**).

When you are sure you can take any individual piece of information from the table and parse it as a natural-sounding sentence, you should practise **interrogating it**. This can involve seeking out pieces of information, comparing pieces of information and making deeper inferences.

Tables can encode many different types of information. They can be used to show the differences between a group of objects, people or places (normally times, distances or costs); they can be used to show how certain groups have scored according to certain metrics (the classic example being the details of how a sports team has performed over a season); they can show the order and the times that certain events occur (a bus timetable being a standard example).

Three examples of how a table can be unpacked and interrogated are given below.

Table 1 Showing the distances between five islands, in kilometres

Renaee				
63	Shola			
20	48	Muna		
25	54	29	Ayesh	
88	35	77	71	Ejiro

Unpack it

To unpack the table it is worth choosing a few random numbers and forcing them into a sentence: for instance, the '54' is explained by the link between 'Shola' and 'Ayesh'. In this case, 'the distance between the islands of Shola and Ayesh is 54 km'.

Interrogate it

1 Find! Give yourself the task of extracting a piece of information from the table. For example, how far is it from Renaee to Ejiro?

2 Compare! Give yourself the task of comparing or contrasting two pieces of information. For example, where is furthest from Muna?

3 Infer! This requires using the information to find a limit, or an optimum. For example, show that it is possible to get round all five islands in 151 km (without returning to the starting point).

Table 2 Showing how eight teams fared in seven football matches

	Played	Won	Drawn	Lost	First goal	Points
Avocets	7	2	2	3	4	7
Dunlins	7	0	2	5	2	7
Godwits	7	3	2	2	4	7
Shrikes	7	3	1	3	3	7
Lapwings	7	2	0	5	2	7
Curlews	7	3	2	2	4	7
Stints	7	2	2	3	2	7
Egrets	7	6	1	0	6	7

Unpack it

Again, choose a few random numbers and try forcing them into a sentence. Here, the '4' in the top row is explained by the link between 'First Goal Scored' and 'Avocets'. In this case, 'the team called Avocets scored the first goal in four of their matches'.

Interrogate it

1   Find! Who won the most matches?

2   Compare! How many teams lost more than half their matches?

3   Infer! How many matches were 0 – 0 draws?

Table 3 Showing the times that five buses reach the bus stops on their journey from Annfield, through Bowes, Chester and Durham, to reach Elton

Bus Timetable					
ANNFIELD	13:08	13:17	14:10	14:32	14:42
BOWES	13:40	13:50	14:30	15:02	15:18
CHESTER	14:13	14:28	14:58	15:23	15:50
DURHAM	14:28	14:50	15:16	15:38	16:06
ELTON	14:50	15:12	15:38	15:56	16:20

Unpack it

Select a few random numbers and force them into a sentence. For example, the '15:16' is explained by being in the third column, in the row labelled Durham. In this case 'the third bus of the day from Durham to Elton leaves at 3:16 in the afternoon'.

Interrogate it

1   Find! When does the first bus reach Elton?

2   Compare! Does the journey from Bowes to Chester take the same amount of time for all five buses?

3   Infer! What is the latest bus you could catch from Annfield if you wanted to spend 40 minutes shopping in Chester and meet a friend in Elton at 16:00?

Practice questions

1   The table below shows the office opening hours (in local time) for a company's offices in five countries. It also shows the time difference from Greenwich Mean Time for each country (+2 hrs means that when it is 12:00 in Greenwich, it is 2 p.m. in that country).

Country	Asinica	Bolsovia	Carbenia	Dervia	Eruthia
+/– GMT	+1 hr	–3 hrs	+7 hrs	+5 hrs	–8 hrs
Opens	8:00 a.m.	9:00 a.m.	8:30 a.m.	9:00 a.m.	7:30 a.m.
Closes	5:00 p.m.	6:00 p.m.	5:00 p.m.	5:30 p.m.	4:30 p.m.

Unpack it

Choose a number and write a sentence about it.

Interrogate it

a   What time is it in Greenwich when the office opens in Asinica?

b   Which office opens earliest?

c   Is there a time when all five offices are open? When can someone in the Asinica office call someone in the office in Eruthia?

(Adapted from Cambridge AS & A Level Thinking skills 8436, Paper 1 Q46, June 2004)

2   The bus from Lincoln to Barnsby Horses runs according to the following timetable:

Lincoln Bus Station	10:15	11:15	12:15		14:15	15:15
Saxilby High St	10:30	11:30	12:30		..	..
Sturton by Stow A1500	10:35	11:35	12:35		..	..
Barnsby Horses	10:45	11:45	12:45		14:35	15:35
Barnsby Horses	10:45	11:45		13:45	14:45	15:45
Sturton by Stow A1500	..	..		13:50	14:50	15:50
Saxilby High St	..	..		14:00	15:00	16:00
Lincoln Bus Station	11:05	12:05		14:15	15:15	16:15

Unpack it

Choose a number and write a sentence about it.

Interrogate it

a   When does the last bus leave Barnsby Horses?

b   What is the longest and shortest times it can take on the bus, to get from Saxilby to Sturton by Stow?

c   The driver complains that it always takes an extra minute to drop off and pick up passengers at each stop, and so he runs late. If what the driver says is precisely true, by how much must the driver shorten his lunch break?

3   The following table shows a summary of the matches played in the Fantasy World Cup. Teams gain 3 points for a win, 2 points for a score draw (1 − 1, 2 − 2 and so on) and 1 point for a scoreless draw (0 − 0). Each team plays each other once.

This is the final table for Group 3:

	Played	Won	Drawn	Lost	Goals For	Goals Against	Points
Narnia	5	3	2	0	10	2	12
Omnia	5	3	1	1	8	2	11
Xanadu	5	2	1	2	8	6	8
Utopia	5	2	1	2	5	6	7
Lilliput	5	1	1	3	2	9	5
Ruritania	5	0	2	3	2	10	4

Unpack it

Choose a number and write a sentence about it.

Interrogate it

a   How many goals did Lilliput score over the five matches?

b   How many of Ruritania's matches were scoreless draws?

c   Use the following newspaper report and the information in the table to determine which team Narnia drew against 2-2 against in their last group match: *"Narnia were losing 2-0 during their last match, but two late goals from Tumus, Narnia's strike, ensured qualification for the semi-finals."*

(Adapted from Cambridge AS & A Level Thinking skills 9694, Paper 12 Q29, June 2013)

Taking it further

4   Eightskate is a sport in which two teams of eight compete on roller skates.

An eightskate match consists of 12 heats. In each heat, three skaters from each of the two teams are nominated by the respective team managers to race around a 300 m circuit. The skater who crosses the line last at the end of the second lap drops out. This is repeated at the end of the third, fourth and fifth laps – these retiring skaters being ranked fifth, fourth and third respectively. The remaining pair continues for a sixth lap to determine first and second positions.

An eightskate match between Grinnon Bears and Lowan Sharks is currently in progress and is about to reach its climax. The two team managers will shortly nominate their skaters for Heat 12.

This is the score sheet as it stands at present:

Grinnon Bears v. Lowan Sharks

BEARS	Points Scored												
Heat	1	2	3	4	5	6	7	8	9	10	11	12	Total
T. Black	2			0		1		3		0			
O. Brown		4		4			5			5			
L. Grizzly	1			1		0		4			2		
E. Honey	5		4		5				2				
R. Kodiak			0			3		0		2			
A. Malay		2			1			2			5		
T. Polar			2			4			1				
E. Ursa		3		5			0			4			
Team	8	9	6	10	6	7	6	6	6	11	7		

SHARKS	Points Scored												
Heat	1	2	3	4	5	6	7	8	9	10	11	12	Total
S. Angel		0			2		4		0				
W. Basking	4		3		5				5		3		
I. Hammer		5		3		1		5					
N. Head				2			3			3			
D. Horn		1			4			1		0			
L. Nurse	0		5			2				4	4		
E. Tiger	3			0			2			1			
R. White			1		3			3			1		
Team	7	6	9	5	9	8	9	9	9	4	8		

Points are awarded as follows:

Position	Heats 1 to 11	Heat 12 only
First	5 points	10 points
Second	4 points	7 points
Third	3 points	4 points
Fourth	2 points	2 points
Fifth	1 point	1 point
Sixth	0 points	0 points

When nominating the skaters for any heat, a team manager must be careful to comply with the following rules:

- All skaters must be nominated for a minimum of 4 heats.
- No skater may be nominated for two consecutive heats.
- The same three skaters may not all be nominated together a second time.

a After which heat did the Sharks first take the overall lead in the match?

b i) What is the maximum total distance (in metres) that one skater could possibly skate during an eightskate match?

   ii) What is the total distance (in metres) that Edward Ursa has skated so far during this match?

c Select a possible line-up of three skaters to compete in Heat 12 for

   i) the Bears

   ii) the Sharks.

d i) Assuming that no skater drops out, is it possible for any eightskate match to end in a draw? Explain your answer.

ii) Rupert, a keen Bears fan, fears that his team can win the match in progress only if they secure first position in Heat 12. Is he right? Explain your answer.

(Cambridge AS & A Level Thinking Skills 9694, Paper 31 Q4, June 2011)

Graphs

On the journey from the real world to an artful problem expressed and solved in an exam hall, raw data is often marshalled into a table, and then presented in a graph. While tables are about ordering the data, graphs are about presenting it, often to support a particular claim.

A good graph is like a fully-formed argument – posing a problem, analysing it and presenting the solution in one go:

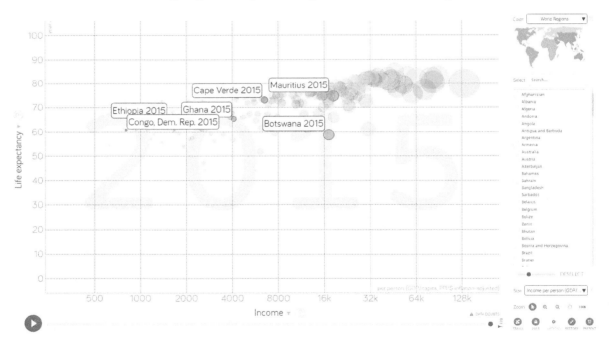

▲ 'Africa is not a country' as presented by www.gapminder.org

This famous graph, created by Hans Rosling (a superstar statistician), demonstrates one of the first laws of graph interpretation: respect the labels, and especially the units, on the axes. They introduce the characters in the story. In this case, the scatter diagram manages to capture four different changing variables for each of the countries: the population (represented by the size of the circle), the income of those in the country (expressed so as to avoid confounding factors such as the relative desirability of currencies, or inflation), the average life expectancy, and the year (the latter visible only when you animate the graph online).

There are four main specialist types of graph:

» Those that aim to compare the frequencies of certain characteristics, referred to as **frequency charts**. These are typically composite bar charts, or cumulative frequency diagrams.

» Those that aim to demonstrate changes over time, referred to as **time charts**, and which include any graph with time as a continuous scale along the horizontal axis.

» Those that aim to demonstrate proportions, referred to as **proportion charts** – the most common being the pie chart.

» Those that aim to demonstrate correlation, referred to as **correlation charts** – the most common being a scatter diagram.

As with the previously discussed tables, the key to understanding is to 'inhabit' the graph and then consider what can be inferred from it. This can be done by converting 'the facts of the matter' into a graph, or by analysing a graph (and establishing what it shows). Looking at the four types of graph in turn, we will now consider how our senses need to be heightened when analysing each one.

Frequency charts

These can be unpacked and interrogated, like the tables. Rather than articulating each piece of data with reference to its row and column heading, you need to take a point and identify its position on the horizontal and vertical axes, before attempting to frame the sentence which it represents.

The graph below shows the cumulative distribution of finishing times in a marathon:

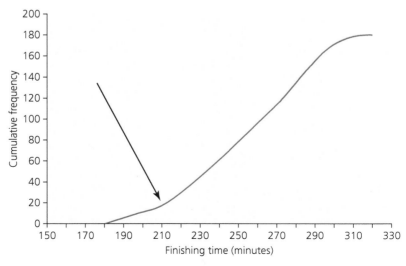

▲ **Cumulative distribution of finishing times in Prudosia**

Unpack it

The point indicated by the arrow – what exactly is it telling you?
Something like '20 people finished the marathon in 210 minutes or less'.

Interrogate it

1 Find! How many people finished in 4 hours or less?

2 Compare! Which group finished closer together – the first 10
   competitors or the last 10 competitors?

3 Infer! My cousin and I finished exactly 100 places apart, and exactly
   50 minutes apart – is it possible to tell where we finished?

Time charts

Time graphs tell a story, and tell them so well that extremists claim
that some stories are actually better when graphed.

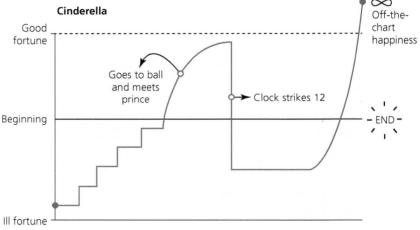

▲ **The fairytale of Cinderella, shown as a graph**

The key to time graphs, as with all graphs, is to reduce them to sets of
key points if the 'story' is unclear.

To think about

Which of these could represent the height of a tree growing over a number of
years?

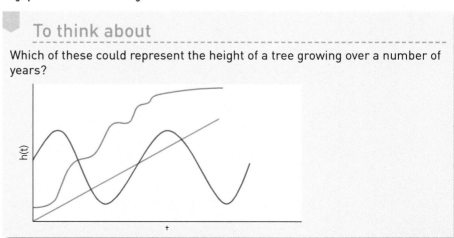

Speed and gradient

The rates at which the variables change will correspond to the gradient of the line. At a descriptive level this just means that the steeper a line is, the quicker it changes over time. At a more precise level, this involves defining the rate of change, and the gradient, as:

$$\frac{\text{Change in vertical variable}}{\text{Change in horizontal variable}}$$

This results in gradient (of a line), rate of change and speed (on a time graph) all being the same. You do not need to meditate too hard on why or how these are the same, but you do need to remember that the speed (on a distance or time graph) can be found by calculating its gradient – there is more on this in Chapter 5.

Sample question

Try this problem yourself, before reading the analysis!

Every Sunday in the town of Handel, there is a free concert in the town hall. Many people of the town walk past the hall during the morning, and decide whether to stay for the concert.

The doors to the hall open 2 hours before the concert starts.

The organisers know, from experience, that people choosing to listen to the concert arrive at a constant rate for the first hour; the rate doubles in the next 40 minutes and then doubles again for the final 20 minutes. No-one is allowed into the hall after the concert starts.

The hall holds 400 people.

   a   What is the smallest number of people arriving in the first ten minutes that would imply there was not enough space in the hall?

The concert lasts for an hour: when it is over everybody leaves at a constant rate of 30 people per minute, until the hall is empty.

   b   Draw a graph showing the number of people in the hall, if 30 people came in the first 10 minutes that the doors were open.

   a   This could be done by 'trial and error' (see Section 2.4) but is most efficiently done with a function machine or algebra (see Section 3.1).

If we call the number who come in the first 10 minutes 'r'

then r × 6 = the number who come in the first hour

(r × 2) × 4 = the number who come in the next 40 minutes

(r × 4) × 2 = the number who come in the final 20 minutes

and these must add together to give more than 400, if there is not enough space

i.e. 6r + 8r + 8r > 400

or 22r > 400

and so r > 18.18.

r must be a whole number : so we can conclude that 19 people in the first ten minutes would be the smallest value to imply the hall is full. It is worth checking that this gives a reasonable answer: $(19 \times 6) + (38 \times 4) + (76 \times 2) = 418$ people, which is marginally greater than the capacity of the hall.

b The rates given (30 per 10 minutes, 60 per 10 minutes, 120 per 10 minutes, 30 per minute) can be used to give snapshots of the graph.

The following list gives the time in minutes (in brackets) and the number of people at that time:

(10) 30, (20) 60, (30) 90, (40) 120, (50) 150, (60) 180, (70) 240, (80) 300, (90) 360, (97) 400, (120) 400, (180) 400, (190) 100, (193) 0

This can then be converted into a time graph:

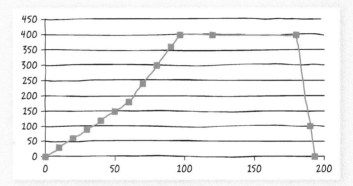

Proportion charts

Pie charts show proportions, not absolute values. This is a simple fact, but one that's easy to be caught out by.

When comparing pie charts (with other pie charts or with data represented in other ways) you need to remind yourself that a bigger slice of the pie does not reflect a big number but a bigger proportion of the whole.

Pie charts have no axes – and often have no numbers on them at all – but there are two ways that you can make inferences from them:

1 The relative sizes of the slices allow you to rank the different categories.

2 The 'easy fractions' visible in a pie chart allow you to decide which slices represent more or less than $\frac{1}{4}$, $\frac{1}{2}$ and $\frac{3}{4}$ of the whole.

To think about

How many precise angles can you create, given only a piece of (rectangular) paper?

- There is a 180° angle-template waiting to be used along the edge of any piece of paper.
- There is a 90° angle-template waiting to be used at the corner.

Can you make a 60° degree angle using only a piece of paper and two folds?

What other angles can you make using just a piece of paper?

Correlation charts

Scatter diagrams expose correlations between two variables. They are wheeled in as pieces of 'showcase statistics' when you are young, and then exposed as instruments of deception when you come of age (with the slogan 'correlation does not imply causation').

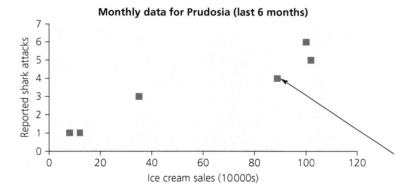

▲ A graph showing number of reported shark attacks, and the number of ice creams sold (in 10 000s) during the last six months in Prudosia

This graph prompts discussion of how correlation relates to causation. The pattern that can be seen in the graph (the fact that the points lie on a roughly straight line going from bottom left to top right) can betray at least three different relationships: A causes B, B causes A, something causes them both. There is little you can actually infer from a trend without knowing about the possible causal mechanisms, however – that is, having some explanation of how changes in one variable can lead to changes in another. This kind of explanation is normally established under close scrutiny in a laboratory.

What is more likely to invite a higher-level problem-solving approach is the interrogation of the individual data points themselves, by applying the same principles as with the other graph.

Unpack it

The point indicated by the arrow – what exactly is it telling you? Something like 'during one month, between January and June, there were four reported shark attacks and approximately 90 000 ice creams sold in Prudosia'.

Interrogate it

1 Find! What was the largest number of reported shark attacks in a calendar month?

2 Compare! How many reported shark attacks were there in the last six months?

If the trend shown was to continue, how many ice creams would you expect to be sold during a month in which there were two shark attacks?

3 Infer! What is the greatest and least number of shark attacks that could have occurred in a 30-day period in the last six months in Prudosia?

Practice questions

1 The number of boxes of apples that can be harvested from a tree depends on its age. The following graphs show the expected yield from *Todd's Tastiest* variety.

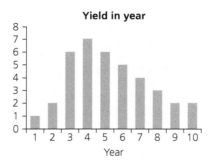
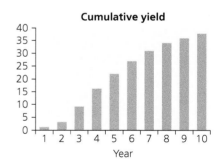

Unpack it

Choose a data point and write a sentence about it.

Interrogate it

a Find! In which year was the yield highest?

b Compare! Between which years was the greatest change in yield?

c Infer! To get the greatest average yield, how often should these trees be replaced?

(Adapted from Cambridge AS & A Level Thinking Skills 9694, Paper 11 Q21, November 2014)

2   The graph below shows, in cumulative form, the estimated salt
    consumption per day of the British public.

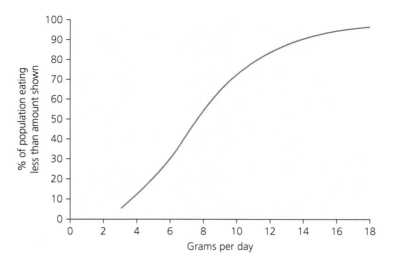

Unpack it
Choose a data point and write a sentence about it.

Interrogate it

a   Find! Roughly what percentage of the population eat less than 8 g
    per day?

b   Compare! If the amount of salt people consumed was rounded to the
    nearest whole number, which amount do the least people consume,
    according to the graph?

c   Infer! What percentage of the British population consume more than
    twice the recommended daily amount, which is 6 g?

3   The winner of the Perfect Piecrust award is about to be announced and
    the presenter stands with the envelopes, including the three runners-up
    and the one winner, in his hand.
    As he pauses for effect, the ingredients for the winning pie are projected
    onto the screen behind him:

Alarmed by the spoiler, the presenter drops the envelopes, spilling their contents and losing the winner amidst the runners–up.

Which one of the four piemakers must have been the winner?

	Gooseberries	Rhubarb	Cherries	Plums
David	200 g	100 g	150 g	50 g
Sally	170 g	100 g	80 g	50 g
Martin	50 g	40 g	30 g	100 g
Anne	100 g	40 g	50 g	210 g

Taking it further

4   The only oil refinery in Bolandia is the small one at Riebeeck. It can produce two grades of oil: 'light' and 'heavy'. All the oil from Riebeeck is sold in Bolandia. The total number of barrels produced per day is constant.

If the percentage of 'light' required is above 75, the cost of production is higher because extra processing is needed.

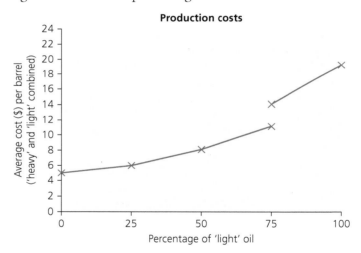

Production costs

(The lines joining the points on the graph are straight.)

Initially, the government sets the selling price at $20 per barrel for 'light' and $10 per barrel for 'heavy'.

a   i)   When producing 25% 'light', the output of 'heavy' is 6000 barrels per day. What is the total daily profit?

ii)   What proportion of 'light' oil should the refinery choose in order to maximise its profits?

The government changes its policy and allows the price of 'light' to be set by the market, whilst keeping 'heavy' at $10 per barrel.

b What is the price for 'light' above at which the refinery's profit becomes greatest by producing 75% 'light' and 25% 'heavy'?

c What is the lowest price for 'light' above at which the refinery's maximum profit would always be gained by only producing 'light'?

(Cambridge AS & A Level Thinking Skills 9694, Paper 31 Q3 (a) – (c), June 2012)

Questions

The final element of problem solving is the phrasing of the question itself.

Obviously there are as many different questions as there are problems, but it is worth considering the axes on which these questions lie, so as to be sensitive to their characteristics.

Two key aspects are the generality and justification expected by the question. The following table offers examples of the different combinations.

	All instances	**Optimal case**	**Single instance**
Prove it	Prove that all integers can be decomposed into one unique product of prime numbers.	Prove that there is no **largest prime number**.	Prove that there is at least one prime number that is even.
Justify it/ Explain it	Are any square numbers prime? Justify your answer.	Explain why **the greatest number of primes** in any consecutive string of 10 numbers is 4.	Explain how you can tell that 511 is not a prime number.
State it	What is the probability that two numbers are relatively prime (that is, have no common factors)?	What is **the lowest string of 10 consecutive numbers,** none of which is prime?	Find a prime number greater than 1000.

Problem solving is normally motivated by getting an answer that works, rather than finding the universal certainty, or the modality, of the answer (known as a proof). The questions that you can expect to face in a problem-solving paper will not require anything as formal as a proof.

And, although some problem-solving questions may ask you just to state an answer, you should always consider what an explanation or justification might be. This is a very good way to check that the answer is sensible, and that you have not missed out any solutions. The importance of this, and the different ways it can be done effectively, are discussed in Chapter 4.

The superficial similarities between the three columns of the previous table hide fundamental differences in the types of answer required.

All instances

» Showing that something is true for *all* cases normally requires the problem solver to explicitly **generalise** the situation. Using algebra is one classic tool for generalising to all cases.

» In contrast, attempting to list all the options is often practically or theoretically impossible (if there are infinite cases). The key feature to appreciate is that even one tiny, non-conforming case destroys an attempt at a 'complete list'. So an attempted solution must begin with completeness built into its plan – not just by starting with proving that 'some cases conform', aiming for 'more cases conform', and then stopping when no more can be found.

» Such **total** demonstrations are rare in problem-solving exam-paper questions – but are clearly useful in real life.

Optimal case

» Showing that a certain case is optimal requires the problem solver to find a boundary value or limit. Identifying a limit is a two-step process: you need to show that one value *is* possible, and that the next one *is not*. To do this you must list your cases in an ordered fashion, so that it is obvious what counts as 'coming next'.

» The key feature here is to order the cases clearly. Only after doing this is it worth trying to find the first value which qualifies/does not qualify.

Sample question

> Try this problem yourself, before reading the analysis!

Key term

Optimisation – Finding the value of a variable which leads to an extreme outcome in a mathematical model. For instance, the number of taxi journeys which leads to the maximum profit for a driver in a day.

During Literacy Week at the Primary school, the pupils are asked to write the date in words, using individual words for each digit (including zero).

For instance, the 7th of the month would be written 'ZERO SEVEN' and the 13th would be written 'ONE THREE'.

◆ What is the minimum number of different letters that could be used on a given day (ignoring the word for the month)?

◆ What is the maximum number of different letters that could be used on a given day (ignoring the word for the month)?

◆ What is the minimum number of days needed for all the different letters used in the 10 number words to be used?

All of the optimisation questions that could accompany this problem require a sense of how the digits are to be ordered. The temptation to place the numbers in numerical order is distracting. They must be viewed in the order of how many different letters they have in them, before the problems of repeating letters and viable dates are considered.

Only after doing this is it worth considering the restrictions imposed by 24-hour time, that is, what are the maximum numerical values for each of the four digits.

Number of different letters:

3: *One*
Two
Six
Nine

4: *Zero*
Three
Four
Five
Seven

5: *Eight*

▲ Considering the optimal number of letters

When considering problems which require a maximum value, it is often useful to approach the answer from two different angles:

» **Find a lower bound.** Begin by trying to find any answer which works. Often it is a good idea to choose the easiest feasible answer, just to check you have understood the restrictions that you need to abide by. In the 'written dates' problem, you might begin by taking one of the examples given (ZERO SEVEN) and counting the number of different letters used (7). Any answer that works is a lower bound for the maximum – 'the maximum must be at least as big as this'.

» **Find an upper bound.** In order to know how big the 'solution space' is, and to enable you to formulate an efficient strategy, you should then try and find an answer that is definitely too big. In the 'written dates' problem, you could consider the total number of different letters in all ten digits (15 in this case).

Key term
- - - - - - - - - - - -
Solution space –
The range of
possible values
which satisfies the
fixed constraints
of the problem.

These two tasks will allow you to home in on the optimum. Normally that involves improving the lower bound until you think you have reached a maximum. When you have reached a potential maximum, you must try and explain (to yourself, in your head) why the next number up is impossible. In the 'written dates' example, it becomes clear that nine different letters is not possible, since it would require numbers with 5 and 4 letters, and the only candidate is ZERO EIGHT (which has 8).

Optimisation problems are dealt with in more detail in Section 4.4.

Single instance

» Showing that a particular case is possible requires the problem solver to search a 'solution space' creatively to find a case that conforms.

This may require a sense of the 'geography' of the space, to enable a speedy solution. Although such cases are easy to check when they are successful, they can be harder to achieve than the two previous types of question, because there may be no simple way of organising the data. An open-minded sweep for 'salient features' may be all one can do to narrow down the search.

Finding the unique correct answer to a problem is a special case of this problem type.

Sample question

Below are the timetables for a Shakespeare Festival which will take place from Wednesday 3 July to Saturday 27 July. A total of 10 plays will be performed at three different venues in the town of Chambet.

Belmont Gardens

	Mon	Tues	Wed	Thurs	Fri	Sat	Sun
Week 1	1	2	As You Like It	As You Like It	As You Like It	Twelfth Night	Twelfth Night
Week 2	Twelfth Night	Love's Labour's Lost	Love's Labour's Lost	As You Like It	As You Like It	Twelfth Night	Twelfth Night
Week 3	Love's Labour's Lost	As You Like It	Twelfth Night	As You Like It	Twelfth Night	Love's Labour's Lost	As You Like It
Week 4	As You Like It	Twelfth Night	Twelfth Night	Love's Labour's Lost	As You Like It	Twelfth Night	28

Corioli Park

	Mon	Tues	Wed	Thurs	Fri	Sat	Sun
Week 1	1	2	Romeo and Juliet	Romeo and Juliet	Othello	Othello	Romeo and Juliet
Week 2	Othello	King Lear	Romeo and Juliet	Othello	Timon of Athens	Romeo and Juliet	Othello
Week 3	Romeo and Juliet	Othello	King Lear	Timon of Athens	Romeo and Juliet	Romeo and Juliet	Othello
Week 4	Othello	King Lear	Timon of Athens	King Lear	Othello	Romeo and Juliet	28

Elsinore Common

	Mon	Tues	Wed	Thurs	Fri	Sat	Sun
Week 1	1	2	The Tempest	Measure for Measure	The Tempest	Measure for Measure	The Tempest
Week 2	The Tempest	The Tempest	Measure for Measure	Measure for Measure	Cymbeline	The Tempest	The Tempest
Week 3	Measure for Measure	Measure for Measure	Cymbeline	The Tempest	The Tempest	Measure for Measure	Measure for Measure
Week 4	Cymbeline	The Tempest	Measure for Measure	Cymbeline	The Tempest	Measure for Measure	28

Try this problem yourself, before reading the analysis!

Richard wants to see all of the plays, but he will not arrive in Chambet until 18 July, when only 10 evenings of the festival remain. He particularly wants to save *Twelfth Night* for the final evening, and he wants to avoid going to the same venue on two consecutive evenings.

Show that it is possible for Richard to choose plays that fit his wishes.

(Adapted from Cambridge AS & A Level Thinking Skills 9694, Paper 32 Q4, November 2014)

The completion of this problem involves narrowing the options case by case, and thus identifying the only possible allocation. The following working shows the order that the plays can be allocated, with brief comments regarding the reasoning below.

Belmont Gardens

	Mon	Tues	Wed	Thurs	Fri	Sat	Sun
Week 1			As You Like It	As You Like It	As You Like It	Twelfth Night	Twelfth Night
Week 2	Twelfth Night	Love's Labour's Lost	Love's Labour's Lost	As You Like It	As You Like It	Twelfth Night	Twelfth Night
Week 3	Love's Labour's Lost	As You Like It	Twelfth Night	As You Like It	Twelfth Night	Love's Labour's Lost	As You Like It
Week 4	As You Like It	Twelfth Night	Twelfth Night	Love's Labour's Lost	As You Like It	Twelfth Night	28

Corioli Park

	Mon	Tues	Wed	Thurs	Fri	Sat	Sun
Week 1			Romeo and Juliet	Romeo and Juliet	Othello	Othello	Romeo and Juliet
Week 2	Othello	King Lear	Romeo and Juliet	Othello	Timon of Athens	Romeo and Juliet	Othello
Week 3	Romeo and Juliet	Othello	King Lear	Timon of Athens	Romeo and Juliet	Romeo and Juliet	Othello
Week 4	Othello	King Lear	Timon of Athens	King Lear	Othello	Romeo and Juliet	28

Elsinore Common

	Mon	Tues	Wed	Thurs	Fri	Sat	Sun
Week 1			The Tempest	Measure for Measure	The Tempest	Measure for Measure	The Tempest
Week 2	The Tempest	The Tempest	Measure for Measure	Measure for Measure	Cymbeline	The Tempest	The Tempest
Week 3	Measure for Measure	Measure for Measure	Cymbeline	The Tempest	The Tempest	Measure for Measure	Measure for Measure
Week 4	Cymbeline	The Tempest	Measure for Measure	Cymbeline	The Tempest	Measure for Measure	28

All performances start at 19:30

➤ Delete all the dates that are not available.

➤ Allocate *Twelfth Night* on the 27th and delete all other performances.

➤ Identify the impossibility of seeing *Timon of Athens* on the 24th because the only two performances of *King Lear* are adjacent to it, and allocate *Timon of Athens* to the 18th.

➤ Allocate *The Tempest* to the 19th, since it is the only alternative after the 18th is *Twelfth Night*.

➤ Allocate *Romeo and Juliet* to 20th, since only available performance.

➤ Allocate *As You Like It* to the 21st, since *Measure for Measure* is the only play that can be watched on the 24th.

➤ Allocate *Cymbeline* (22nd), *King Lear* (23rd), *Measure for Measure* (24th), *Love's Labour's Lost* (25th) and *Othello* (26th) as the only way of completing the remaining evenings.

Explanations and logical relations

Finding an optimum, or finding a solution that satisfies a given requirement, are problems that are focused on the end result. However, some problems ask you to explain why something can (or cannot) be. Problems like this depend on you first understanding the relationship that generates or underpins the solution, and then explicitly explaining it (in relation to the solution you are giving).

One element of these explanations involves what information is logically necessary or sufficient for a solution.

The key distinctions are laid out below.

Key term	Rule of thumb	Example problem
A is sufficient for B	The truth (or the occurrence) of A is *all that is needed* to establish the truth (or the occurrence) of B.	If you want to know what number someone has thought of between 1 and 10, is it *sufficient* to know the product of their number and the number of letters in the word for their number?
		(e.g. EIGHT has five letters, and the product would be 8 5 = 40.)
A is necessary for B	The truth (or the occurrence) of A is *vital* to establish the truth (or the occurrence) of B.	If you want to know what number someone thought of between 1 and 10, and they will answer only 'yes' or 'no' to your questions, is it necessary to ask them at least four questions?
		(e.g. Is it bigger than 5? YES/NO Is it even? YES/NO)

Key term	Rule of thumb	Example problem
A is irrelevant to B	The truth (or the occurrence) of A *has no effect on whether* B is true (or whether it will occur).	If you want to know what number someone thought of between 1 and 10, is it relevant to ask them if the number describes how many letters it has in itself (when written in English)?
		(e.g. The word EIGHT does not have 8 letters, so does not describe itself.)

The mantra that must accompany these refined logical relations is:

» if A is sufficient for B – it *must* be B, if it is A

» if A is necessary for B – if A doesn't happen then B doesn't happen.

For example:

In order to work legally in the United States of America (B) ...

It is sufficient that you are president (A). There is no way you can be an illegal worker if you are president.	It is necessary that you have a visa (A). You cannot work legally in the USA without a visa.

Sample question

The average weight of a particular group of people is 72.1 kg. The group is joined by Wilf and Zak.

What is the minimum number of pieces of information from the following list that would be sufficient to calculate the average weight of the new group including Wilf and Zak?

A The number of people in the original group.

B The weight of Wilf.

C The weight of Zak.

D The combined weight of Wilf and Zak.

E The total weight of the people in the original group.

F The total weight of the group including Wilf and Zak.

G The percentage increase in the number of people when Wilf and Zak join.

H The percentage increase in the total weight when Wilf and Zak join.

I The average weight of Wilf and Zak.

J The weights of all the individual people in the original group apart from one.

(Adapted from Cambridge AS & A Level Thinking Skills 9694, Paper 13 Q16, June 2011)

Try this problem yourself, before reading the analysis!

This question requires you to consider combinations of pieces of information that will be enough to calculate the average of the new group. Central to answering this is the relationship between the mean and the total weight (see Section 5.3 for a reminder of this).

$$\frac{\text{Original } T}{\text{Original } N} \longrightarrow \frac{T + W + Z}{N + 2}$$

$$72.1 \longrightarrow \text{New average}$$

The new average weight is shown as a fraction on the right of the diagram.

The various pieces of information offered in the question can be placed into three groups:

➤ B, C, D and I all allow the additional weight (W + Z) to be calculated. F fits with this group, since it can be combined with knowledge of the original weight (T) to find the average.

➤ A, E, J and G all provide the number of people and the weight of those in the original group (using the average given in the question as a 'key'): T and N.

➤ Together, one piece from the first list and one from the second are sufficient to find the new average.

➤ H is a perplexing piece of information which is only really useful if combined with F to find the original weight (T) and then the average.

When offering an explanation, you should keep the following precepts in mind:

» Your audience is an intelligent **outsider**. You should not assume that they know the logic of the question intimately, and are looking for a few tell-tale confirming clues that you understand it too. Your teacher will only read the words and diagrams you have put down on the page: it is up to you to check that they show all the key aspects that you have thought about clearly.

» You should always aim for as much **detail** as possible. If you are asked to show something is possible, give a precise numerical example.

» When you offer an explanation, consider what the **alternative outcomes** are. Your explanation should explain why this outcome has occurred rather than a possible alternative.

The times taken by the daily train between Tinseltown and the next stop at Rideaux are shown below.

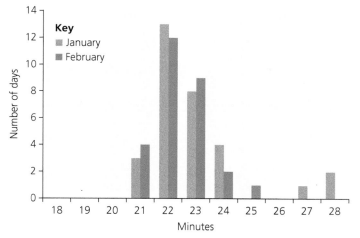

Explain what may have caused the change in the distribution from January to February.

(Adapted from Cambridge AS & A Level Thinking Skills 9694, Paper 12 Q29, June 2014)

Statements which appear to explain what caused the change but do so inadequately:

a *Adverse weather caused the train journeys to take different amounts of time.* **This may be true, but it has not identified what caused the significant difference between the two months.**

b *The train took longer on a few occasions in January.* **This identifies the significant difference, but simply describes it rather than offering a possible cause.**

A statement which explains a possible cause: In January three trains took substantially longer than in February – and this could be explained by snowfall or extreme weather on three days in January.

1 I am sending out invitations to my daughter's wedding – and wish to buy stamps so I can send one to each address. She has given me the following information:

a the names of the 50 individuals she wishes to invite

b the list of five from those 50 who she thinks will not accept the invitation

c a list of the 10 married couples who live at the same address as each other

d a list of those who are likely to bring young children, even though the children are not invited

e a list of those who live close enough to deliver their invitations by hand.

Which of these pieces of information are not necessary if I am to work out how many stamps to buy?

2 Giles works at his local shop in his spare time. He always works the maximum number of hours, which remains constant each week, but some of those hours are in the daytime and some are in the evening. There is a different rate of pay for working in the daytime than in the evening. Both rates of pay are a whole number of dollars per hour. If he earns $126 this week, and earned $114 last week, which of the following could NOT explain this difference?

a Giles worked for 3 extra hours in the evening this week.

b Giles is paid $4 per hour more for working in the evening.

c Giles worked for 5 extra hours in the evening this week.

d Giles is paid $6 per hour more for working in the evening.

(Adapted from Cambridge AS & A Level Thinking Skills 9694, Paper 12 Q19, June 2013)

3 Aristotle drove his car at a constant speed from Metropolis to Supercity. He observed that every 30 minutes he overtook a bus travelling the same route. He knows that all buses travel at the same constant speed as each other, and leave at precise regular intervals from the bus station.

Give an example of a speed of travel for Aristotle and the buses and how often the buses depart which could explain this.

(Adapted from Cambridge AS & A Level Thinking Skills 9694, Paper 11 Q24, June 2016)

Taking it further

4 The following details of the suspects for a crime are available to Detective Inspector Rory Kilmartin.

	Suspect A	Suspect B	Suspect C	Suspect D	Suspect E
Gender	Female	Female	Female	Male	Male
Eye colour	Blue	Brown	Green	Blue	Brown
Handedness	Left	Right	Right	Right	Left
Hair	Dark	Dark	Dark	Dark	Dark

DI Kilmartin wants to know the height of the suspects, but is only able to access summary data, because of a technical problem in the database. He is able to get the median height of any group referred to by a descriptor in the table (e.g. the median height of the blue-eyed suspects).

Below is the summary data that is accessible to DI Kilmartin:

Median (Female) = 168	Median (Male) = 181	
Median (Blue) = 185	Median (Green) = 155	Median (Brown) = 170
Median (Left) = 176	Median (Right) = 168	
Median (Dark) = 172		

He realises that only one suspect has green eyes and so is able to deduce that the height of suspect C is 155 cm.

a DI Kilmartin believes that the fact that the median (Female) and the median (Right) are both 168 must mean that suspect B has a height of 168 cm.

   i) What alternative hypothesis about some suspects' heights would be consistent with these two medians?

   ii) Identify one of the other medians which confirms that DI Kilmartin was in fact correct.

b DI Kilmartin uses another median to conclude the height of suspect E. State which median he uses and the height of suspect E.

c Explain how the heights of the remaining two suspects can be found, stating clearly which medians are used.

A colleague working on another crime has five suspects with the following data, and there is the same problem with the raw data of their heights.

	Suspect H	Suspect I	Suspect J	Suspect K	Suspect L
Gender	Male	Female	Male	Male	Male
Eye colour	Blue	Blue	Brown	Blue	Brown
Handedness	Left	Right	Right	Right	Left
Hair	Dark	Fair	Fair	Dark	Dark

Median (Female) = 181	Median (Male) = 182	
Median (Blue) = 181	Median (Brown) = 177	
Median (Left) = 173	Median (Right) = 168	
Median (Dark) = 172	Median (Fair) = 183.5	

d Suspect K is the tallest of the five. Explain why it is not possible to deduce his height from the medians.

e Deduce the heights of the other four suspects.

(Cambridge AS & A Level Thinking Skills 9694, Paper 32 Q2, November 2015)

Whenever you have solved a problem, try to formulate another problem which could be derived from the same situation. This will allow you to experience the process of problem creation, and allow you to explore the logic of the question more deeply. Most importantly, if you did not manage to solve the problem without guidance (from the book, the mark scheme, a teacher or a friend), this gives you another chance to wrestle with the problem (or a cousin of the original problem), and defeat it.

▶ ACTIVITY

Problem variants

At a networking event, six delegates are sitting around a circular table, engaging their immediate neighbours in conversation. When the whistle blows, they must all get up and then sit down again so that no-one is next to anyone they have sat next to before.

What is the maximum number of times the whistle can blow?

Some examples of variants to the 'rules' are:

» 'No-one can have exactly the same two neighbours as before' instead of 'No-one is next to anyone they have sat next to before'.

» 'Exactly one person must sit next to the same neighbours as before each time' instead of 'No-one is next to anyone they have sat next to before'.

» 'Six people sit along one side of a straight table' instead of 'Six people sit around a circular table'.

» 'Five people sit round a circular table' instead of six.

This process – of reviewing a problem creatively by considering what happens when the question or the variables are altered – can accompany all problem solving. You should aim to create three problem variants for the Practice questions below.

Practice question

Igor Toreadors is the leader of the Great National Party (G), the largest party in the Bognovian Parliament which has 123 seats. The allocation of seats between all the parties is shown below (initial letters for the parties are used).

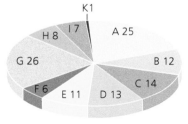

He needs to ally his party with other parties to form a coalition government with a majority in parliament (more than half the seats) but will not ally his party with the second largest party because they have incompatible policies.

He also wants to have the fewest number of parties in his government as experience shows that the more parties are involved, the more likely the government is to break down.

However, while having the fewest number of parties, he also wants to have the smallest government possible, so that his party will dominate it.

With which parties should Igor attempt to form an alliance?

(Adapted from Cambridge AS & A Level Thinking Skills 9694, Paper 13 Q5, June 2011)

Looking back and looking forward

In this chapter you have looked at how a problem solver needs to interact with a problem critically, while respecting the many decisions that will have been made on its journey from the real world to the page in front of you.

In particular, this has involved considering:

» what problems can be posed about a given situation
» how the problem can be interrogated
» how the problem has been modelled
» what kind of question is being asked.

For each of the following more developed questions, you should explicitly consider these four elements as you progress through the question.

Practice questions

1 When making puff pastry, a block of pastry is cut into two. One half is then placed on top of the other and the pastry is pressed down until it makes the original shape. This process of 'rolling out' is repeated many times.

We can model this by considering a cross–section of the pastry, viewed from the side, represented by a square of one unit by one unit. Points in this cross–section can be referred to using (x, y) coordinates.

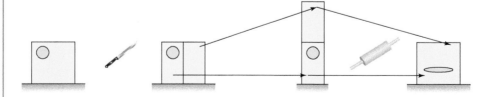

In this model, the right-hand half of the pastry block is always placed on top of the left-hand half. So, for example: $(0.2, 0.2)$ moves to $(0.4, 0.1)$ and $\left(\frac{7}{8}, \frac{7}{8}\right)$ moves to $\left(\frac{3}{4}, \frac{15}{16}\right)$

a i) Give the coordinates of a point that ends up in the same place as it started, after one roll-out.

ii) Where does the point $(0.4, 0.1)$ move to after a roll-out?

iii) Where does the point $\left(\frac{3}{5}, \frac{3}{5}\right)$ move to after a roll-out?

Rolling out mixes up the ingredients as well as introducing the desired texture to the pastry. Ground spice has been sprinkled all over the top of the pastry.

b i) How many layers of ground spice will there be after three roll-outs?

ii) How many roll-outs are needed before all points are within $\frac{1}{10}$ of a unit from some spice?

A lump of butter is represented in the diagram above by the dark blue disk. Before the first roll-out, its left-hand edge was at $x = 0.1$ and its right-hand edge was at $x = 0.4$. As shown, it changed shape, but remained as one piece. However, it will be in two pieces after the second roll-out.

c i) Into how many pieces will the butter have been cut after the fourth roll-out?

ii) Draw a pair of diagrams to show how two lumps of butter, of any simple shape, could combine to form one lump during a roll-out. One diagram should show the position of the two lumps before the roll-out, and the other diagram should show the single combined lump after the roll-out.

(Cambridge AS & A Level Thinking Skills 9694, Paper 32 Q3 (a) & (c), November 2014)

2 Universal Time (UT) is the standard time at 0° longitude (which is the imaginary line running from pole to pole through Greenwich, UK). Throughout the world, the local time is defined relative to UT.

The table below gives the times of sunrise and sunset (UT) on June 8th each year along the 0° line of longitude at selected latitudes.

Latitude	Sunrise	Sunset
60° North	02:41	21:18
50° North	03:52	20:07
40° North	04:31	19:27
30° North	04:58	19:00
20° North	05:20	18:38
10° North	05:39	18:20
0° (Equator)	05:55	18:03
10° South	06:12	17:46
20° South	06:31	17:28
30° South	06:51	17:07
40° South	07:17	16:41
50° South	07:53	16:05
60° South	08:56	15:02

All locations at the same latitude have the same amount of daylight (the time between sunrise and sunset) on any particular day of the year. The UT sunrise and sunset times are always 4 minutes later for every 1° of longitude further west at the same latitude (and therefore 4 minutes earlier for every 1° of longitude further east).

a   Piedra del Aguila in Argentina is situated at latitude 40°S, longitude 70°W. The local time here in June is UT−3 (i.e. 3 hours behind UT).

   i)   What are the UT sunrise and sunset times in Piedra del Aguila on June 8th?

   ii) What are the local times of sunrise and sunset in Piedra del Aguila on June 8th?

The line of latitude 40°N runs for 4200 km through China: from Jigenxiang in Xinjiang Province at longitude 74°E to Dandong in Liaoning Province at longitude 124°E. The same line (40°N) also runs for 4200 km through the USA: from Mantoloking in New Jersey at 74°W to Shelter Cove in California at longitude 124°W.

The whole of China uses UT+8 all year round, whereas the USA uses a number of local time zones. In June, the local time in New Jersey is UT−4 and the local time in California is UT−7.

b   How much later is sunrise in Jigenxiang than it is in Dandong?

c   What is the local time of sunrise on June 8th in

   i)   Mantoloking?

   ii) Shelter Cove?

The graph below shows how the amount of daylight varies between latitudes 30°N and 50°N on June 8th.

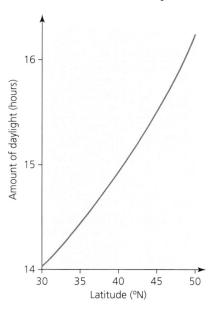

d Harrison in Michigan, Rochester in Minnesota and Eugene in Oregon all have 15 hours 23 minutes of daylight on June 8th. What is the latitude of these three cities?

The Four Corners Monument marks the point where the states of Arizona, Colorado, New Mexico and Utah meet. It is the only point in the USA where the boundaries of four states meet. The local times of sunrise and sunset at the Four Corners Monument on June 8th are 05:56 and 20:34 respectively. The local time here in June is UT−6.

e Use the graph and the previous information you have been given to deduce the latitude and longitude of the Four Corners Monument.

(Cambridge AS & A Level Thinking Skills 9694,
Paper 31 Q4, June 2013)

2 Tackling the problem (I)

By the end of this chapter you will be able to:

★ use '2358' as a problem-solving strategy
★ use 'diagramming' as a problem-solving strategy
★ use 'systematic listing' as a problem-solving strategy
★ use 'trial and error' as a problem-solving strategy
★ select which strategy is appropriate.

In Chapter 1, you were introduced to the process by which 'real-life' problems become formal written problems. You have been introduced to some of the aspects of formulating a problem which require specialist care; and some of the points on the journey of the problem solver which demand particular scrutiny.

In order to become a competent problem solver, you must ensure that you reflect upon and learn from your mistakes.

Here are three classic mistakes that you may have made, and what you should learn from them.

Mistake 1

You ask someone to show you how a problem can be solved before you have tried it yourself.

The lesson learned: a problem explained is a problem destroyed.

Once you have been shown a correct answer to a problem, you cannot be 'unshown' it. It is a mistake to think much can be gained by studying the 'finished product' (a solved puzzle, with exemplary working), without having engaged with it first. You must resist the temptation to be shown how a problem is solved: if you are stuck and have access to someone who has solved it, try to find out how they made initial progress by asking them questions with yes/no answers – the technique introduced in Section 1.2.

An analogy could be made between the art of problem solving and the art of conversation. To become an expert conversationalist, you must engage in conversation. It is true that you may benefit from developing your viewpoint on various issues or likely topics, and that this may require study – but the art of conversation is focused on interaction. It is a profound mistake to think that you can become an expert conversationalist by studying great conversations of the past (in literature, or on CCTV). Similarly, the art of problem solving is focused on interaction: you, interacting with the problem. It is a mistake to think you can become an expert by studying the solutions to great problems.

Mistake 2

You just cannot see how to reach the final answer to a problem, so you do not begin.

The lesson learned: you can't get anywhere if you don't do anything.

Most problems that you will encounter are much harder to solve if you try to do them 'mentally' – without writing anything down. Our brains can only hold a few bits of information clearly, and even when we do hold all the relevant information to solve a problem in our heads, clearly, we are as easily distracted as butterflies. Someone coughs, and we drop the lot.

A blank piece of paper and a writing implement are the main weapons that you have as superheroes of problem solving. When a problem is difficult to access, or difficult to progress with, you need to present it on the page and then dissect it.

Mistake 3

You think that the next problem will be just like one you have seen before.

The lesson learned: the problems are endless.

There is a temptation to think, 'If I could just memorise all the problems (and their solutions) that have occurred so far, then I will be able to find a solution that fits the one you give me tomorrow.' But it is plain wrong – as you will continually find, when a new problem turns up (and you can be heard muttering into your sleeve, 'Ah! this must be the last one – I have them all now'). As long as you approach problem solving with this attitude, you will be faking it.

In this chapter, the focus will be on a toolkit of strategies which you can call on when you don't know what to do. These tools will boost your problem-solving powers, but they must be part of an alert, experimental, reflective approach. That is how you will develop your personal heuristic.

2.1 '2358'

The '2358' problem-solving strategy uses manageable numbers to work out how the parts of a problem are related to each other.

One of the primary difficulties encountered when engaging with a problem is the destabilising effect of big or unwieldy numbers. The first strategy for dealing with a problem whose structure is unclear is to try to tame it by reducing it to a set of numbers which is concrete, easy to visualise, and straightforward to deal with.

If you can establish the logic that governs a simpler version of the problem then you can normally scale up to the problem in hand – or sometimes just apply the 'solution' from your simpler problem directly to the more complex one.

This strategy is a tool for exploring the logical structure of a problem. It does not always get you the answer straight away. It can be used deftly, and it can be used clumsily – if you are aiming for the former, you need to appreciate the variations on the theme discussed below.

Sample question

Try this problem yourself, before reading the analysis!

Using 2, 3, 5 and 8

27 people came into the sports centre this morning: 17 used the gym and 14 used the swimming pool.

What is the largest number that could have used neither the gym nor the swimming pool?

(Adapted from Cambridge AS & A Level Thinking Skills 9694, Paper 12 Q16, June 2014)

The strategy recommends that you try replacing any numerical values in the problem with 'easy numbers' – such as 2, 3, 5 and 8, in rank order (that is, replace the smallest number in the problem with 2, the next smallest with 3, the next with 5 and so on).

Why have you not recommended 1, 2, 3 and 4? There is no 'easy rule' which copes with all cases – but the number 1 is often 'too basic' (in particular, if you divide or multiply by 1 then nothing changes) and the fact that 4 and 6 are multiples are of 2 and 3 may accidentally make the problem seem simpler than it is. Try some numbers, and if it seems that some element of the original puzzle has been lost, try some different ones. But keep them low, so you can represent them easily on the page.

The rephrased problem:

➤ **5 people came into the sports centre this morning**

➤ **3 used the gym**

➤ **2 used the swimming pool**

What is the largest number that could have used neither the gym nor the swimming pool?

With small numbers like these, it is easy to recreate the situation on your desk (with pieces of stationery) or on your page (using stickmen/symbols).

➤

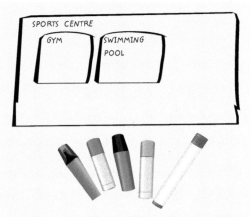

Trying to find less obvious answers reveals that an alternative is to send three to the gym, and then two of those three to the pool – leaving two who did neither.

There is one further alternative – three go to the gym, of whom one goes on to the pool, and one goes to the pool having not been to the gym – leaving one who did neither.

Having established the options in the simplified case, you can see that the maximum number who could use neither is simply 5 − 3, or the total take away the largest number. You can now take this generalisation and apply it to the original case: in the original, this means 27 − 17 = 10 people.

As suggested in Chapter 1, you should try to get the maximum out of a problem (if you have been shown the answer) by considering problem variants.

In the original problem:

- ›› What is the minimum number who could have used neither?
- ›› What is the maximum number who could have used both?
- ›› What is the minimum number who could have used both?

This problem-solving strategy is a classic tool for reducing 'number-blindness' and magnifying our capacity for inferences. Even simple relations between numbers, such as the rate at which something occurs, are easy to mishandle, or use 'the wrong way round'. And our ability to survey the possible landscape of potential inferences, given such simple relationships, takes a lot of practice. The 2358 approach should enable you to avoid the errors, and to gain confidence in making inferences.

Try this problem yourself, before reading the analysis!

During the Second World War, many ships crossed the Atlantic from the USA to Europe, bringing supplies to Britain and her allies. To protect themselves from hostile submarines, these supply ships would cross in a convoy – escorted by a squadron of naval ships.

A convoy of ships could cross the Atlantic in 10–16 days, depending on the speed of the slowest ship. The convoys would transport between 30 and 40 (inclusive) ships at a time, protected by naval vessels. Any fewer ships, or any more, made the process more dangerous and so was avoided.

After the convoy had reached safety, the naval vessels would return to the USA where the next batch of supply ships would be waiting. This return journey could be done predictably in 10 days.

The following table shows the number of ships gathered to cross at a particular time in the USA, classified according to how long it takes them to cross:

Number of days to cross	Number of ships
10	25
11	45
12	60
13	55
14	52
15	30
16	14

What is the minimum time it would take to escort them all across – assuming there is only one squadron available? You can ignore any time spent 'in port' at each end of the journey.

The 2358 strategy offers to make the dynamics of the question manageable by making the numbers easy enough to diagram or model on your desk. Ranking the numbers and pairing with 2358 gives the following redrafting of the problem:

Initial description	Value	2358	Rewritten
A convoy of ships would take 10–16 days	10	2	A convoy of ships would take 2–3 days
	16	3	
... escorting 30–40 ships (inclusive)	30	5	... escorting 5–8 ships (inclusive)
	40	8	
Frequencies ranging from 14 ships to 60	14–60	4–9	Frequencies ranging from 14 ships to 60
	The original frequencies range beyond the minimum and maximum sizes of the convoys – so it is worth choosing simplified numbers which also do this		

With these more manageable numbers, you can consider how to transport 4 fast ships and 9 slow ships across.

The number of 'long journeys' needs to be minimised – and so all the slow ships should go together. In the simplified case, the journeys could be as follows:

Ships on USA side	Ships in convoy	Ships on European side	Time taken
4 fast and 1 slow	8 slow		3
4 fast and 1 slow	Squadron returns	8 slow	2
	4 fast and 1 slow	8 slow	3
Total			8

This process allows the dynamics of the problem to be exposed: the trips need to include the maximum numbers of ships, and they travel at the pace of the slowest. The convoys must aim to cluster the slow boats together.

When considering each row, it becomes obvious that the second column needs to be completed in order to decide how many are left.

This insight can then be applied back to the original numbers:

Ships on USA side	Ships in convoy	Ships on European side	Time taken
24/45/60/55/52/30/14			
24/45/60/55/52/4/0	26/14		16
	Squadron returns	26/14	10
24/45/60/55/16/0/0	36/4		15
	Squadron returns	36/30/14	10
24/45/60/31/0/0/0	24/16		14
	Squadron returns	24/52/30/14	10
24/45/51/0/0/0/0	09/31		13
	Squadron returns	09/55/52/30/14	10
24/45/11/0/0/0/0	40		12
	Squadron returns	49/55/52/30/14	10
24/16/0/0/0/0/0	29/11		12
	Squadron returns	29/60/55/52/30/14	10
0/0/0/0/0/0/0	24/16		11
Total			151 days

Sample question

Try this problem yourself, before reading the analysis!

Use 2358 to solve this problem.

A band wishes to promote a concert to its most devoted fans, and so sends out promotional emails to its 10 most devoted fans three days before the concert, which is happening on a Thursday evening.

◆ On Tuesday, two days before the event, those 10 fans each send out 5 emails to other fans.

◆ On Wednesday, each of the fans who received an email on Tuesday sends out 4 emails to their friends.

◆ On Thursday, the day of the event, everyone who received an email on Wednesday sends out 12 emails to people they thought might want to come to the concert.

◆ Surprisingly, on Monday, Tuesday and Wednesday the emails all went to different people: no-one received two emails about the event.

◆ But on Thursday, two-thirds of the fans received two emails, and the rest just received one.

How many people received two promotional emails on Thursday?

You may consider the following:

➤ **If you rewrite this question, using 2358, you will be faced with a diagram which attempts to show five initial emails (on Monday)**

➤ **three emails sent on Tuesday**

➤ **two emails sent on Wednesday**

➤ **eight emails sent on Thursday.**

These numbers are just about manageable on a diagram:

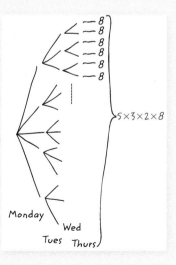

This supports the conclusion that you multiply the numbers together to find the total number of emails sent on Thursday: in this case 10 × 5 × 4 × 12 = 2400 emails in total.

The tricky bit is to know what to do with the information about the two-thirds who received two emails on Thursday. The tempting option, to find two-thirds of 2400, is not appropriate.

You can see this by working backwards from that conclusion: if two-thirds of 2400 (= 1600) received email from two other fans, then there must have been at least 3200 sent (1600 people × 2 emails). But there were only 2400.

One way to study the logic more carefully is to use 2358 again.

If only 5 emails were sent and two-thirds of the recipients received two emails, while one-third received one email, then that must have involved two people receiving two and one person receiving one:

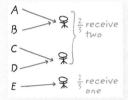

Applying this to the original, with larger numbers: one-fifth of the emails went to one person, and the four-fifths went to two people. That means that $\frac{2}{5}$ of the people received two emails. So 480 (of 2400) people received one email, and 960 received two.

Check: 960 + 960 + 480 = 2400

Practice questions

Choose manageable numbers to simplify these problems.

1   In a certain village, there live 800 women. Three per cent of them wear one earring. Of the remaining 97 per cent, half wear two earrings, and half wear none.
    How many earrings are being worn by the women in total?

2   Two missiles speed directly towards each other, one at 9000 mph, and the other at 21 000 mph. They start 1317 miles apart.
    How far apart are they one minute before they collide?

3   In Prudosia, the streets are constructed from 10-metre pieces. A lamp post must be placed at both ends of every completed street and at points every 10 metres along its length. Additional lamp posts must also be placed at every noticeboard along the road.

Einstein Street, in Prudosia, has 7 noticeboards, and 42 lamp posts were needed altogether.

How long is Einstein Street?

(Adapted from Cambridge AS & A Level Thinking Skills 9694, Paper 13 Q2, November 2015)

4   When Mary won $3360 on a TV quiz programme she decided to give it to her two grandchildren, Susan and Luke, to be shared between them in the ratio of their ages.

5-year-old Luke complained that it wasn't fair that his older sister should get more than him. His mother sympathised, but told him to be thankful that his grandmother hadn't won the money next month (after Susan's birthday) when he would have received $70 less, or last month (before his birthday) when he would have received $160 less.

How much of Mary's $3360 did Luke receive?

(Adapted from Cambridge AS & A Level Thinking Skills 9694, Paper 12 Q27, June 2013)

Taking it further

5   Roger's cleaning company calculates its prices for cleaning buildings in the following way:
   * There is a fixed charge of $20.
   * $0.50 is charged for every square metre of floor area in the building.
   * An additional $10 is charged for every room in the building.

In this question, assume that all rooms in buildings have a floor area that is a whole number of square metres.

a   What would be the price for Roger's company to clean a building containing 5 rooms and having a total floor area of 50 square metres?

Trevor is planning to set up a cleaning company, but only wants to calculate his prices based on the floor area to be cleaned. He will not have a fixed charge or add any extra to the price for the number of rooms.

b   What should he charge per square metre of floor area to match the price of Roger's company for a building containing 5 rooms and having a total floor area of 50 square metres?

Trevor has decided to set his charge at $1.50 per square metre to be cleaned.

c   If a building has 6 rooms and would cost the same to clean with either company, what is the total floor area?

Trevor also intends to offer an 'Express' service in which he will have 3 cleaners clean the building, rather than just 1. He wants to set the price for this service so that he earns twice what he would from the standard service, after paying his cleaners. Trevor pays each cleaner $0.90 per square metre to be cleaned.

d   How much should Trevor charge per square metre of floor area for the 'Express' service?

➤

As soon as Trevor announced his prices, Roger's company reduced their prices by making the extra charge per room just $5. One of the bookings that Trevor had received was cancelled because Trevor's price at the standard rate had been cheaper but was now $15 more expensive than Roger's price.

e i) What is the minimum number of rooms that could be in such a building?

ii) What is the floor area of a building with this minimum number of rooms?

(Cambridge AS & A Level Thinking Skills 9694, Paper 32 Q3 (a) – (e), June 2015)

A variation on the strategy: 'make one number extreme'

An alternative way of exposing the logical relationships in a problem, if it is obscured by clouds of numbers, is to make one key number relatively large, so that its influence stands out. This is like magnifying one 'corner' of the problem.

Sample question

> Try this problem yourself, before reading the analysis!

An example of a problem in which this can be useful.

Three men in a cafe order a meal that costs $15 in total. They each pay $5, and the waiter takes the money to the chef, who recognises them as friends and tells the waiter to give $5 back to them.

The waiter sees a chance to make a quick buck and gives them back $3 (to split three ways) and pockets $2 for himself.

This means that the men paid $4 each ($12 in total) and the waiter pockets $2 … so where did the missing dollar go?

This problem is confusing, even though the numbers are all fairly small.

They are small enough to 'play out' the scenario. And it is clear that what is described could happen – but it is not very clear why we end up with $12 + $2 and $15.

The logic is obscured by the similarities between the numbers.

If we rephrase the problem to involve nine men at the cafe, ordering a meal which costs $90 in total, and we imagine that the chef offers to give them $10 back, the waiter sees his chance and gives $1 to each of the men and pockets $1 for himself.

This mimics the situation of our sample question.

If we now try to articulate the final 'missing dollar' statement we are faced with: the men pay $81 in total (9 × 9) and the waiter pockets $1 … where have the missing $9 gone? This makes it clearer – we are not expecting 81 + 1 = 90 but 81 − 1 = 80. The chef takes $80, the men pay $81 and the waiter takes $1.

Paradox explained.

▲ Monty Hall

To think about

Research The Monty Hall problem on the internet.

This is a famously puzzling game, which problem solvers and statisticians have argued over.

Try applying the 'make one number extreme' strategy: imagine that there are not just two doors with goats behind them and one door with a prize, but 99 doors with goats behind them and one door with a prize. And then consider what you would do if Monty opened 98 of the doors, each revealing a goat. Would you change your mind?

When to use it

» Simplifying the numbers is only useful *if you are not sure how to combine the pieces of information you have been given.* It can seem like a long-winded process: why create another new problem to solve, on top of the old one? Isn't there enough to do? As a result you may find it is more useful when in training than actually in a time-constrained environment (such as an exam).

The process enables you to deal with unfamiliar situations, tapping into your intuition. It tames the problem by choosing low numbers that make the problem easy to manage and *easy to present on the page.*

How to use it well

» You want to choose low numbers – but avoid the number '1' if any multiplication or division is involved. '1' is unique in leaving the answer unchanged when you multiply or divide by it. This can make the simplified problem look different to the original.

» If you are dividing one value by another, check to see whether the numbers in the question are multiples of each other. As in the convoy of ships sample problem from earlier, the question may offer you numbers which divide nicely (18 and 6), in which case you should use numbers which divide nicely too (9 and 3).

You don't need to represent the whole of a problem with 2358: it is often useful to reduce a small part of a problem to simple numbers, in order to understand its logic. The part of the earlier problem in which 'two-thirds of the colleagues received two emails' is a good example of this.

2.2 Diagramming

If information is given in the 'right' way then the solution 'announces' itself.

This bold claim is true in a facile sense – if you arrange the information so that it is clear what to do next, then all that is needed is processing skills to complete the task. This *is* true, but it's not very useful when problem solving since 'what to do next' is precisely the problem!

But the claim is true in a more useful sense – laying out the information in a way that is clear, and in a way that allows different elements of the problem to be shown by different parts of the diagram, often reveals the solution (even when the problem solver is not sure what they are looking for). Problems are often presented in linear sentences, as if spoken, and it is the first job of the problem solver to re-present the information in an appropriate way.

To become adept at diagramming, you need to know what 'design classics' there are to use, and also be willing to experiment. The design classics include:

»» network diagrams
»» tables
»» Venn diagrams (dealt with in Section 3.4)
»» function diagrams (dealt with in Section 3.1).

The first two are both very user-friendly, and applicable in a huge range of circumstances.

An example of how each of these can shed light on a messy-looking problem follows.

Network diagrams

A network is simply a collection of objects (known as nodes) connected by lines. The nodes can represent places or people or tasks or any variety of things depending on the problem. The lines show how the nodes are connected, and can be accompanied by measurements or costs or limitations on direction or diverse data about the connection.

They are one of the most flexible and useful forms of diagram – and are particularly useful when a problem presents a number of options, only some of which are possible.

Sample question

Ashwinder is a courier who works for a bank – his work involves carrying important documents between the bank's offices. He gets paid per journey, and so wishes to complete as many possible during his shift (09:00 until 13:00).

He always begins the day at the bank's sorting office, and there are always documents to be delivered between the nine depots.

The times it takes him to travel the standard journeys is as follows:

Sorting office to HQ	20 mins	HQ to south (commercial)	10 mins
HQ to central	15 mins	South (commercial) to south (private)	5 mins
HQ to east (commercial)	30 mins	North (commercial) to north (private)	10 mins
HQ to west (commercial)	45 mins	South (private) to north private	30 mins
HQ to north (commercial)	25 mins	Central to sorting office	20 mins

It takes him 15 minutes to sign for and collect a document from any of the depots. It takes a negligible amount of time to deliver it at its destination.

What is the maximum number of journeys that Ashwinder can make?

Try this problem yourself, before reading the analysis!

It is immediately clear that success with the question depends on exactly which destination is connected to which. This is what the network diagram was designed to present, in as clear a form as possible.

Nine different destinations are listed, and it is often easiest to lay these out as if spaced around a circle, so that all connections are equally easy to draw:

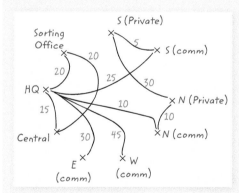

The beauty of the diagram is that it allows our eyes, or fingers, to trace out a route, and minimises the chance of choosing a list that is not possible to achieve. We still have to make choices about what will maximise the number of journeys in a given time, but we can reduce the strain of mentally performing the three tasks simultaneously. Of the three key tasks – checking that the journey is feasible, summing the times, checking that the return to the sorting

office is possible – the first is much reduced by the network; the second can be recorded in a list; and that leaves our brain to focus on the third, and perform meta-tasks (such as checking that we have not oversimplified the problem – see Section 4.1).

The solution:			
09:00	SO arr	11:10	S (comm) dep
09:15	SO dep	11:15	S (private) arr
09:35	HQ arr	11:30	S (private) dep
09:50	HQ dep	11:35	S (comm) arr
10:15	S (comm) arr	11:50	S (comm) dep
10:30	S (comm) dep	12:15	HQ arr
10:35	S (private) arr	12:30	HQ (dep)
10:50	S (private) dep	12:50	SO arr
10:55	S (comm) arr		

A quick check is needed to ensure that no extra trip is possible, but the next best alternative (back and forth between north (commercial) and HQ) exceeds the journey time when six trips are done.

This means that the total maximum number of journeys possible is 8 (arrivals highlighted).

Practice questions

1 When out driving I came across the two signs shown below uprooted and on the ground by a crossroads. Clearly one of the signs did not belong to the crossroads at which I had stopped. I had just come from Kaali and had not been through any of the other towns.

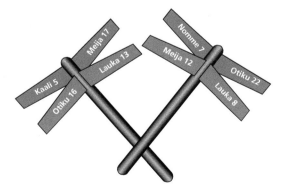

Assuming that one of the signs belonged at the crossroads where I found them, which direction should I go for the shortest route to Nomme – left, straight on or right?

(Adapted from Cambridge AS & A Level Thinking Skills 9694, Paper 11 Q9, November 2011)

2 The table below shows the average journey time by car, on the fastest roads, between four Italian towns.

	Arezzo	Firenze	Pisa	Siena
Arezzo	–			
Firenze	1 hr 00 min	–		
Pisa	2 hr 00 min	1 hr 05 min	–	
Siena	1 hr 15 min	1 hr 10 min	1 hr 55 min	–

Sylvia, starting from Pisa, wishes to visit Arezzo, Firenze and Siena and return to Pisa on the same day. She wants to spend as little time in her car as possible, and chooses a route that minimises her expected time in car travel.

How long does she expect to spend travelling in her car?

(Adapted from Cambridge AS & A Level Thinking Skills 9694, Paper 12 Q9, June 2012)

3 Four women (Ada, Babs, Cath and Dee) and four men (Mac, Nick, Oscar and Pete) are sitting evenly spaced around a circular table. No woman sits next to another woman. Pete is opposite Nick, who is sitting next to Ada, and she is opposite Babs, who sits next to Mac. Oscar is next to Dee. Who is Cath between?

(Adapted from Cambridge AS & A Level Thinking Skills 9694, Paper 11 Q11, November 2011)

Tables

Tables attempt to lay out the information two-dimensionally, where looking across the page means one thing, and looking down the page means another. When laid out with due care, tables allow patterns hidden within rows and columns to become obvious, and allow you to concentrate on, or disregard, cells of the table as is necessary.

Sample question

Each morning what Sebastien has for breakfast depends precisely on the number of minutes until his bus is scheduled to leave, when he first sees the clock on the kitchen wall. The alternatives are to eat a piece of fruit (this takes 2 minutes to eat and walk to the bus stop), a bowl of cereal (this takes 7 minutes to eat and walk to the bus stop), or a boiled egg (this takes 15 minutes to eat and walk to the bus stop).

➤

Try this problem yourself, before reading the analysis!

If he has 10 minutes or less then he always has a piece of fruit.

He eats a boiled egg only if there is *more than* 20 minutes until the bus is due to leave.

On Monday, Tuesday, Wednesday and Thursday this week Sebastien has arrived at the bus stop 3 minutes, 10 minutes, 5 minutes and 6 minutes before the bus was due to leave (in that order).

What is the largest amount of time Sebastien could have spent eating breakfast this week?

As with the previous question, it is not vital to tabulate the information, but doing so frees up your mind to perform meta-tasks (such as checking that you have not oversimplified the problem or made numerical errors).

A simple table showing Sebastien's choices (F, C or E), according to how many minutes he has until his bus arrives:

Minutes until bus arrives	Arriving at bus stop (minutes early)
2	0 (F)
3	1 (F)
4	2 (F)
5	3 (F)
And so on until ...	
10 8 (F)	
11 9 (F) or 4 (C)	
12 10 (F) or 5 (C)	
13 11 (F) or 6 (C)	
14 12 (F) or 7 (C)	
And so on until...	
20 18 (F) or 13 (C)	
21	19 (F) or 14 (C) or 6 (E)
22	20 (F) or 15 (C) or 7 (E)
23	21 (F) or 16 (C) or 8 (E)

The table appears complete and fully formed now it is written down here on the page, but the table evolved as the problem was being solved. As can be seen from the omitted rows, it shows a balance between careful precision and efficiency with time and space. (See Section 4.3 for more on this.)

With the complete table you are able to identify possible occurrences of 3, 10, 5 and 6 in the right-hand column. Given the question, it becomes clear that numbers under 4 must have involved fruit for breakfast, and numbers under 8 can only have

involved fruit or cereal. **Larger numbers could have involved any of the three breakfasts.**

The longest time he could have spent eating breakfast was (2 + 15 + 7 + 15) = 39 minutes.

Practice questions

1 Clark makes frequent journeys between the towns of Axeford and Barcastle. For the journey he can choose between the bus services named 'Direct' and 'Loyalty'. Direct charges the same fare of $40 to all passengers at all times. Loyalty has a 'frequent user' discount system and charges $50 for the first journey a passenger takes, $49.75 for the second journey, $49.50 for the third and so on. Each journey is 25 cents cheaper than the previous one until the fare reaches $20, when there are no further reductions.

At what point would it become cheaper overall to use Loyalty rather than Direct?

(Adapted from Cambridge AS & A Level Thinking Skills 9694, Paper 12 Q12, June 2012)

2 Four teams competed in a balloon race of 150 kilometres. The teams flew at varying speeds by catching the wind at different altitudes. The data below shows how long each team spent flying at different speeds, starting from the beginning of the race.

Team	Speed (km/h)	Time (hours)	Speed (km/h)	Time (hours)	Speed (km/h)	Time (hours)
Arrow	30	1	35	3	20	2
Flame	35	3	40	1	5	2
Hurricane	10	3	40	2	80	1
Velocity	20	2	30	3	20	1

Which team was the first to travel 150 kilometres?

(Adapted from Cambridge AS & A Level Thinking Skills 9694, Paper 12 Q18, June 2014)

3 A photograph shows five brothers standing side by side. Dmitri is the tallest of them all. Ivan is taller than both his neighbours in the line. Alyosha and Fyodor are the same height. Pavel has his arm round Fyodor. The very shortest of all the five is at one end of the line.

What order are they standing in?

Freestyle diagramming

Many questions cannot be easily structured as tables or networks, and bespoke diagrams must be created.

When creating a diagram to represent you will need to:

» ensure that you give yourself enough space.

» use abbreviations – but ensure that you can tell which objects are which. Consider using a key if your abbreviations are unclear. Your diagram needs to be understandable by others too.

» not be afraid to start with one type of representation and then morph into another. Such changes show your perception of the problem is growing.

Sample question

> Try this problem yourself, before reading the analysis!

At the Prudosia zoo, four different animals must be temporarily placed in two separate enclosures. Animals must not be placed in the same enclosure if one of them will prey on another.

Girbras prey on antelions but not on rhinolopes.

Antelions will prey on tigaffes, but only if there are no rhinolopes present.

Rhinolopes prey on girbras but not on antelions or tigaffes.

Tigaffes prey on girbras but not on antelions.

Which animal must be placed on its own (in an enclosure with no other animals)?

(Adapted from Cambridge AS & A Level Thinking Skills 9694, Paper 12 Q14, June 2014)

The following diagram is an attempt to encode all the relevant information: black lines equate to 'prey on' and red lines to 'will not prey on'.

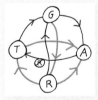

It is not 'transparent' – in the sense of immediately revealing the correct answer to the question.

The question asks which animal must be placed on its own, something that depends upon the animal not preying on other animals, nor being preyed on itself. Reviewing the diagram we

can see that the girbra appears to be the solution to the problem. This possible solution is worth verifying, and another simple diagram will suffice:

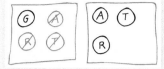

▲ A possible solution

By drawing the two enclosures and populating them with the animals we are able to perform a quick check to see if the solution works. It does, and we can confidently conclude that the answer is: the girbra must be placed on its own.

Sample question

Try this problem yourself, before reading the analysis!

The retirement age in Prudosia will be raised from 66 to 67 over two years: every six months the minimum age will jump up by 3 months. Anyone over the retirement age on the date they apply will immediately get a free retired-person's bus pass.

How much **younger** could one person with a free retired-person's bus pass be than someone not able to get one?

(Adapted from Cambridge AS & A Level Thinking Skills 9694, Paper 13 Q24, November 2015)

The following diagram shows an attempt to pin down the changing ages and retirement ages as time passes over two years:

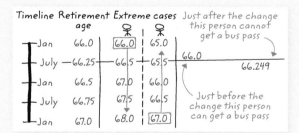

This diagram shows the months – January and July of each year – in which the retirement age increases over the two-year period. The retirement age at that time is also shown, as well as the ages of people who are at the limits of the retirement age at that time (the final two columns).

What the diagram allows you to see is that the ages of people who are at the limits of the process do not end up qualifying for a bus pass and being significantly younger: the person who just qualifies for a bus pass at the beginning of the change is a year older than the person who just qualifies at the end. The area to focus on in fact is just before the change of retirement age. The two cases in the diagram show someone who just qualifies for a bus pass immediately before the change, and someone who just does not qualify immediately after the change.

The diagram is not perfect, but it does allow you to consider the key people, and to home in on the critical point (the youngest and oldest people, before and after one of the quarterly changes). The oldest and youngest people on either side of the boundary are $\frac{1}{4}$ of a year apart in age and on the 'wrong sides' of the boundary.

The answer is: a person with a bus pass could be just under 3 months younger than someone unable to claim it.

Sample question

Try this problem yourself, before reading the analysis!

In a cycle time trial, the riders set off at two-minute intervals over a fixed 50 km route and are timed individually. The winner is the rider who completes the course in the shortest time.

In one time trial of 64 riders, one cyclist managed to overtake three of the riders who had set out before her, four cyclists overtook two riders, and seven overtook one rider. No cyclist suffered the humiliation of being overtaken by more than one rider, and all riders completed the course.

How many riders, in this time trial, started and finished the course with the same number of riders in front of them?

(Adapted from Cambridge AS & A Level Thinking Skills 9694, Paper 11 Q29, November 2016)

The key to the question is simply to list the riders from the back.

If the cases are then considered one by one: 'one cyclist managed to overtake three riders who set out ahead of her …' The overtaken cyclists now have a different number of cyclists in front of them, so they can be crossed out. The case when one cyclist overtook two riders is then considered and, again, all those cyclists who were overtaken are crossed out.

If this process is continued, including the last two who overtook two riders, and the seven who overtook one rider, there are 34 unaffected cyclists.

This layout and the modelling of the situation enables the answer to 'fall out'.

The choice of a correct re-presentation of the information occurs whenever information is given as text. Sometimes it requires a bespoke layout (as occurred with the cyclists); at other times you can use one of the 'design classics' which enable patterns and solutions to announce themselves.

1 The members of Purlone knitting club decided recently to knit scarves to sell for charity. Their goal was to create a chain one kilometre in length along Purlone promenade by knotting scarves together.

All 50 members of the club pledged to knit 10 scarves, each 2 metres long. This has now been successfully achieved, except that one member got confused and has only produced 2 scarves, but both are 10 metres long.

It has become clear, however, that **laying** the scarves end to end will be the only way to achieve one kilometre, because each knot in a chain of scarves would reduce the overall length by 40 centimetres.

If Purlone knitting club were to make a knotted chain with their scarves, how far short of one kilometre would it be (to the nearest whole metre)?

(Adapted from Cambridge AS & A Level Thinking Skills 9694, Paper 11 Q13, November 2012)

2 2 men and 2 women escaped from a yacht just before it sank. The life raft only has space for 3 people. The longest time a man can survive in the water is 3 hours but a woman can survive for 4 hours. After being in the water, they need 10 hours out of the water to recover or they will die immediately. Each time they go back into the water, the time they can survive is reduced by 1 hour.

How long can all 4 people stay alive?

(Cambridge AS & A Level Thinking Skills 9694, Paper 11 Q13, June 2016)

3 A club's football field has a playing area of 105 m × 70 m. Outside the playing area there is a surround, 5 metres wide, which is not used for play. The club uses the playing area for junior games, which are played on pitches of 34 m × 24 m but with a 2 metre gap between them for safety.

How many junior pitches can be fitted into the playing area?

(Adapted from Cambridge AS & A Level Thinking Skills 9694, Paper 11 Q15, November 2012)

Taking it further

4 A laboratory technician is asked to look after his colleague's collection of Cloning Nanobots, while she is away at a conference. The collection is kept in isolation, in a sealed container. He is told nothing about how many are in the container, but is told their 'rules of cloning':
- cloning always occurs precisely at 6am
- each nanobot will produce an exact replica of itself every day – apart from during its first 3 days of 'life'. So its first clone occurs exactly 4 days after it was 'born'.

➤

a If a single 'newborn' nanobot was in the container, how many would be there after 7 days?

b If a single 'newborn' nanobot was in the container, how many days must pass before there are more than 20?

The technician is told the population has been altered many times during the timescale of the experiment, so the nanobots in the container are of many different 'ages'.

On the first day he looks into the container and sees 50 nanobots:

c i What is the maximum number there could be on the second day?

   ii What is the minimum number there could be on the second day?

On the second day he looks into the container and sees 88 nanobots

d i What is the maximum number there could be on the third day?

   ii What is the minimum number there could be on the third day?

e How many will be born at 6am on the fourth day?

When to use it

Diagramming works best when some element of the question's structure is captured in the diagram. For example, you may capture the placement of the different objects spatially, show their connections, note the different directions used for different variables, use ticks and crosses for whether options are permissible or not, or represent numerical patterns as visual patterns. When the diagram carries some of the structural logic it frees your mind to concentrate on the other aspects, allowing you to engage with meta-tasks of verification and sceptical self-scrutiny.

If you are despairing of a question and can't see how objects are related, sometimes the act of trying to get them on the page makes things clearer. This was the case with the retirement age question discussed previously – the diagram was not particularly useful or appropriate, but it ruled out certain options, and that allowed a fruitful path to emerge.

How to use it well

» Practise using networks when a problem involves numerous connections between objects. Networks are a classic case of 'the picture carrying some of the logic of the question'. It is important to make the network big enough and sufficiently neat, because that allows your pattern-seeking pictorial eye to pick out details.

» Using tables, or two-dimensional arrays, is another classic means of presenting a problem to your pattern-seeking eye. Often the numbers in a question are sufficiently large to make a full table daunting, or prohibitively long, but most of the work is done in the first line or two: look for patterns, and check for oversimplification.

» When you struggle to frame a problem diagrammatically, consult your peers/teacher and allow them to try it (without seeing your attempt, obviously). Creative diagramming is something that comes with effort, and with exposure to diverse viewpoints.

2.3 Systematic listing

A systematic list is a list of possible answers that have been arranged in a clear and methodical order. Any problem which demands an optimal answer from a finite collection of possible answers could be theoretically answered by a systematic list; however, when problems involve lists that are lengthy, they can often seem like a test of endurance.

The art of the systematic list is to avoid writing the whole thing out, while still ensuring that nothing could have escaped. As such it is always accompanied by the meta-task of 'rooting for escapees': trying to imaginatively identify or locate where a case could have been missed.

Systematic listing requires that you have a plan before you begin; often that plan is to change the components of your list one at a time.

The next problem exemplifies this.

Sample question

Try this problem yourself, before reading the analysis!

The letters of the word 'ASTER' can be arranged in 120 different ways. If these are arranged in alphabetical order (starting with AERST), where does the word RATES come?

(Adapted from Cambridge AS & A Level Thinking Skills 9694, Paper 12 Q17, June 2014)

This question can be answered by scrutinising this table:

AERST	EARST	RAEST	SAERT	TAERS
AERTS	EARTS	RAETS	SAETR	TAESR
AESRT	EASRT	RASET	SARET	TARES
AESTR	EASTR	RASTE	SARTE	TARSE
AETRS	EATRS	RATES	SATER	TASER
AETSR	EATSR	RATSE	SATRE	TASRE
AREST	ERAST	REAST	SEART	TEARS
ARETS	ERATS	REATS	SEATR	TEASR
ARSET	ERSAT	RESAT	SERAT	TERAS
ARSTE	ERSTA	RESTA	SERTA	TERSA
ARTES	ERTAS	RETAS	SETAR	TESAR
ARTSE	ERTSA	RETSA	SETRA	TESRA
ASERT	ESART	RSAET	SRAET	TRAES
ASETR	ESATR	RSATE	SRATE	TRASE

ASRET	ESRAT	RSEAT	SREAT	TREAS
ASRTE	ESRTA	RSETA	SRETA	TRESA
ASTER	ESTAR	RSTAE	SRTAE	TRSAE
ASTRE	ESTRA	RSTEA	SRTEA	TRSEA
ATERS	ETARS	RTAES	STARE	TSAER
ATESR	ETASR	RTASE	STAER	TSARE
ATRES	ETRAS	RTEAS	STEAR	TSEAR
ATRSE	ETRSA	RTASE	STERA	TSERA
ATSER	ETSAR	RTSAE	STRAE	TSRAE
ATSRE	ETSRA	RTSEA	STREA	TSREA

Artful use of the systematic list will enable you to get the correct answer (53rd) in the list after considering only a few cases.

It is worth appreciating why the list can be called 'exhaustive'. Here, words are ordered alphabetically in columns and, within each column, coloured sections are used to group together words which begin with the same two letters. The remaining three letters of these words can be ordered in six possible permutations. Doing this allows you to demonstrate the completeness of each of those coloured sections (for example, for words beginning AE, the permutations are: RST, RTS, SRT, STR, TRS, TSR), and means you then need only consider the coloured groups as a whole.

One can quickly see that the words in the left-hand column are all the cases which begin with A (AE, AR, AS, AT), and that the columns cater for all the different beginnings. This approach is what allows you to say that there are only 120 options (or permutations), and means you can easily identify the position of the word 'RATES' within the complete list.

The short-hand way of remembering how many permutations there are for a given number of n (distinguishable) letters is that it is $n!$ Or $n \times (n - 1) \times (n - 2) \times \ldots \times 2 \times 1$

For the five letters of our sample question there are $5! = 5 \times 4 \times 3 \times 2 \times 1 = 120$ permutations, also known as '5 factorial'.

As the questions bring in different aspects and restrictions it is highly recommended to develop a habitual way of listing these – alphabetical listing works well, and often coincides with listing in numerical order (when does it not?). A good approach is to keep all the letters the same and change the last letter. When this is done, change the second last letter and list again. When all of these are done, change the third last letter and so on.

Key term

Permutations
(noun) – An
arrangement of
objects where the
order of them is
significant.

Combinations
(noun) – A
collection or
selection of
objects where the
order of them is
not significant.

Key term

Limit case (noun)
– An example
that lies at
the boundary
of possibility
according
to defined
conditions.

Sample question

To think about

Finding permutations of letters which make actual English words.

Challenge

- Can you find any collections of letters, which are more likely to make a comprehensible word than not, if you arrange the letters randomly? Show your answer in a systematic list.
- Which four letters produce the most words when rearranged? Show your answer in a systematic list.

You are not expected to become expert on the permutations and combinations (a mathematical area known as combinatorics), but it is important to see why such orderly listing is powerful.

Lists can quickly become unmanageable.

There are two particular types of problem that emerge from the world of combinatorics: those that involve using lists and shortcuts to find the number of cases that fit a certain requirement, and those that involve using lists and shortcuts to find a limit case.

A limit case is one that lies at a boundary defined in the question, such as 'the latest date on which this will occur', 'the first word with no vowels in', 'the next time that all digits from 1 to 10 will be showing'. The sample question in search of RATES involved both aspects. The question below involves the use of systematic listing to find a limit.

Using six digits to represent a date can be done in different ways. The international standard system (ISO 8601) is to use the order year–month–day (YYMMDD), so 1st February 03 would be 030201. This makes them easiest to sort.

The normal usage in some countries, including Britain, is DDMMYY, giving 010203 instead. In Belize, the United States and Palau, the form MMDDYY is used, giving 020103 for the same date.

What is the largest possible difference (in the same century) between dates corresponding with a 6-digit date that would be valid in all three systems?

(Adapted from Cambridge AS & A Level Thinking Skills 9694, Paper 11 Q29, November 2014)

Try this problem yourself, before reading the analysis!

An initial layout of the problem might look something like this:

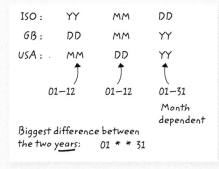

To decide what should go in the middle, it is probably easiest to try maximum and minimum values and compare the differences:

01/01/31 gives 31 Jan 2001 (ISO), or 1 Jan 2031 (GB) – a gap of 29 years and 11 months.

01/12/31 gives 31 Dec 2001 (ISO), or 1 December 2031 (GB), or 12 Jan 2031 (USA) – a gap of 29 years and 11 months (or 29 years and 12 days).

Therefore, the largest possible difference is 29 years and 11 months.

To think about

Is the desk calendar shown on the right able to show all the dates necessary to accompany the months using only two regular cubes for the numbers?

APRIL

1 Ismahan said she was a special child because she was born on 1st January 2000.

Adrielli, who was a year older than Ismahan, said that she was even more so.

At the precise minute she was born, the time (HH:MM) and date (DD/MM/YY) used ten different digits. She admitted, this did involve using the 24-hour clock.

a Give a possible time and date at which Adrielli could have been born.

Farha was younger than them both, and said that she felt even more special. At the precise minute she was born, the time (HH:MM) and date (DD/MM/YY) were all exactly the same digit.

b On how many occasions could this happen in a millennium?

2 A computer's filing system uses a label with each file to determine who is allowed to use that file, and in what way. A label consists of nine characters: the first three for the user; the next three for the user's group; the last three for everyone. Each set of three covers the three functions 'read', 'write' and 'execute'.

For example, r w x r w – r – – would permit the user to read, write or execute; any member of the group could read or write; and others could only read the file.

It is not valid to allow the group to do something but forbid the user. It is also not valid to allow everyone and forbid the group. All other combinations are valid, although these include some options which are unlikely to be useful.

How many valid labels are possible?

(Adapted from Cambridge AS & A Level Thinking Skills 9694, Paper 12 Q30, June 2013)

3 A bus season ticket costs $9 for 12 single trips. A standard single ticket costs $1.20 whilst a return ticket costs $1.60. A visitor to the area plans to make 7 return trips; he also plans to walk to the beach and get the bus back on 4 occasions.

What is the cost of the cheapest ticket combination he can purchase?

(Adapted from Cambridge AS & A Level Thinking Skills 9694, Paper 12 Q27, June 2012)

Taking it further

4 Carla manages a local store and wants to work out how long the queues are likely to be at different times of the day.

There is only one queue for the checkouts and customers go to the next available checkout once they have reached the front of the queue. Carla assumes that it takes two and a half minutes to serve each customer.

The store opens at 09:00. Carla assumes that one customer joins the queue every 2 minutes, starting at 09:02:00. Therefore, customer 1 arrives at the checkouts at 09:02:00 and is served immediately; customer 2 arrives at 09:04:00 and starts a queue.

The number of customers in the queue for each 30-second period of the first 5 minutes is shown in the diagram below:

	09:00:00		09:01:00		09:02:00		09:03:00		09:04:00		09:05:00
Queue	0	0	0	0	0	0	0	0	1	0	
	No customers at checkouts				Customer 1 being served						

The first time that there is one customer in the queue waiting to be served is at 09:04:00.

a How long will customers 2 and 3 each have to wait to be served?

b At what time will customer 5 have finished being served?

c At what time will there first be two customers in the queue?

A second member of staff begins work at the second checkout at 10:32:00.

d How many customers will be in the queue at 10:31:00?

e At what time will there first be no customers in the queue, after the second checkout has opened?

Carla would like to change the time that the second member of staff starts work. The start time must be either on an hour or at half past an hour and Carla wishes this time to be as late as possible, whilst ensuring that there will be no queue at 14:00:00.

f i) What time should the second member of staff start work at the second checkout? Justify your answer.

ii) What is the longest time that a customer would have to wait to be served if the second member of staff starts work at this time?

(Cambridge AS & A Level Thinking Skills 9694, Paper 32 Q3, November 2016)

When to use it

Systematic listing is a strategy that caters for problems in which it is easy to generate some solutions, but difficult to find all the solutions. The type of problem must generate options (from a finite list), which can be combined in a number of ways. Such problems can often be visualised as occupying a number of blank boxes which need to be filled – with letters, numbers, or options:

The problems become manageable by considering what goes in each of the boxes independently, and then multiplying the number of alternatives that could occupy each box together. When considering how many ways people can be chosen from a list of 10, for instance, there are 10 alternatives for the first box, 9 for the second, 8 for the third, 7 for the fourth and 6 for the fifth.

The total number of possible ways is $10 \times 9 \times 8 \times 7 \times 6 = 30\,240$.

How to use it well

» When making this decision it is useful to remember the decreasing multiplication rule: if you are filling a series of boxes and there are 'n' choices for the first box, then the number of choices in the first two boxes will be $(n) \times (n - 1)$, in the first three boxes $(n) \times (n - 1) \times (n - 2)$, and so on. This produces the factorial formula given below the RATES sample question on pages 101–2: if you have four items to arrange in four boxes, there will be $4 \times 3 \times 2 \times 1 = 24$ ways of doing it.

» Do write out your list formally.

As with many of these strategies, you are aiming to free up the sceptical, creative part of your intellect so that it can criticise your proposed solution and check it for potential errors. This is possible only if your listing process leaves a physical pattern on the page.

2.4 Trial and error

The technique known as trial and error will be familiar to many of you as a part of your standard Maths course: it is a highly formulaic method for finding solutions to difficult equations, to a given degree of accuracy. What is being recommended here as a problem-solving strategy is *not* the same thing.

Trial and error is a slightly more pro-active version of the instruction given at the beginning of this chapter: you can't get anywhere if you don't do anything. Trial and error instructs you to explicitly offer a potential answer to the problem, and then learn from the mistake.

There are many problems where:

1 the essential logic is difficult to grasp
2 the 2358 technique has not helped
3 it is not clear how to diagram what you have
4 there is no obvious list emerging.

In cases like these, you need to consider what an answer to the problem looks like and, when your attempt fails, try to improve your mistake. This process will enable you to gain a perspective on how the problem works.

| Sample question | The annual Twitchers Quiz at the North Warren Wetlands Centre involves 50 multiple-choice questions in which teams attempt to identify birds by their mating calls. |

Teams score 3 points for a correct answer, they lose 1 point for a wrong answer, and there is no penalty for not answering.

The winning team scored 110 points. The runner-up scored 107, despite having answered 2 more questions correctly.

How many questions did the runner-up leave unanswered?

> **Try this problem yourself, before reading the analysis!**

When using trial and error, the best initial 'guess' you can make is one that manages to conform to some of the restrictions. In this case, ensure that the winning team does score 110 (fairly easy to do), and that the runner-up scores 2 more correct answers. The remaining details can be filled in without much thought.

Take 1:

Winning team = 38 correct; 4 incorrect; 8 omitted = 110 points

Runner-up = 40 correct; 5 incorrect; 5 omitted = 115 points

Increase the number of incorrect answers for the runner-up, and this will decrease their score. Consider the maximum case for this.

Take 2:

Winning team = 38 correct; 4 incorrect; 8 omitted = 110 points

Runner-up = 40 correct; 10 incorrect; 0 omitted = 110 points

There is no more room for incorrect answers: 110 is the lowest the runner-up can score, from this starting point. So reconsider and try a different number of correct answers for the winning team.

Take 3:

Winning team = 37 correct; 1 incorrect; 12 omitted = 110 points

Runner-up = 39 correct; 5 incorrect; 6 omitted = 112 points

This does allow room for manoeuvre and 5 more incorrect

questions will lead to the required scores.

Take 4:

Winning team = 37 correct; 1 incorrect; 12 omitted = 110 points

Runner-up = 39 correct; 10 incorrect; 1 omitted = 107 points

This does fulfil all the requirements, and so the runner–up must have omitted one question.

This solution shown here does work, and 'one omitted answer' would be an acceptable answer to the question. However, because we have not exposed the logical entrails of the problem in our working, the solution is unsupported, and fragile. Its fragility is obvious when we ask ourselves whether it is the only correct solution. Nothing we have done allows us to answer this question. As you can see, the strategy does have its limitations for real-life problem solving as a result.

On the other hand, the strategy does allow aspects of the problem's logical entrails to be inspected. For example, one aspect that we have uncovered of the problem's internal working is the fact that one more correct answer for the winner affects the runner-up's minimum by three marks. In this way trial and error can be used as a tool for understanding the nature of the problem, as well as just solving it.

Sample question

> Try this problem yourself, before reading the analysis!

A teacher needs to buy at least 31 doughnuts so that each person in her class can have one. The doughnuts come in two different pack sizes:

Number of doughnuts in pack	Price per pack
5	$2.00
8	$3.10

All the doughnuts are identical.

What is the least amount of money she needs to spend?

(Adapted from Cambridge AS & A Level Thinking Skills 9694, Paper 13 Q9, November 2013)

As with the previous question, the rates involved in this question are not easy to diagram, and not something the 2358 method will help with.

It is tempting to find a combination of packs that adds up to 31 (although this is not necessarily the cheapest way to do it).

Take 1:

16 + 15 = 31, so we can use 2 × 8 packs, and 3 × 5 packs.

This will cost (2 × $3.10) + (3 × $2) = $12.20

It is not clear how good this answer is yet, however. To find this, we need to alter something and study the effect. When doing this

it is important to limit the changes as much as possible, so that we can identify their effects.

Take 2:

Increase the number of 8 packs by one, and reduce the number of 5 packs by one.

3×8 packs and 2×5 packs = 34 doughnuts, giving us the 31 doughnuts we need.

This will cost $(3 \times \$3.10) + (2 \times \$2) = \$13.30$

This takes us further from our target. Let's try something else.

Take 3:

Try four packs of 8, giving 32 doughnuts (so no packs of 5 are needed).

This will cost $(4 \times \$3.10) = \$12.40$

It feels as if our first attempt – of $12.20 – might be the solution, but it is difficult to verify.

All that can be done is to complete the list of solutions according to the number of packs of 8 needed.

Take 4:

We have tried four, three and two packs of 8.

One pack of 8 will require five packs of 5 to reach the 31 doughnut target.

This will cost $(1 \times \$3.10) + (5 \times \$2) = \$13.10$

To achieve a confident solution …

Take 5:

Seven packs of 5 will suffice, with no 8 packs needed.

This will cost $(7 \times \$2) = \$14$

We can now confidently conclude that the least she can spend on doughnuts is $12.20.

Practice questions

1   I have 30 water jugs which I am using for a party. I would like to put a piece of lemon in each one. I do not mind how small the pieces of lemon are. I can provide for all 30 jugs using the lemons that I have, and 21 cuts of the knife. Each cut will divide a whole lemon into two pieces, or divide a section of lemon into two smaller pieces.

How many lemons do I have?

2   Junior and Ibrahim drive from their street to their mother's house in separate cars.

Junior travels the whole distance at 70 km/h, on clear roads.

Ibrahim travels exactly half the distance at 60 km/h and half at 80 km/h. Ibrahim arrives 3.75 minutes later than Junior.

How far is it from their street to their mother's house?

3 Roma makes scented candles, which she sells for $5 each or $11 for 3. Yesterday she took 200 candles with her to a craft fair and sold them all, taking a total of $788.

How many of her candles did Roma sell for $5 at the craft fair?

(Adapted from Cambridge AS & A Level Thinking Skills 9694, Paper 11 Q25, November 2016)

4 A printer provides calling cards, charging a flat fee for setting up the graphics (which remains the same for any number of cards greater than 5) and a rate per card.

You know that the flat fee is a whole number of dollars, and that the rate per card must be more than 10¢ per card.

You overhear the printer charging one customer $4.80 for some calling cards, and then another customer $5.75.

How many cards did the first customer order?

Taking it further

5 The gold ducat is a coin currently worth 40 silver pennies, but, because of the scarcity of gold, King Offa is going to decree an increase in its value relative to the silver penny. Ethelred knows that this will be done overnight on one of the next four nights (Mon, Tue, Wed, Thu), and that the value will go up once by 1, 2 or 3 pennies. All possibilities are equally likely.

Ethelred only has 30 silver pennies. He could get one or more overnight loans, but it costs a halfpenny to get a loan of 10 pennies from one day to the next.

His first thought was to take a loan of 10 pennies to obtain a ducat and renew the loan each night until the revaluation. Then he would convert the ducat back to pennies.

a i) What is the most he could gain with this strategy?

  ii) What is the most he could lose?

Ethelred tells Greta that the value of the ducat will change. She also has 30 pennies, but cannot afford to lose any money. She selects the strategy which gives the best chance of making some gain whilst ensuring that she will not lose any money.

b i) Describe the strategy that Greta selects.

  ii) What is the probability that she will make some gain?

  iii) What is the most that she can gain?

  iv) **On Monday**, what is the probability that she will have gained the maximum possible by Friday?

(Cambridge AS & A Level Thinking Skills 9694, Paper 31 Q1 (a) & (b), June 2012)

When to use it

Like with '2358', the trial and error strategy is designed for cases when the logic of the question is not easy to see or diagram. It succeeds by prodding the question, and then studying the response. As shown in the examples, one can learn from the process only by trying one case, and then another in which one of the variables is changed.

Unlike those cases that succumb to systematic listing, the strategy works when there are infinite possible options.

How to use it well

>> The trial and error strategy depends on laying out which examples you are using clearly, for formal inspection. The reason for this is twofold: first to enable you to inspect your investigation easily; second to give someone assessing your solution a chance of understanding what you are doing. You may well be trying answers which are far from the goal, and not following the path that the problem setter, or the assessor, has in mind. And without some guidance, you will lose your audience.

>> Ensure that you precisely control what you change when you choose a new case to study. It is always tempting to seek shortcuts, especially when problem solving in high-pressure situations, such as exam conditions, but if you alter two variables from Take 1 to Take 2, you may well confuse the effect of one with the effect of the other. In this lies the art of efficient trial and error.

3 Tackling the problem (II)

By the end of this chapter you will be able to:

★ use 'functions and algebra' as a problem-solving strategy
★ use 'sequence generation' as a problem-solving strategy
★ use 'particular solutions' as a problem-solving strategy
★ use 'Venn diagrams and logic' as a problem-solving strategy
★ select which strategy is appropriate in exam situations.

The last chapter covered four general problem-solving strategies which were designed to cope with unfamiliar problems, and to be useable in diverse situations. We also noted some general rules that accompany any problem solving:

>> A problem explained (to you) is a problem stolen (from you). You learn most about a problem when you are struggling with it, so ask for an explanation only as a last resort.

>> You cannot get anywhere if you don't do anything. Rather than being immobilised by a problem, some of the techniques we're learning will help give you an idea of what you might do, or where you might begin.

>> The variety of problems you can face is endless. At its heart, the subject of Thinking Skills is 'The Unknown Problem', and you must keep this in mind whenever you are practising the techniques that constitute the course.

In this chapter you will learn four further strategies to call on when trying to solve a problem. These strategies are more refined, more specialised, and often more powerful than the four we've looked at already.

3.1 Function machines and algebra

'Function machines' in the context of this chapter are an informal diagramming of the relationships that make up a problem (rather than the formal language of functions used in A Level Maths courses and beyond). Function machines may have been introduced to you when you first encountered algebra; however, function machines in Thinking Skills are more flexible, and have fewer rules.

References to 'algebra' are to the familiar topic from your Maths course; however, within Thinking Skills the key problem-solving skill is the expression of the problem in algebraic terms. This can be a challenging task, requiring art and imagination, and is separate from the manipulation of algebraic symbols (for example, solving equations, factorising expressions, writing the expressions in different formats). The focus in Thinking Skills is on the use of algebra as an aid to problem solving, although some brief notes on the manipulation of algebraic symbols are included in Section 5.1 for your reference.

The two parts of this problem-solving strategy – function machines and algebra – both offer the same kind of response to a problem: they aim to clearly lay out, on the page, the logical structure of a problem involving a number of unknown quantities. Once the problem is laid out unambiguously, you can then use appropriate techniques to find the unknown quantities.

Function machines

Function machines are just diagrams which encode the different moving parts of a problem and how they relate. They use boxes and arrows to represent objects and processes, but they are meant to be adaptable. You should aim to develop a few good habits which will allow your diagramming to work, and be willing to break those habits if the problem needs it.

Sample question

Try this problem yourself, before reading the analysis!

Charles' journey from his home to his school takes a varying amount of time depending on when he leaves, the volume of traffic on the roads, the weather, and how late the bus is when it arrives. The longest bus journey time is 35 minutes, the average 25 minutes, and the shortest 20 minutes. The bus, which is timetabled to run every 15 minutes, can be as much as 12 minutes late. He has to arrive at school no later than 08:00 to ensure he is able to go on a school trip.

Given that his walk to the bus stop takes just under two minutes, at what time must he leave home to make sure he is able to go on the school trip?

(Adapted from Cambridge AS & A Level Thinking Skills 9694, Paper 11 Q28, November 2016)

➤

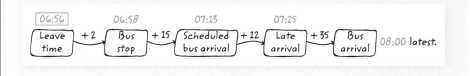

The question involves an unknown value (the times he must leave) subject to a number of varying constraints. This can be easily represented as a function machine, according to the basic principles:

◆ *Start with the answer*, if it is unclear. In this case, the time he must leave home.

◆ *Box the number along the way*. In this case, the times he will be at the different points in his journey.

◆ *Write the processes by the connecting arrows*. In this case, the relevant times that each event could take.

This gives something like the diagram above.

Some of these values take care and thought – and you may leave a couple of options. For example, is the maximum time until the first bus 14 minutes or 15 minutes? Do we need the average time for a bus journey or the longest time?

Once the information has been codified it is worth checking that all the relevant restrictions and times have been selected. It is possible to work backwards to the answer (diagram below).

This gives the answer: the latest time he can leave to be sure he is in time for the trip is **06:56**.

Many problems involve more options than this, often without a linear chain of events. The next sample question involves a collection of interrelated quantities and rates, and is difficult to hold in your mind 'in one go'.

A teacher's contract requires her to spend 800 hours in contact with students during the school year. The school year lasts 40 weeks and each lesson lasts 1 hour. This is her timetable for the new academic year.

Day	Period 1	Period 2	Period 3	Period 4	Period 5	Period 6
Monday	3B	2J	1H	–	2H	1A
Tuesday	–	3B	–	4G	3T	5L
Wednesday	1A	–	6L	2P	–	2T
Thursday	2J	–	5L	2T	4G	–
Friday	1H	–	2P	3T	–	6L

> Try this problem yourself, before reading the analysis!

Within the 40 weeks of the school year, students get a week's study leave in January and three weeks in June. However, the teacher is expected to do 9 hours of invigilation during each week of study leave, which also counts as contact hours.

The teacher checks whether the school is giving her too much contact time.

How many hours over or under her contracted time is she due to work?

(Adapted from Cambridge AS & A Level Thinking Skills 9694, Paper 11 Q25, November 2012)

Applying the basic principles described above:

➤ **Start with the answer, if it is unclear. In this case, the total number of contact hours.**

➤ **Box the number along the way. In this case, the component parts of the school year, and the hours of contact in each.**

➤ **Write the processes by the connecting arrows. In this case, the addition and multiplication of relevant values.**

These connections yield a diagram looking like this:

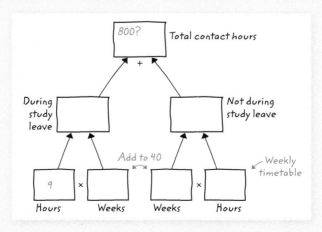

In this diagram you must not be concerned if you are unsure what a value is – there will always be some 'unknowns', to be filled in later.

Having laid out the structure, you need to add in as many pieces of information as you can from the text. This will give you something like this:

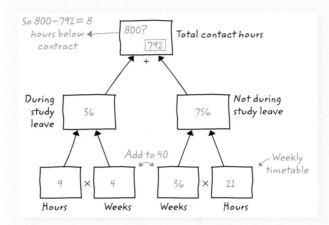

The final stage of the problem is to find out what the missing boxes must be. Normally it is obvious in problem-solving questions whether the answer should be unique or a range of answers. In this case, 'How many hours over or under her contracted time is she due to work?' makes it clear that we are expecting one answer – which will depend on the number of hours she is in contact with students in a year.

As the second diagram shows, she will be scheduled 36 hours of contact time during study leave, and 756 hours during the rest of the year. This leaves her $(800 - 792) = 8$ hours under her contract.

Practice questions

1 Five friends take Zebedee out for his birthday.

The return train tickets to the local town costs $10 each.

They bought a cake to share between them.

They then paid for 4 rounds of 'crazy snooker' ($0.50 per person per game).

And then ordered 4 ice creams to share (which were $1 each).

They then played frisbee until the Sun went down and finally returned home.

When they got back they added up the total they had spent, and decided to cover the costs of the day out as a birthday present to Zebedee – so they split the total five ways, and ended up paying $16.80 each.

How much did the cake cost?

2 Ben hires a van to help his friend move house. He knows that the round trip is 350 km and the van hire company tells him that the van does

100 km per $10.00 worth of diesel fuel (the diesel costs 70 cents per litre). He asks them to put $36.00 worth of diesel into the van. However, the pump is faulty and actually puts in extra fuel at a rate of 51 litres for every 50 litres shown on the pump. On the return journey he encounters a fallen tree across the road and has to make a detour. There are no filling stations on the remainder of his journey, but he decides to get as near to his destination as he can.

What is the maximum distance the detour could have added to his journey if he still manages to make it back?

(Adapted from Cambridge AS & A Level Thinking Skills 9694, Paper 11 Q20, November 2012)

3 George's consultancy firm has a large number of employees who use their own cars when travelling to customers. The company pays 10¢ per kilometre travelled towards the cost of the journey, plus an additional 25¢ for each visit made. Because many employees have complained that this is not enough to cover the cost, George has decided to change the policy. He can only afford to increase the total cost for an average week (40 visits covering a total of 300 kilometres) by 10%. The new policy will still offer a rate per kilometre, plus an amount per visit (both of which will be a whole number of cents), and George wants the rate per kilometre to be as high as possible.

What will be the amount paid for a visit involving travel of 20 kilometres?

(Adapted from Cambridge AS & A Level Thinking Skills 9694, Paper 11 Q17, November 2012)

When to use it

Function machines show processes, and allow you to track how a variety of inputs is transformed by these processes. So any problem that involves a series of processes being applied to an input, to yield an output, can be presented using boxes and arrows.

How to use it well

» Make sure you write down the processes carefully, so that you are able to 'reverse them' to find missing values. Your default approach to the diagramming of function machines should be to use boxes for the values (which may change as you work towards a solution) and arrows for the processes (which normally do not change).

» Be flexible. Different problems may require you to consider multiple inputs combining to produce outputs which are subject to various conditions, with processing values that change; they may require you to change a value in the middle of the diagram, in order to find another one which is obscurely linked to the first. The key principle for diagramming a function machine is that you should try to represent all relevant connections and processes, even if the resulting network is a mess. And that you should represent any missing values with a '?'.

» Don't be afraid to restart your diagram from a different perspective if you are struggling to draw it.

Algebra

Consider where you stand on the following scale:

At one end you may be algebra-phobic; in the middle, you may be used to it only in Maths assessments (and think it should stay that way); at the other end you may be an eager practitioner, already competent and keen to push your understanding.

This section is written with those in the middle of the scale in mind.

If you are mildly algebra-phobic, you may wish to refer to Section 4.1 which reminds you of the basic principles. If you are an eager practitioner, then feel free to focus on the problems themselves with only a cursory look at the discussion of how algebra may be used as a problem-solving tool.

As with function machines, algebra attempts to capture the relationship described in a problem. The structure is much more rigid and prescriptive, but the mechanisms for extracting the answer are more predictable. If one is to use algebra to solve a problem, it is vital to:

» define your variables. Always begin with a sentence like: 'Let x = the new distance travelled'. If you introduce other variables, define these too.

» make sure your equations have an equals sign.

» separate out the equations you create.

» state your answer as a sentence, in the context of the question, at the end.

Sample question

Two different types of cake are on sale at prices of 30¢ and 40¢ each. The cakes that are being sold for 30¢ cost 20¢ to make and the ones for sale at 40¢ cost 25¢ to make. No cakes can be kept to be sold the next day, so all of the cakes are reduced to half price 2 hours before the sales finish.

All of the 30¢ cakes sold out before any of the prices were reduced, and all of the 40¢ were eventually sold, even though only half had been sold when the price was reduced. The overall profit at the end of the day was $30, but it could have been $40 if all of the cakes had sold before the prices were reduced.

How many of each type of cake were there in the sale?

(Adapted from Cambridge AS & A Level Thinking Skills 9694, Paper 13 Q23, November 2015)

You can prepare for creating the equation as follows:

Let T = number of 30 ¢ cakes on sale

Let F = number of 40 ¢ cakes on sale

$$\text{Overall profit} = 3000 = (T \times (30-20)) + (\tfrac{1}{2}F \times (40-25))$$
$$+ (\tfrac{1}{2}F \times (20-25))$$

$$\text{Profit if all sold before prices reduced} = 4000 = (T \times (30-20)) + (F \times (40-25))$$

The profits in dollars have been converted into cents, in order to make all the units correspond. This is easy to forget when phrasing relationships algebraically.

With all the information encoded into two equations, the problem solver needs to reflect on how to solve the pair simultaneously. This requires simplification of the algebraic relationships, and strategic decisions about how to eliminate one of the variables.

The following shows one way to do this.

The answer: 100 40¢ cakes were for sale, and 250 30¢ cakes. This can be checked by trying those numbers in the two original statements. See Section 4.3 for more on 'jigsaw-piece verification'.

Simplified $10T + \frac{15}{2}F - \frac{5}{2}F = 3000$

$10T + 15F = 4000$

Subtract top from bottom $10F = 1000$

$\boxed{F = 100}$

Substitute into second equation $10T + 1500 = 4000$

so $\boxed{T = 250}$

Sample question

Try this problem yourself, before reading the analysis!

Heraclitus and Parmenides have a weekly argument, which continues until one of them agrees that the other has won. They have records of who won:

11 weeks ago Heraclitus had won exactly $\frac{3}{4}$ of the battles. However, Parmenides has won 8 times in the last 11 weeks, and now has a success rate of 60 per cent.

How many times has Heraclitus won the argument?

In this sample problem there is a choice about what to use as the variable (either the number of times Heraclitus has won 11 weeks ago or the number of times that Heraclitus has won now or the total number of times they have argued). The default position is to let x equal the thing you are trying to find; here that is: 'The number of times that Heraclitus has won the argument.'

Sometimes it is worth stepping back to consider which relationships are easiest to express algebraically first – in this case, it is easier to begin with the number of arguments won by each person 11 weeks ago.

Let H = number of times Heraclitus has won now

Let P = number of times Parmenides has won now

$$\frac{P}{H+P} = 0.6$$

Present success rate: 60%

$$\frac{H-3}{H+P-11} = \frac{3}{4}$$

11 weeks ago H had won $(11-8)$ 3 less arguments

Let H = number of times Heraclitus had won 11 weeks ago

Let P = number of times Parmenides had won 11 weeks ago

$$\frac{H}{H+P} = \frac{3}{4}$$

Success rate 11 weeks ago

$$\frac{P+8}{H+P+11} = 0.6$$

Success rate (when P has won 8 more arguments)

The diagram shows how the two compare.

The relationships on the right-hand side are easier to phrase algebraically.

If the two equations are solved simultaneously, they produce the results: $P = 1$ and $H = 3$

This means that Parmenides had won one argument 11 weeks ago and Heraclitus had won three. This means that Heraclitus has now won $(3 + 3) = 6$ times while Parmenides has won $(1 + 8) = 9$ times.

Practice questions

1 Photographs of students are taken and offered for sale in various packages.

2 large and 3 small: $8

3 large and 2 small: $9

4 large and 2 small: $11

These prices include the same amount for postage and packing.

What is the cost of postage and packing included in these prices?

(Adapted from Cambridge AS & A Level Thinking Skills 9694, Paper 11 Q5, June 2015)

2 Peter is laying out his vegetable plot, which is $3\,\text{m} \times 3\,\text{m}$. He wants to divide it into four sections, as shown, all of equal area.

How long should the line marked 'x' be?

(Adapted from Cambridge AS & A Level Thinking Skills 9694, Paper 11 Q16, June 2015)

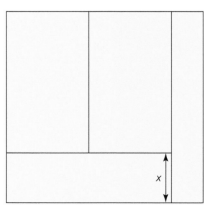

Not to scale

3 The Prudosian Rail Company is buying some new trains. The trains

must have an engine carriage at each end, and a number of passenger carriages in between.

A train with 3 passenger carriages costs $360 000.

A train with 5 passenger carriages costs $480 000.

How much will a train with 6 passenger carriages cost?

4 Simon and his two friends buy tickets from a low-cost airline to fly to Rome. The return flight costs $10 less than the outgoing flight and the airport tax for each flight is $20 on top of the airfare. One of Simon's friends will not return and only has an outgoing ticket. The overall cost of the flights was $320.

What is the price of the outgoing flight?

(Adapted from Cambridge AS & A Level Thinking Skills 9694, Paper 12 Q21, June 2012)

Taking it further

5 Package holidays to *Costa Natura* are priced per person.

The current brochure only gives departure dates up to December 17th, but holidays continue after that date.

The **total** price per person is made up from the flight price for the outbound flight, the flight price for the flight back, and their cost for the room.

The room price does not depend upon the number of people sharing the room, but may change from week to week.

The flight price changes frequently, but is the same in both directions on any date.

There are no discounts.

The prices in the brochure (shown below) are **total** prices, **per person**, given in dollars; they refer to holidays starting on the date shown.

Someone has put a coffee mug on my brochure, and I can't read some of the figures.

Departure date	1 person 1 week	1 person 2 weeks	2 sharing 1 week	2 sharing 2 weeks
Nov 5th	550	660	500	560
Nov 12th	570	730	520	630
Nov 19th	640	750	590	645
Nov 26th	710	760	655	65.
Dec 3rd	650	760	595	
Dec 10th	590	710	535	
Dec 17th	600	710	545	6.

a What is the price of a room for the week beginning Nov 5th?

b Considering only holidays which begin on one of the dates shown in the table, for which week or weeks will it not be possible to be sure of the room price?

c What is the highest weekly room price, for the weeks for which it can be determined?

d What is the cheapest date for an outbound flight, and what is the (one-way) cost per person on that day?

(Cambridge AS & A Level Thinking Skills 9694, Paper 31 Q1 (a) – (d), June 2013)

When to use it

Phrasing a problem algebraically works well if there is a clear unknown value and a collection of restrictions that it must conform to. Many of the function-machine questions can be phrased algebraically.

For instance, the earlier sample question about teacher contact hours can be phrased as:

$$(H_1 \times W_1) + (H_2 + W_2) \ ? < 800$$

$$W_1 + W_2 = 40$$

where H_1 = the number of contact hours per week during study leave, W_1 = the number of weeks of study leave in a year, H_2 = the number of contact hours during a normal school week, and W_2 = the number of normal school weeks in a year. The '? <' symbol means 'is it less than?'

Whether you wish to perfect the art of phrasing problems algebraically or expressing them as function machines will depend on how strong your algebraic manipulation skills are (that is, how confident you feel in solving the equation that is produced).

How to use it well

Phrasing a problem algebraically depends upon you being very clear about what any letters you use stand for. It is vital that you state briefly what they mean, for instance 'H_1 = contact hours during study leave', and it is a good habit to do this with absolute precision, for example, stating what units you are using: 'Let H_1 = the number of contact hours per week during study leave.'

One of the benefits of stating a problem algebraically is that it is normally possible to see whether an equation is solvable. As a rule of thumb, you can find a unique answer to *one* equation involving *one* unknown, *two* equations involving *two* unknowns and *three* equations involving *three* unknowns. Anything more than that gets messy.

If you find yourself with more unknowns than equations, then you will not find a unique solution – but this may mean that you have a 'degree of freedom', and can choose a value for one of the unknowns. Often this allows you to 'Let $x = 1$' (or 'whichever letter you like' = 'whichever number you like').

If you find yourself with more equations than unknowns, you can use one equation to check the answer that you get from solving the others. If you find that you get two answers that disagree, then you have inconsistent equations, and you may have made a mistake in the way you have phrased the equation.

There are some brief reminders about how to solve equations and how to phrase them in Section 5.6.

3.2 Sequence generation

Sequence generation is another specialised problem-solving strategy. This strategy aims to find patterns in problems which involve a large number of objects, building up from the simplest cases (involving as few objects as possible). Sequence generation ignores the mechanism and context particular to the problem it is being used on and, instead, reduces the problem to just an input and an output. These can then be studied separately from the distracting details, and patterns can be sought. Once the nature of the pattern has been found, you can precisely predict cases which occur 'further down the list'.

If the input and output are related by a **linear** formula then it is easy to predict the output for any given input. If a formula is **quadratic** in nature (involving squaring the input), it will require more sophisticated maths to be solved. A reminder of how this process can be carried out efficiently for linear cases is given in Section 5.7.

Key terms

Linear – A linear relationship exists between two variables if there is a formula involving only multiplying the input by some number and/or adding to it. An example would be taking the input and adding 10 to it; or taking the input and doubling it; or taking the input, halving it and then adding 100. One aspect of linear relationships that allows them to be easily identified is that they always have a 'common difference', that is, the difference between any pair of adjacent terms is always equal.

Relationships that are not linear (and which are much harder to identify, and to predict) include those involving squaring the input, and dividing a number by the input.

Quadratic (adjective) – Involving squared values, but not higher degrees (like cubes).

Sample question

Try this problem yourself, before reading the analysis!

A set designer is constructing a stepped platform for a choir to stand on. The platform will be constructed of cubic boxes, arranged to form steps. A section of the platform, on which five rows of choristers could stand, four on each row, is shown on the right.

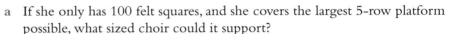

The set designer needs to ensure that all the parts that are visible to the audience before the choir come in are covered in black felt. The flat sides (with 15 squares shown on the diagram) will be visible, as well as the fronts and tops of the rows where the choir will stand. The faces which stand against the back wall and on the floor will NOT be visible.

a   If she only has 100 felt squares, and she covers the largest 5-row platform possible, what sized choir could it support?
b   Find the number of felt squares needed to cover the platform if it is to be capable of supporting 5 rows with 50 choristers on each.

An appropriate input and output are fairly easy to spot here: the number in each row (input) and the number of squares of felt needed (output).

A table allows you to concentrate on each case one by one, and to store them to review later.

Number in each row	Number of squares needed
1	15 + 10 + 15 = 40
2	15 + 20 + 15 = 50
3	15 + 30 + 15 = 60
4	15 + 40 + 15 = 70

a   It is easy to see that this sequence leads to 7 in each row, needing 100 squares. This means $(7 \times 5) = 35$ choristers.

b   In this question it is necessary to state the relationship between the number in each row and the number of squares formally. Because each person per row adds on 10 more squares, and the end pieces require 15 squares each, the following formula is reached:

(number of people per row $\times$ 10) + 30 = total number needed.

If there are 50 people in a row, then that will require $(50 \times 10) + 30 = 530$ felt squares.

Practice questions

1   In a certain family, the father gives out pocket money to his children in the following way.

Every month he chooses a number between 1 and 100, and then shares that amount of money equally between the seven children, giving them whole-number sums of money, and giving anything left over to charity.

For instance, if he chose the number 30, he would give $4 to each child ($4 × 7 = $28) and $2 to charity.

If the father realises after 100 months that every number between 1 and 100 (inclusive) has been used once, how much has he given to charity?

(Adapted from Cambridge AS & A Level Thinking Skills 9694, Paper 13 Q24, November 2013)

2   A school chess competition involves 20 players. In the first part of the competition, all of the players play each other once. On the basis of the results of these games, the top ten players qualify for the championship. In the championship, players play each other twice.

How many games do you play if you reach the championship?

3   A builder is supplying one hundred new beach huts to the town of Seasideville. They will be positioned in a row along the seafront and will be numbered consecutively from 1 to 100. The builder wants to provide a colourful display and so he paints the huts according to the rules given in the following table.

Colour of hut	Number
Purple	A multiple of both 3 and 5
Red	A multiple of 3, but not a multiple of 5
Blue	A multiple of 5, but not a multiple of 3
Yellow	One more or one less than a multiple of both 3 and 5

The remaining huts are painted green.
How many huts will be painted green?

(Adapted from Cambridge AS & A Level Thinking Skills 9694, Paper 11 Q22, November 2016)

4   Margaret is making name cards for guests at a wedding, and decides she will cut up a plastic checked tablecloth to do this.

The tablecloth is a 3 m square, covered in black and white squares, each of width 5 cm. The top left-hand corner of it is shown here.

She wishes to cut out cards which look like this, to write the names of guests on.

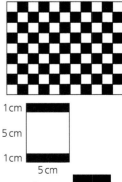

a   How many name cards can she cut from the tablecloth?

Margaret considers cutting out cards which include 1cm of black border on each of the four sides:

b   How many name cards of the second kind can she cut?

Taking it further

5   Gwen runs a company called *Lance-a-lock* and wishes to reassure her customers about the security of the locks she sells. The most basic type of lock is defined by a 5-digit code. The digits of the code represent the shape of the 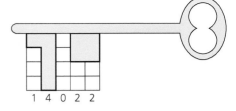 key that matches the lock by describing it as the lengths of 5 columns of squares, each of which can be up to 4 units long. An example is shown above. The columns of the key can be any integer length from 0 to 4 – except that the extreme case of **0 0 0 0 0** is not permissible because it would not turn any lock.

a   How many different keys of this sort can be made?

The Guild of Locksmiths places restrictions on what locks and keys are permitted. One is that no lock should have a 'low-security code' – one which could be opened by a key with a code that does not match the lock, by partially inserting the key.

An example of a lock with a low-security code is **0 2 0 0 0**. This could be opened by the key with code **2 0 0 0 0**, partially inserted so that the 2 lines up with the appropriate part of the lock.

You should assume that the key cannot be inserted further into the lock than intended – so the key with code **0 2 0 0 0** cannot open the lock with code **2 0 0 0 0**.

b   Which five locks could be opened by the key **3 0 0 0 0**?

c   Give an example of a key, with a code containing no more than two 0s, that could open more than one lock. List all the locks that this key could open.

For some locks (such as door locks) the key can be inserted from either side. In these cases the shape of the key needs to match the shape of the lock whichever side it is put in.

d   How many locks, including low-security locks, are permissible given this restriction?

Considering also the restriction on low-security locks, Gwen concludes that there are only 100 locks available using this kind of key, and thinks that this may worry some of her customers. She therefore considers using locks with 7-digit codes.

e   Subject to all the restrictions, how many locks with 7-digit codes are permissible?

(Cambridge AS & A Level Thinking Skills 9694, Paper 32 Q2 (a) – (c), (e) & (f), June 2016)

When to use it

Sequence generation depends upon the reduction of the problem to an input and an output. This does not mean that there can only be two 'relevant numbers' in the processing – but all other values must be 'held steady' while the chosen input and output are investigated.

This is possible only in certain problems.

As was alluded to at the beginning of this section, the maths required to identify the key numbers in the relationship is easily manageable when it is linear, feasible when it is quadratic (if you know the techniques) and increasingly time-consuming when other relationships are involved.

How to use it well

Identifying when a relationship within a problem is likely to be linear is important. The linear relationship makes it easy to predict the output for any given input, and appreciating this allows you to make the most use of the sequence-generation technique, especially when faced with time pressures.

As with the other abstract techniques discussed in this chapter, it is vital that any predictions made by sequence generation are given an independent check at the end (for more detail on this see Section 4.2).

3.3 Particular solutions

Certain problems can be disorientating because of their generality. The 'particular solutions' strategy can be applied to these kind of problems. In such problems where you are considering a general case (covering all possible values), it is often possible to select a single arbitrary value to represent all possible values.

On the surface this strategy looks a little like '2358' (see Section 2.1), and 'trial and error' (see Section 2.4), in that it involves choosing simple values for key variables in the question. However, the intention here is different – you are choosing your 'random' values as exemplars of 'any number'. As such, the answer that you find will be the answer to the 'general case'.

Sample question

> Try this problem yourself, before reading the analysis!

When banks enable customers to withdraw money using a bank card and a simple four-digit Personal Identification Number (PIN), they must balance the security of their customers with the likelihood that customers will make occasional mistakes. The number of possible PINs created from any of the ten digits in any of the four positions acts as the main security guard. And most people make only occasional mistakes.

One solution is to withdraw any bank card from circulation if, and only if, at least two of the digits are entered incorrectly. If the correct number is entered then the customer is allowed to withdraw money. If a PIN with one incorrect digit is entered, the customer is informed that an error has occurred and asked to try again.

If this system is applied, how many different PINs would result in a customer being asked to try again?

> **This question is off-putting because it is so general. All possible four-digit codes flash before your eyes, and it is difficult to focus on what is being asked.**
>
> **However, it is implicit in the question that the answer is not dependent on what the PIN is.**
>
> **So, it is true for all PIN numbers.**
>
> **And so it is true for any PIN number.**
>
> **So let us choose a number: let us consider the PIN 4261.**
>
> **What would constitute 'one incorrect digit'? Beginning with the first digit:**
>
> **5261, 6261, 7261, 8261, 9261, 0261, 1261, 2261 and 3261 would all involve one incorrect digit, and thus a request to try again. There are nine options.**
>
> **A similar consideration of the next digit (4361, 4461, 4561, 4661, …) reveals nine alternatives.**
>
> **And you can hopefully see that there will be nine for each digit. There will be no overlap between these miskeyed codes, and so the total number is 36 PINs.**

In some cases where a general problem is considered, choosing an arbitrary value, or set of values, does not shed much light on the problem. In problems like this it is worth considering what an extreme case is for one of the variables, since this may make the logic of the problem more stark. One example is to consider what happens when a variable equals zero (if that is a permissible value) since that can reveal how the other variables are related. Alternatively, considering the largest possible value can allow its influence on other variables to become clearer.

Once again, the reasoning goes:

- if the claim is true generally
- then it is true for all values of the key variable
- and then it is true for any values
- so you can choose whatever you like for the variable
- so you can choose the most extreme value.

Sample question

> **Try this problem yourself, before reading the analysis!**

An airplane flies in a straight line from airport A to airport B, then back in a straight line from B to A. It travels with constant engine speed, and there is no wind. Will its travel time for the same round trip be longer, shorter or the same if there is a constant wind which blows from A to B during the whole return journey?

This question has the tell-tale lack of detail which often allows for a particular solutions approach. Implied in the question is the claim that the travel time will be longer, shorter or the same *regardless of what the engine speed is, and what the wind speed is.*

One could make up some simple numbers for these, for example: the plane goes at 100 km/h and the wind blows at 10 km/h.

But this still leaves us with some careful analysis of distances, speeds and times to perform.

If, following the reasoning discussed previously, it is true for any speeds, then we should consider extreme speeds, to see if this makes the problem simpler. What is the extreme case, in terms of movement? Well, an extreme would be for the wind to be going the same speed as the plane. In that case, the plane will go fast in one direction but, in the other direction, the speed of the wind will cancel out the speed of the plane – so the plane will go nowhere! As a result, the round trip will never be completed. This result shows that a round trip with a constant wind will definitely take longer than a round trip with no wind.

Practice questions

1   This year the local supermarket has offered a 'special' 25 per cent discount on the noodles that I like. At New Year, it invites me to 'Buy one and get one free', as well as applying the usual discount.

    What is the overall reduction from full price if I buy noodles at New Year?

2   I am marketing a new app and trying to maximise the profit I make. I find that when I drop the price by 10 per cent, the number of people buying it goes up significantly, and the profit I make goes up by 10 per cent.

    By what percentage did the number of people buying it increase?

3   A caretaker wished to cordon off a rectangular area of a playground using a piece of rope.

    The playground is bounded on two sides by the school buildings.

➤

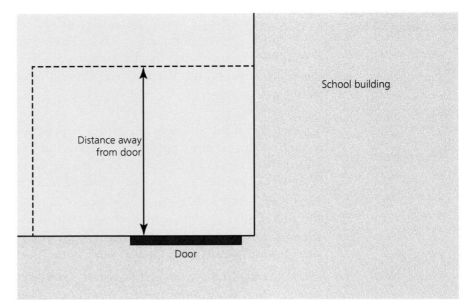

School building

Distance away
from door

Door

Draw a graph showing how the area changes as the distance from the door changes.

4   A commuter is in the habit of arriving at her suburban station each evening at exactly 5 o'clock. Her husband always meets the train and drives her home. One day she takes an earlier train, arriving at the station at 4 o'clock. The weather is pleasant, so she decides to start walking down the route her husband always drives. They meet somewhere along the way, and he drives them home, arriving home 10 minutes earlier than usual. Assuming that he always drives at the same speed, and that he left at his normal time to meet the 5 o'clock train, for how long did she walk (in minutes) before being picked up?

Taking it further

5   The *Qualis?* magazine uses a five-star rating in its reports on consumer goods: 1 star indicates barely adequate; 5 stars indicate perfection. Items which would get no stars in at least one category are simply not listed. Jack and Jill are considering which bucket to purchase. The available choices are:

Name	Capacity	Handle	Pouring	Base	Price
Kova	5 litres	★ ★ ★	★ ★ ★	★	$11
Pail	5 litres	★ ★	★ ★ ★ ★	★ ★ ★	$12
Seau	4 litres	★ ★ ★	★ ★	★ ★ ★ ★	$11
Emmer	6 litres	★ ★	★	★ ★	$13
Ndoo	5 litres	★	★ ★ ★ ★ ★	★ ★	$15
Kopp	6 litres	★ ★ ★	★ ★ ★	★ ★ ★ ★	$14

Jack's priorities are to have both the largest capacity and the best handle.

a   Which one would Jack select if he ignored other considerations?
Jill wants to pay the minimum, but also wants the pouring to be the best available.

b   i)   What stops Jill having both her priorities?

   ii)   Which one would she select if her main requirement was cost, and she was then to look for best pouring given minimum price, ignoring Jack's preferences?

Jack and Jill make a joint decision, and agree to take a bucket that gives the best available score for at least one of Jack's priorities and at least one of Jill's.

c   Which one do they select? Explain why.

Mervyn suggests that the best way to look at the information in the table is by showing each option as a pentagon, where the five ratings are displayed on five axes. For example:

It is normal to arrange the ratings along the axes so that being further away from the centre represents being 'better'. Here, having a larger capacity is considered to be better.

d   Since a lower price is a better price, suggest what to do with the rating for price.

e   i)   Bucket A is better than bucket B in precisely two categories and bucket B is better than bucket A in precisely two categories. Sketch, on one set of axes, two possible pentagons for buckets A and B.

   ii)   If the pentagon for bucket C touches but does not go outside that of bucket D, would any customer be disadvantaged if bucket C were no longer available? Explain your answer.

f   Give an example of ratings for a seventh bucket, the *Spand*, which doesn't have the worst rating of any of the buckets in the table for any factor, but which nobody would choose to buy based on the *Qualis?* assessment. Explain why they would not.

(Cambridge AS & A Level Thinking Skills 9694,
Paper 32 Q1, November 2015)

When to use it

Particular solutions are possible to introduce only when you are being asked to find a solution that is generalised and which applies over a range of values. These types of problem are often daunting because they are general, and there is little that is concrete enough to diagram or tabulate or list.

The key to selecting this strategy is to realise that such problems which are true for all values are therefore true for any values – and that places the power back in your hands.

How to use it well

As has been exemplified in the sample questions, when choosing a particular input you should either aim for numbers that are 'easy', or ones that are in some sense 'extreme' (therefore making the logic of the question easier).

3.4 Venn diagrams

Venn diagrams show how different concepts can overlap by forcing you to consider the exhaustive list of possibilities. For example, if A and B are two closely related properties:

1 Could an object be both A and B?
2 Could an object be A but not B?
3 Could an object be B but not A?
4 Could an object be neither A nor B?

The diagram forces these decisions upon you, while also enabling you to concentrate on other things.

One thing to note, and which is often forgotten, is the 'universal set'. This is generally drawn as a large rectangle, and contains all of the elements that are being considered in the problem.

Example

Venn diagram in action

Consider the descriptors A = {prime numbers} and B = {factors of 30} applied to the universal set = {positive integers less than 10}.

Integers less than 10

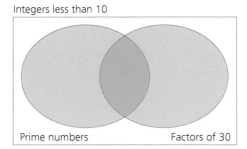

Prime numbers   Factors of 30

When completing a Venn diagram it is natural to begin with the central section, as this is usually the easiest part of the diagram to state a qualifying definition for. In our above example, the central section contains 'positive integers less than 10, which are both prime numbers, and also factors of 30'.

In a problem-solving context it is normally easiest to consider the central intersection of a Venn diagram first, but there is no 'objective necessity' to do so.

Consideration of all the objects in the universal set yields the following classification:

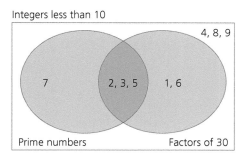

When you have allocated a number to every section, it is worth checking that the elements in the sections add up to what you are expecting. In this case, that there are nine digits on the diagram (hopefully you have considered '0' and rejected it as not being a positive integer).

> ## ACTIVITY
>
> For each of the following pairs of properties, try to find an example of an object/word which could go in each of the four sections of the diagram.
>
> 1 A = {objects that you are capable of lifting}, B = {objects that are too big to fit in an average car}, universal set = {physical objects}.
>
> 2 A = {names appropriate for a baby boy}, B = {names appropriate for a baby girl}, universal set = {written words}.
>
> 3 A = {fractions made up of two single digits}, B = {numbers that can be written as finite, non-recurring decimal numbers}, universal set = {numbers less than 1}.
>
> 4 A = {carnivores}, B = {mammals}, universal set = {animals}.
>
> 5 A = {carnivores}, B = {animals that you personally have eaten}, universal set = {animals}.
>
> 6 A = {nationalities}, B = {ethnic group}, universal set = {words}.
>
> 7 A = {animals}, B = {things that can move themselves around independently}, universal set = {physical objects}.

In problem-solving situations, it is often the case that you are asked to find a maximum or minimum value that could conform to a Venn diagram restriction.

1 Moby is a border guard at Passport Control. On his shift, he notices that 20 of the first 30 travellers wear reading glasses, and 12 of them carry a briefcase.

What is the smallest number that could wear glasses but not carry a briefcase?

2 In Tamlandia, there are four daily newspapers – The Tribune, The Morning Gazette, The Headline News and The State Herald.

180 Tamlandians were asked which of the four newspapers they had bought on a specific date in a survey.

Of the 122 people who said they had bought newspapers on that date:

53 had bought The Tribune

55 had bought The Morning Gazette

39 had bought The Headline News

17 had bought The State Herald.

a What is the largest number of residents who could have bought all four newspapers?

b What is the largest number who could have bought three?

c What is the smallest number who could have bought four?

3 The diagram below shows eight students, represented by dots, and which of three courses – Financial skills, Ethics in business, and Marketing – they are studying at a university.

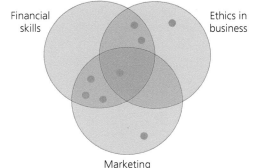

Financial skills

Ethics in business

Marketing

Complete the following table showing the courses that the students took:

	Financial skills	Ethics in business	Marketing
Alex			
Leillah			
Mark			
Nick			
Radiyah			
Rita			
Stef			
Tim			

(Adapted from Cambridge AS & A Level Thinking Skills 9694,
Paper 13 Q21, November 2015)

4 I asked the guests at my uncle's birthday party whether they used a newspaper, the radio and television on a daily basis when keeping up to date about current affairs.

Half of those I asked used none of those media on a daily basis.

The number who used exactly two of the three media was more than the number who used exactly one and at least one guest listened only to the radio.

And the number who used all three was twice the number who used exactly two.

What is the minimum number of people I must have asked?

Taking it further

5 Telescopes now come with software which picks out the brightest three stars, and from the angles of the resulting triangle they can work out which stars they are, and thus exactly in which direction they are pointing. Each circle in the diagram below shows the field of view for one setting of a telescope.

In the first position shown below the stars labelled A, B and C are used. In the second position it uses D, E and F.

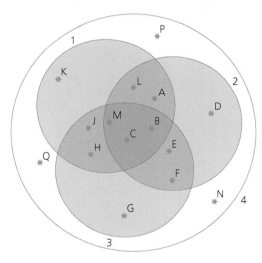

a Which stars could be used in the third position?

b Which stars could be used in the fourth position?

(Adapted from Cambridge AS & A Level Thinking Skills 9694, Paper 31 Q10, November 2010)

When to use it

Venn diagrams are designed to show how a set can be split up into overlapping subsections. The drawing of circles and the box round them (often forgotten) offers the problem solver a menu of options (where to place the objects in the problem) which excludes the possibility of error.

How to use it well

It is possible to misuse a Venn diagram – but only if you are casual in your reading of it.

Two classic errors

1 Thinking that any numeral in the question can go somewhere on the diagram.

Every object in a problem (be it a person, or a vegetable, or a toy car) must be placed somewhere on the diagram, but often this will involve splitting up the numbers given in the question, and dividing them between two or more sections of the Venn diagram.

Sample question

300 monks are worshipping in a monastery. 150 of them have a shaved head. 250 of them are barefoot. What is the greatest number that could be neither barefoot nor have a shaved head?

> Try this problem yourself, before reading the analysis!

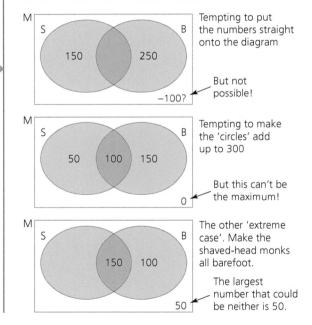

Tempting to put the numbers straight onto the diagram

But not possible!

Tempting to make the 'circles' add up to 300

But this can't be the maximum!

The other 'extreme case'. Make the shaved-head monks all barefoot.

The largest number that could be neither is 50.

2 Forgetting about those objects outside the rings!

Every Venn diagram should have a box around it, representing the 'universal set': this defines the objects which are being considered in the problem. Every object *in this set* must go somewhere on the diagram. If you don't draw it, you may forget it is there, and then you will forget that there are probably objects that should be placed in the box (but outside of the 'rings').

4 Answering the problem

By the end of this chapter you will be able to:

★ consider the meta-tasks involved in solving a problem
★ avoid common misinterpretations of a problem
★ choose and evaluate strategies for problem solving
★ check the solution is correct, where possible
★ engage with a problem-solving question.

When you are working on a problem, you need to take full advantage of your split brain.

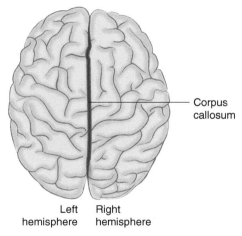

Corpus callosum

Left hemisphere   Right hemisphere

▲ The two hemispheres of the brain

Your brain has two hemispheres: the left hemisphere evolved to specialise in detailed, logical, systematic tasks, and the right hemisphere evolved to be alert to new inputs, and to deal with the unknown. To picture how these different halves work, think of a bird picking up and eating seeds (left hemisphere) while being alert for unexpected predators (right hemisphere).

For more on the neurological basis of the divided brain, see
https://www.ted.com/talks/iain_mcgilchrist_the_divided_brain.

It is easy, when immersed in a problem, to find your thinking dominated by the left hemisphere's approach – you organise the data, list the options, and work your way through the calculations. The detail is important, the precision of your movements (writing and diagramming) is important, and the overriding of all distractions is important. Focus and persistence are vital parts of what is needed for successful problem solving.

The strategies discussed in Chapters 2 and 3 essentially build on a left hemisphere approach.

But to be an efficient, adaptable problem solver you also need to nurture the right hemisphere. To do this you should try to survey the scene 'from above' in order to consider the scope of your approach, whether there are alternatives to your approach, and to verify that the approach and answers found along the way are reasonable.

Actively considering different interpretations of the problem, evaluating different strategies for solving the problem, checking you have not made any of the common mistakes in your processing and checking your answer are all meta-tasks that must accompany the intellectual labour of problem solving.

Meta-tasks

Most problems are comprised of a collection of explicit tasks that you are required to complete in order to reach an answer – such as listing the options and selecting the highest value, or drawing a network and finding a route that satisfies the restrictions. While your left hemisphere is working on these tasks, it is useful for your right hemisphere to oversee in the role of a sceptical companion, considering questions such as:

>> Where might you have *misinterpreted* the question?
>> How do you *evaluate strategies* for solving a problem?
>> Where are you most likely to make *unforced errors*?
>> Is it possible to *check* whether the answers you have found are correct?

In this textbook these are referred to as meta-tasks: 'meta' is a Greek prefix, meaning 'beyond', and you may know it from words like metaphysics, metamorphosis, meta-analysis and metadata. It is sometimes used to mean a supervisory, critical approach to the word it is attached to.

You need to imagine being your own critical companion, who is watching your progress, knowing your weaknesses and keeping an eye on your overall goal.

4.1 Misinterpreting the question

When encountering a problem for the first time, you should keep in mind the journey it has undergone prior to its presentation on the page in front of you. The key elements of modelling a problem for the page were discussed in Section 1.3, and are noted below for reference:

- » discrete and continuous variables
- » rounding
- » time and speed
- » relative measures
- » representing 3D
- » units and bases.

The decision to use these aspects of the modelling process is an important one, which requires precise articulation. You should consider what alternatives may have been available when the problem was formalised.

The range of possible situations, and the range of possible values for variables, is referred to as the 'problem space'. The formal problem that you face defines the problem space in which you can search for a solution. Two aspects of this space need to be appreciated before you begin: the scope of any restrictions on this problem space and the range of any variables.

1 The scope of any restrictions

Are the restrictions articulated in the problem true for the whole 'problem universe', or temporarily true, or true just in certain defined cases? This will be made clear in the formal presentation of the problem, but you need to be sensitive to it in case the definitions given are not what you are expecting. It is easy to read what you want the problem to say, rather than what it actually says. For example:

Sample question

Try this problem yourself, before reading the analysis!

You are given four cards from a deck, all of which have a letter on one side and a number on the other. You wish to check whether these cards conform to the rule: 'If there is an even number on one side then there is a vowel on the other.'

Turning over which of these cards would help you to check this?

The most common answer to this famous puzzle is '4' and 'A', or 'all four cards', but neither of these answers is correct.

> **The reason these answers are popular is that it is common to understand the rule as meaning: 'If there is an even number on one side there is a vowel on the other, *and if there is an odd number on one side then there is not a vowel.'***
>
> **The rule does not state this. It does not state anything about what odd numbers might be paired with. As a result, the correct cards to turn over are 'A' and '7'. If 'A' is paired with an odd number then the rule is proved false. If '7' is paired with a vowel then the rule is proved false. The other two cards could not confirm or disprove the rule.**

In the sample question just discussed, the statement, '... all of which have a letter on one side and a number on the other' is intended to apply to the whole situation, and does not invite your scrutiny. Obviously, if you needed to check that aspect of the question, you would need to turn over all four cards. This illustrates the differences in *scope* that can occur in the restrictions imposed:

» Some limitations are built into the infrastructure of the problem.

» Some limitations apply to particular sections of the problem but not others.

» Some limitations explicitly invite the sceptical problem solver to work out whether they are true at all.

An example of how the scope of certain restrictions can change is discussed below.

| Sample question |

Try this problem yourself, before reading the analysis!

The rate of reported crime in Einrossdorf is said to be exceptionally low, but no figures have been published to support this, so Edward, an investigative journalist, tries to get an estimate. He knows that each crime report is given a sequence number, starting from #1 every morning. He assumes, and it is true, that all reports made by townspeople are of real crimes and that the townspeople have all gone to bed by 10 p.m. So each day he selects a random time between 11 p.m. and midnight, makes a false report, and is then given a sequence number.

His false reports are #6/Monday, #5/Tuesday and #6/Wednesday.

a   What does Edward think the total number of genuine reports of crime over the three days was?

> **There are layers of 'reality' embedded into this problem: there is the number of actual crimes committed, the number that are discovered, the number that are reported, and the rumours about the number of reported crimes. As the problem is stated, there is no need to concern yourself with these layers of certainty and uncertainty: the layer *you* are interested in is the number of reported crimes, as evidenced by the false reports made after 11 p.m. The inference that the reporter makes is based on the**

assumption that all the crime reports made before his false report are of real crimes. This is not explicitly stated, but is clearly what Edward imagines to be true (since that is why he is submitting the false reports).

So, the answer to Question a is 5 + 4 + 5 = 14 genuine reports.

The plot thickens …

Unknown to him, or to each other, other journalists were doing exactly the same: each putting in one false report between 11 p.m. and midnight on the same days.

Kim obtained reference numbers #3/Monday, #6/Tuesday and #4/Wednesday. Anthony obtained #2/Monday, #7/Tuesday and #8/Wednesday.

b   What is the minimum (total) number of investigative journalists that could be working on this story?

This new information does not undermine what you have already established, but it will affect any problem solving you engage in from now on. The range of false report numbers (#2 to #6 on Monday, #5 to #7 on Tuesday, #4 to #8 on Wednesday) enables you to deduce how many investigative journalists are working on the story.

There are five false reports on Monday and Wednesday, so there must be at least five journalists.

The tale continues …

There might have been more journalists; unfortunately, we do not know and cannot tell.

c   What are the minimum and maximum of the total number of genuine crime reports over the three days?
d   What are the minimum and maximum of the total number of genuine crime reports over the three days, if there are only the minimum number of journalists?

This statement, and the questions that follow, exemplify the different scope that a restriction can exercise. Now we are told that there is no way of knowing how many investigative journalists there are, subject to the answer we found for Question b (when we deduced that there are at least five). The new statement does not ask you to revisit or change your previous answer, but it does require you to use it in your consideration of further problems.

Question c asks you to consider what can be deduced given this restriction: the minimum and maximum number of actual crime reports depends on whether there is a maximum or minimum number of investigative journalists. If there was a minimum

number of journalists, then there could have been 1 + 4 + 3 = 8 actual reports (one less than the first false report each night). If there was a maximum number of journalists, then every report could have been false (in which case there were no actual reports).

Question d then offers a problem with a temporary limitation: for this question only, consider what is possible if there was a minimum number of journalists. The restricted scope of this situation is made clear by the fact that it is expressed inside the question, and as part of the question ('if this is true, what would be the case?'). If there were five investigative journalists, then they could submit their false reports as early as possible (starting with the 2nd, 3rd and 4th on successive nights) or as late as possible (starting with the 2nd, 5th and 4th on successive nights). This gives the minimum 1 + 2 + 3 = 6 and maximum 1 + 4 + 3 = 8 number of actual reports.

This example illustrates how the scope of a restriction imposed on a problem can vary. You need to watch out for this!

(Adapted from Cambridge AS & A Level Thinking Skills 9694, Paper 32 Q2 (a) – (d), Nov 2016)

2 The range of variables

The second aspect of the 'problem space' you must consider is the range of variables, that is, the precise limitations that are placed on any unknown quantities in the problem.

When you are told that a number can be, for example, between two values, or bigger than this number, or an integer, or at least this quantity, then a special level of care is needed to ensure that you stay precisely within the boundaries that have been set. Restrictions such as these are often dealt out carelessly in everyday speech, but their boundaries can be critical in solving a problem. A list of the most common descriptions and what values they permit is given below.

How it is described	A list of what is permitted	How it is written formally
'At least five people were involved.'	5, 6, 7, …	$p \geq 5$
'At most five people were involved.'	5, 4, 3, 2, 1, 0	$p \leq 5$
'More than five people were involved.'	6, 7, 8, …	$p > 5$
'Fewer than five people were involved.'	4, 3, 2, 1, 0	$p < 5$
'No more than five people were involved.'	5, 4, 3, 2, 1, 0	$p \leq 5$
'No fewer than five people were involved.'	5, 6, 7, …	$p \geq 5$
'Between 5 and 10 people were involved' or 'Between 5 and 10 people were involved (inclusive).'	5, 6, 7, 8, 9, 10	$5 \geq p \leq 10$
'Between 5 and 10 people were involved (exclusive).'	6, 7, 8, 9	$5 > p < 10$

How it is described	A list of what is permitted	How it is written formally
'Only whole numbers ...'	Also known as integers. For example, 4 or 42	$p \in \mathbb{Z}$
'Only consecutive numbers ...'	'One number coming straight after the next.' For example 12, 13, 14	
'Only adjacent numbers ...'	'Next door': which could mean 12, 13, 14 if all the numbers are arranged in numerical order, for example, or 12, 14, 16 if they are arranged with all the even numbers on one line, for example	

When faced with limitations placed on unknown numbers in a problem, you should list the possibilities using an ellipsis (three dots, ...) to show a list continuing so that you establish clearly whether the endpoints are included or not. You do not need to use the formal notation offered in the right-hand column – although it is designed to make the differences clear and easy to express.

Sample question

Try this problem yourself, before reading the analysis!

A restaurant serves between 100 and 200 people every evening. Each customer buys either the 'Meal of the day' at $20 or the 'Gourmet meal' at $40. No more than 25% of the customers on any evening buy the 'Gourmet meal'. All drinks cost $5, and everybody has at least one drink, but nobody ever has more than four.

On the basis of this information, what is the difference between the smallest total amount and the largest total amount customers might spend in any evening?

(Adapted from Cambridge AS & A Level Thinking Skills 9694, Paper11 Q18, Nov 2014)

The ranges expressed in the question can be laid out formally like this:

Guests: 100, 101, ..., 199, 200

Meals: $20 or $40

Gourmet: ≤ 25%   For example: 25, 24, 23, ..., 0 if there were 100 guests

50, 49, 48, ..., 0 if there were 200 guests

Drinks: 1, 2, 3 or 4 each

Smallest total amount: selecting the smallest number of guests (100), the least number choosing the Gourmet meal (0) and each having the minimum number of drinks (1) gives

100 × (20 + 5) = $2500

Largest total amount: selecting the largest number of guests (200), the greatest number choosing the Gourmet meal (50) and each having the maximum number of drinks (4) gives

(150 × (20 + 20)) + (50 × (40 + 20)) = $9000

So the difference is $9000 − $2500 = $6500.

It is important that you are able to identify and understand these two key aspects (scope and range) which often occur in formal problems, but you should also never forget how easy it is to misread text and overlook critical aspects of it, especially under time pressure.

The following text illustrates this:

> *One amniazg ascpet of how our our barins peeircve txet is shwon hree. We can oetfn unandrsetd txet wehn olny the fsirt and lsat leterts of the wrod are ceocrrt. Our barins msut soomhew flil in the the rset!*

As this text illustrates, sometimes our brains 'chunk' the information in the processes of cognition, rather than ingesting it letter by letter. This helps us to quickly digest information, but also means we can miss key details. Our brain has been designed to dismiss information that it thinks is not wanted, especially when we are focusing hard on something else. For example, did you notice the two unwanted repeated words in the above example?

Look again, which two words were repeated?

We have only a finite amount of attention, so, when our focus and attention are on one aspect, our attention to other aspects is reduced. As a consequence, it is very easy to be mistaken even when we think we have witnessed something first hand, in plain sight.

For you, the problem solver, the invisible gorilla experiment acts as a warning to ensure that you continually:

» question yourself when reading a problem, and recording it

» look for ways that you might have made a mistake

» look for ways to verify your solution.

In order to avoid the common misconceptions and mistakes that are made when solving problems, you need to be alert to them. You should spend some time considering the most likely errors, and the tempting wrong answers, as well as the right ones. The best training ground for practising this process is a collection of problems for which **distractors** have been created. Distractors are wrong answers that are based on classic errors, offered as part of a list, to disguise a correct answer.

The 'invisible gorilla' experiment clearly demonstrates the impact of focus and attention just discussed:

http://www.theinvisiblegorilla.com/gorilla_experiment.html

Practice questions

In the following exercises, you have been given the correct answer for each problem, on the page 305. Your task is to explain what errors you would have had to make in interpreting the problem to produce each of the four wrong answers.

1 A new residential development is being planned on the outskirts of a city. The plans are for 5 high-rise blocks, each containing 20 residential units (apartments), with an average occupancy of 4 persons per unit. The 5 buildings will cover a total ground space

of 0.6 hectares (ha), which is equivalent to 6000 m². Government regulations require that any new development must allow 80 m² of open space (for example, play areas) per resident in addition to that covered by buildings.

How many hectares of land will be needed for the whole development?

(Adapted from Cambridge AS & A Level Thinking Skills 9694, Paper 11 Q8, June 2016)

2   We have always applied the strict rule that the number of children coming to a birthday party should be equal to the age of the child: seven for a seven-year-old and so on. Each guest brings a present to each party. Our children are now 3, 6 and 7.

How many presents have been received in all?

(Adapted from Cambridge AS & A Level Thinking Skills 9694, Paper 1 Q23, Nov 2007)

3   Cynics would say that you can tell a restaurant that claims to be one of the top five restaurants is in fact the fifth, because otherwise it would call itself one of the top four, or whatever.

It's not so simple when there are three local schools that claim to be in the top 100 (in a list with no equal placements).

What is the greatest difference in the position in the list of the second and third of these local schools?

(Adapted from Cambridge AS & A Level Thinking Skills 9694, Paper 1 Q32, Nov 2007)

Taking it further

4   Rectangular interlocking roof tiles are available as Standard (S) 20 cm × 30 cm for $1, or Large (L) 30 cm × 30 cm for $3. The dimensions are given as width × height. Each tile has a top and a bottom, so only fits in one way.

Tiles need to be laid next to each other in rows, touching those either side but with an overlap of 10 cm over the row below. The roof must be two tiles thick for the entire length of such an overlap. The joins in adjacent rows must not line up.

The example here shows a partially-tiled roof of area 100 cm by 70 cm.

This tiling arrangement is described by writing:

SS
LSS
SSSS

a   i)   What is the minimum cost to tile a rectangular area of 120 cm × 110 cm?

    ii)   What is the minimum cost to tile a rectangular area of 130 cm × 110 cm?

    iii)   What is the minimum cost to tile a rectangular area of 700 cm × 390 cm?

Tiles are never cut vertically to create smaller tiles. However, not all areas to be tiled are rectangular, so some tiles may need to be trimmed at an angle. Where tiles are trimmed, it is important for the top of the tile to be **more than** 10 cm across.

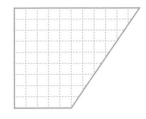

One piece of roof is shown (above right) with a 10 cm grid superimposed.

b   The bottom left tile can be Large or Standard. Which of these enables the cheaper overall cost? Justify your answer, describing the arrangements and calculating the costs.

Another piece of roof is shown (below right).

c   Identify a part of this roof that cannot be tiled, even if the rules are relaxed to allow the top of the tile to be **at least** 10 cm across.

(Adapted from Cambridge AS & A Level Thinking Skills 9694, Paper 31 Q2, June 2013)

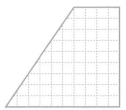

4.2 Choosing and evaluating strategies

When you are tackling a thoroughly unfamiliar problem, often the greatest challenge is beginning the problem. A number of the strategies you have encountered in Chapters 2 and 3 are explicitly directed at overcoming this – trial and improvement (Section 2.4) is one obvious example.

A second challenge is being willing to stop and change direction once you have begun. The tendency not to do this has been studied and is well recognised in the process of medical diagnosis, where the consequences of proceeding down the wrong track can be fatal. There are a number of classic biases in medical diagnostic reasoning, but two of the most striking are called **anchoring** and **confirmation bias**.

Anchoring describes the tendency to stick with our hypothesis rather than alter it when new information arrives. It takes effort to switch strategy, and often we will ignore the evidence that suggests our present strategy is wrong when to accept this means we will have to start again.

Confirmation bias describes our tendency to seek examples that confirm the hypothesis that we think is correct, rather than those which might disprove it.

These two biases tend to occur in combination; when you are problem solving, when you are theorising about the world, and when you are making a diagnosis.

A memorable example of our confirmation bias can be seen in the following map-reading activity.

> **ACTIVITY**

Imagine you have become completely lost while crossing wild country, but are confident you are somewhere on the map shown on the right. Each grid square on the map is 1 km wide. You have managed to lose your compass. You are on a path, but you don't know which one. You come to a Y-junction, one path branching to the left and one branching to the right.

You think you might be approaching the junction marked with an arrow, arriving from the bottom of the map (the area by Hangingstone Hill).
Look at the map, and consider what information about the landscape you would use to check whether this is where you are.

In this activity you may have been tempted to imagine walking down the right-hand path, looking out for the first noticeable feature.

From the map you will see that the first feature is another fork along that path, indicated by the arrow.

You might theorise: 'If I find another forked path after about 1 km, I will conclude that the original junction I was at was probably by the Tinner's hut.'

Such logic is a classic example of **confirmation bias**. In fact, almost all the Y-junctions on the map are followed by another fork about 1 km afterwards.

The logically correct approach is to hypothesise about where you think you are, and then look for where else you might be, and what features would distinguish that.

For instance, if you were at the junction by the Tinner's hut and followed the left-hand path, you would encounter a chicane after two or three hundred metres (turning left, then right, then left again), and there appears to be nowhere else on the map where a path does this. This would be an effective test of your theory – not because it happens here, but because it doesn't happen anywhere else.

When you are pursuing an approach to any problem, you must remain alert to your brain's tendency to anchor and to seek confirming instances. An example of this action follows.

Sample question

Try this problem yourself, before reading the analysis!

The ingredients written on a jar of beetroot and orange chutney are listed in order of their percentage by weight and read as follows:

Beetroot (34%), Sugar, Malt Vinegar, Oranges (14%), Onion, Apple, Modified Starch, Salt, Ginger.

Given values are rounded to the nearest 1%.

What is the narrowest range we can put on the amount of Malt Vinegar?

(Adapted from Cambridge AS & A Level Thinking Skills 9694, Paper 12 Q3, June 2012)

You may have been tempted to conclude that it must lie between 14% and 34%.

If you tested the lower end of this interval, you would have found that this was entirely possible. For example: Beetroot 34%, Sugar 15%, Vinegar 14%, Oranges 14%, the rest 23%.

This confirms that your theory is correct.

The tendency you must develop is to look at the 'worst case' scenario rather than the best – try to prove yourself wrong, rather than prove yourself right.

If you test the upper end of the interval, you will realise that it is not possible: Beetroot 34%, Sugar 34%, Malt Vinegar 34%, Oranges 14%, … which adds up 116% already. This consideration of the 'worst case' scenario leads to the following insight: the two ingredients in between Beetroot and Oranges must add up to a maximum of 52%, and the maximum that Malt Vinegar can be is ($\frac{52}{2}$ =) 26%.

To check this: 34 + 26 + 26 + 14 = 100.

The remaining ingredients can be 'trace ingredients' with tiny percentages that 'fit in' to the space left by rounding.

Practice questions

For each of the following questions an answer is suggested, with supporting evidence, on the page 305. This answer is *incorrect*, having considered only the 'easiest' scenario. It is subject to confirmation bias – some evidence confirms the answer, but insufficient care has been put into trying to disprove it. You need to consider what the worst case scenario is, show that this contradicts the answer given, and then find the correct solution.

1 The Requin Loan Company charges a flat-rate monthly interest on money borrowed. Interest is added to outstanding balances on the first day of every month as follows:

Outstanding balance on first of the month	Interest
Less than $500	$10
$500 or more	$20

I took out a loan for $750 from Requin on May 9th this year. Interest has been added since June 1st and I have been repaying $50 on the 9th of every month since June 9th.

How much will I still owe immediately after my monthly repayment on May 9th next year?

(Adapted from Cambridge AS & A Level Thinking Skills 8436, Paper 1 Q40, Nov 2005)

2 A football league is comprised of 22 teams. Over the course of a season, each team plays each of the other teams twice (home and away). For every game that is played, 3 points are awarded to the winning side, 0 points to the losing side, and 1 point to each side if the match is drawn (equal score). (There are no other possible outcomes to a game.) Each team's total points from all their matches played are added together at the end of the season and the three clubs with the fewest points are relegated to a lower league. If two or more clubs finish with the same number of points, their positions are decided by goal difference, that is, the difference between the total number of goals they have scored and the total number scored against them over the course of the season. A side with a higher goal difference finishes above one with a lower one.

What is the **lowest** number of points that a club can get in one season and not be relegated?

(Adapted from Cambridge AS & A Level Thinking Skills 9694, Paper 1 Q12, June 2007)

3 Harry lives at the top and Joe lives at the bottom of a hill 6 km long. Each Saturday they meet at a bench on the hill somewhere between their houses. They find that, if they both leave their houses at 10 a.m., they arrive at the bench at the same time. They both walk at 2 km/hr uphill and 6 km/hr downhill. After talking for an hour they each return home.
How much earlier does Joe arrive home than Harry?

(Adapted from Cambridge AS & A Level Thinking Skills 8436, Paper 1 Q10, June 2005)

➤

4   A door has a lock which is operated by entering a four-letter code into an electronic keypad. There are 4 buttons on the keypad, labelled A, B, C and D. The programme in the keypad operates by moving between five different states.

Every time that a button on the keypad is pressed, the programme either moves to a different state or remains in its current state. When it moves into state 5, the door is released and the programme moves back to state 1.

The table below shows the next state for the programme when different inputs are made while it is in states 1 to 4.

		Input			
		A	B	C	D
State	1	1	1	2	1
	2	3	1	2	1
	3	1	1	4	1
	4	3	1	2	5

The correct first character of the code is C (which moves the programme from state 1 to state 2).

Mark attempted to unlock the door by entering the sequence C B C A. When the C button was pressed for the first time, the programme moved to state 2.

a   Show that Mark has left the programme in state 3. Write down which state the programme was in after each time Mark pressed a button.

b   What two further button presses would unlock the door?

If the programme is in state 2, then pressing either B or D will return the programme to state 1, as neither is the correct second character of the code. C is also incorrect, but returns the programme to state 2 because C is the correct first character of the code.

c   Explain why the programme is designed so that it will always be in state 1 after B is pressed.

d   Explain why the programme is designed so that pressing A while the programme is in state 4 will return the programme to state 3, rather than state 1.

Another lock is programmed to open only when the code AABDAC is entered. The programme for this lock uses seven states. When it moves into state 7 the door unlocks and the programme immediately moves back to state 1.

e   Draw a table to show the next state for the programme when different inputs are made while it is in states 1 to 6.

4.3 Unforced errors

You have probably made an error at some point in your life as a problem solver.

You have probably made an error, at some point, which was entirely 'by mistake' – you knew how to get to the answer, you had the right method, but you made a mistake along the way.

And when you did this, you probably thought, 'I was basically right. I was unlucky. There is not much to learn from this, because I knew how to solve it.'

In one way, such a resigned response is justified. You may have tried your hardest.

But most of these 'unforced errors' can be avoided by:

a developing *good habits* in the way you lay out a solution
b knowing the areas where you tend to make *mistakes*
c being *vigilant*.

Good habits

As has been stressed in Section 2.2, if you have a system which you are used to, which you can accomplish semi-automatically, then you free up your mind to perform active meta-tasks (such as being generally vigilant of unforced errors).

Examples of good habits that you should cultivate across your problem-solving life include the following:

» highlighting key information, particularly key numbers and key words, in the problem
» highlighting the question that is being asked
» labelling your diagrams so they can be understood by someone else (like yourself, looking back at the problem, after five minutes lost in thought)
» linking your working together with appropriate words or symbols. Common examples are given below:

Symbol/link word	Significance
'Let number of people = 10'	If you choose a value for one of the aspects of a problem, write it down clearly. You are likely to want change it, or give another aspect a different value, and it won't take much for you to forget what you've done.
The equals sign, =	If you are stating that two things are equal then that is important. You need to be able to depend on it. So get into the habit of using the sign, and using it carefully. Avoid 'dodgy chains': $12 + 5 = 17 - 7 = 10 + 1 = 11$
'Therefore' ∴	If you are claiming that one statement leads to another then write 'therefore', 'implies' or 'or'.
Use units!	When you are giving an answer or a partial answer, bother to write whether the number you have reached is, for example, people, $, kg or baskets of fruit.
~~Crossing out~~	Cross out any wrong working, neatly so that you can still read it (in case you need to backtrack) but so that you (and anyone reading your work) knows that it is not part of your argument.

» underlining your answer

» checking that you have not omitted any information from the original question in reaching your answer

» expressing your answer as a clear English sentence – written on the page ideally, or in your head if not. If you cannot express your answer clearly as a sentence, then you do not understand what you have found – and it probably needs re-evaluating.

Knowing your weaknesses

The list of decisions and processes where *you* are likely to make an unforced error is a highly personal thing. It is like a mirror that shows up all your worst features.

You must study this mirror in order to polish your problem solving, and your chance to 'study the mirror' occurs whenever you tackle a problem (especially when you do it under time pressure). You need to do this regularly, identify where you slip up, analyse it and make a note of it.

► ACTIVITIES

Here are four processes which may make it onto your list, and a problem to tackle to help you remember each of them.

Reversing digits: writing 13 as 31. Easy to do. Easy to watch out for.

1   The local shop has an offer on DVDs. All DVDs are priced at $15, $20 or $22. When you have chosen your DVDs, if the total price is a two-digit number and not a multiple of 10, then you can reverse the digits of the price before you pay (so, a price of $65 would become $56, but you would not be able to change a price of $80).

Henry has just bought some DVDs. What is the largest saving that he can possibly have made from this offer?

(Adapted from Cambridge AS & A Level Thinking Skills 9694, Paper 11 Q13, June 2015)

Reversing operations: adding when you should subtract, multiplying when you should divide.

2   Alf and Bede are comparing their football teams' results at the end of the season. There have been games in which many goals were scored and games in which no goals were scored, wins, losses and draws, highs and lows for both teams. They decide to compare the entire season by either adding all the goals scored by their team in every game and comparing the results, or multiplying all the goals scored by their team in every game and comparing. Which method is more likely to lead to Alf's team beating Bede's?

Reversing inputs and outputs: when you are given a chain of operations and are trying to work out one of the missing values, it is easy to lose track of which numbers are inputs and which are outputs. A function machine (see Section 3.1) is designed to organise this information.

3   A detective investigating a murder is trying to pin down the time when the victim was killed in his own home.

The pathologist examined the body at 16:50 and found that the body temperature was 2.0°C below normal; bodies lose between 1°C and 1.5°C every hour. He also looked at the state of rigor mortis and decided from the degree of stiffening that death occurred between 1.5 and 2.5 hours ago. The victim had caught a train to his home at 13:45, a journey which took 45 minutes, and lived 25 minutes' walk from the station. Mr Jones found the body in the victim's hallway at 15:35.

When did the man die, according to the evidence?

(Adapted from Cambridge AS & A Level Thinking Skills 9694, Paper 12 Q18, June 2012)

Proportional shortcuts: treating a relationship as if it was proportional, when it is linear. Two variables are linearly related if one is linked to the other by multiplying and adding $(y = ax + b)$. Two variables are proportionally related if one is linked to the other by multiplying. It is easy to mistake the former for the latter.

4   A caterpillar is climbing out of a well which is 5 m deep.

After five hours he has to rest for an hour – and while he rests he slips 10 cm back down.

How many hours will he take to climb out?

Be vigilant

This feels like a mindless piece of advice. 'Obviously I will try to be careful! The problem is that when I am not being careful, I forget to be careful!'

It is not much use having 'be vigilant' as an instruction. But you can train yourself to stay vigilant.

One way is to take part in exercises or challenges where your **reliability** is more important than your problem-solving skills.

One such exercise is a Precision Speed Test. Competing against your peers, and the clock, your aim is to score the longest stretch of answers without an error. To do well you need to go fast – but without making any mistakes.

▶ ACTIVITY

Your task in the Precision Speed Test is to count up the number of dots in each numbers box. The numbers go down the page, so make sure you begin counting downwards – a blank counts as 'wrong' so there is no point in missing any out. There are 44 boxes of dots to count.

For this activity to be genuinely competitive, you should all start at the same time (no peeking!) and stop when the first person finishes.

Mark your answers. Your score is the longest stretch without a mistake. For instance, if you get number 3, 10 and 29 incorrect, your score will be 18 (having answered 18 questions, 11 to 28, without error).

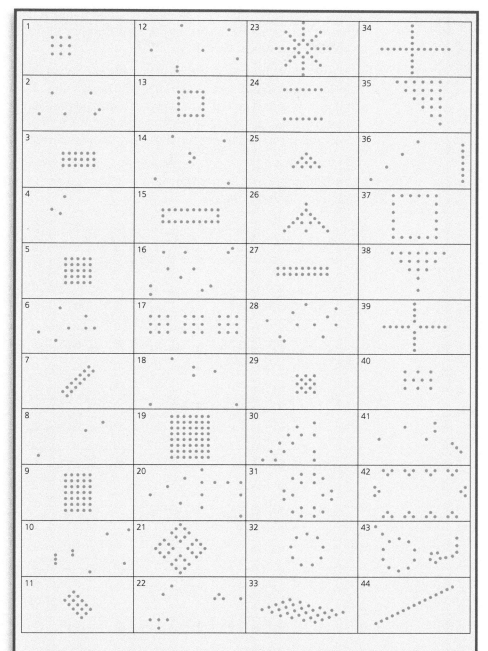

If you did well at this activity, then you have a refined sense of your own precision. Or you are surrounded by hasty, clumsy, easily distracted buffoons!

Two other tests that can be used to assess your reliability and align it with your speed of processing are the Symbol Digit Modality Test and the Stroop Colour Word Test.

The Symbol Digit Modality Test is designed to be used by psychologists wishing to assess someone's speed of processing. It should be administered in the same way as the dotty Precision Speed Test above – against time, stopping when the first person is finished, scored according to the largest number of unbroken correct answers.

The top line contains a key, identifying what each symbol means. Participants must select the right number for each symbol, working left to right, line by line.

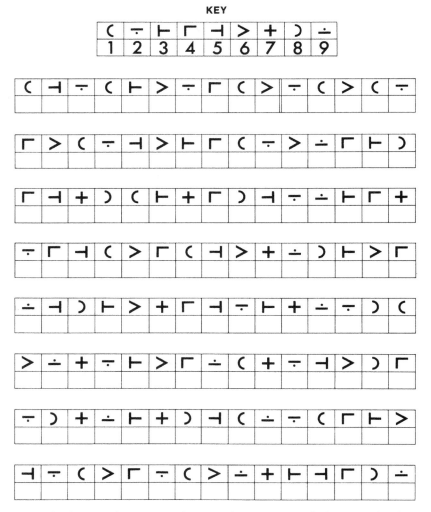

As with the Precision Speed Test, the purpose of the exercise is to calibrate your speed of answering with your reliability at answering. If you made mistakes in either test, you are going too fast!

And you are likely to go too fast when you are processing data in timed problem-solving assessments.

▶ ACTIVITY

A Shuttle Competition is another type of activity that hones vigilance and reliability. In this activity, two-person teams pass answers between each other in order to solve four problems. One member of the team has problems 1 and 3, the other team mate has problems 2 and 4. The answer to problem 1 is a vital part of problem 2, and the answer to problem 2 is a vital part of problem 3. Once problem 1 has been solved, the answer is passed on for use in problem 2, and so on.

Once all four questions are answered, the answers are submitted to the adjudicator/teacher who marks them. Any incorrect answers are identified and the answer sheet is passed back to the team. They can then return to them and try to repair their errors, if needs be. Get into pairs now and try the following problems.

Problem 1

How many different triangles can be made by joining up three corners of a regular pentagon, if you consider triangles that are reflections of each other as being the same?

Pass on your answer.

Problem 2

The answer you have been given from problem 1, referred to as 'A' below, tells you how many senior citizens are in the group in the following puzzle.

A group of 6 people, including 'A' senior citizens, go to a restaurant for a meal.

→ Three people have meals costing $12 each.

→ Two people have meals costing $13 each.

→ One person has a meal costing $14.

The restaurant has two special offers:

→ Groups of 6 or more can have one of the cheapest meals free.

→ Senior citizens get a reduction of $4.50 each.

Only one special offer may be used at a time.

If they take the better special offer for the group, how much is the total bill?

→ If your answer is $58.00 then pass on the letter T.

→ If your answer is $62.50 then pass on the letter N.

→ If your answer is $64.00 then pass on the letter E.

→ If your answer is $71.50 then pass on the letter O.

(Adapted from Cambridge AS & A Level Thinking Skills 9694, Paper 12 Q6, June 2013)

Problem 3

The answer you have been given will tell you which letter you are looking to avoid in the display in the following puzzle.

The individual digits on my digital clock appear as words rather than numerals. For example, at 18:07 the display is as shown below.

How many times each day does the letter given to you from problem 2 **not** appear on the display?

Pass on the number of times.

(Adapted from Cambridge AS & A Level Thinking Skills 9694, Paper 12 Q7, June 2013)

Problem 4

The answer you have been given will tell you how many minutes '(M)' Deena leaves home after Callum in the following puzzle.

Deena takes 15 minutes to cycle to school, and her brother Callum walks there, taking 30 minutes. Normally, Deena leaves home 'M' minutes after Callum.

For how long does Deena cycle until she catches up with Callum?

Pass on the time it takes Deena, and your answers to problems 1–3, to your teacher.

(Adapted from Cambridge AS & A Level Thinking Skills 9694, Paper 12 Q12, June 2013)

Taking it further
Problem 5

A games designer is trying to create rectangular mazes made up of identically-sized square rooms, and needs to quantify how complicated they are. In order to do this, he defines the longest path of a maze as the number of rooms that a participant would visit in completing the maze, if she were to take a wrong door whenever faced with a choice. Rooms visited more than once are counted for each visit.

The rooms all consist of four walls with closed doors in one or more of them. As a result the participant cannot know whether she has reached the exit until she opens the 'exit' door. The designer assumes that the participant marks each door that she tries, and will not repeat any pathways that she has already fully explored.

Because the maze designer is considering mazes of different sizes, he decides to use the complexity coefficient of the maze as the measure of its difficulty, which he defines as the longest path divided by the size of the maze (the number of rooms it consists of).

a Show that the complexity coefficient of the maze shown here is 1.44 (rounded to 2 decimal places), and complete the path that the participant takes: 1, 2, 1, 4 ...

Mazes must not have loops in them. A loop is where a pathway leads a participant back to a room already visited without retracing her steps. The entrance and the exit must be in different rooms. A participant must be able to reach all rooms in the maze.

b Draw a different maze involving a 3 × 3 grid of rooms, which also has a complexity coefficient of 1.44 and which has its entrance and exit in the same places as the maze above.

c i) The maximum complexity coefficient for a 3 × 3 maze is 1.78. Draw an example. (The entrance and exit may be in different positions to those in the example above.)

ii) Find the maximum complexity coefficient for a 5 × 5 maze.

The designer also wants to consider the shortest way out of a maze. He defines the simplicity coefficient as the shortest path from the entrance to the exit divided by the size of the maze. In considering this, the designer restricts his investigation to rectangular mazes whose entrances and exits are in the rooms at diagonally opposite corners of the maze.

d Consider rectangular (including square) mazes made up of no more than 18 rooms. What is the lowest simplicity coefficient for such mazes? Give an example of a maze with this simplicity coefficient.

The designer thinks it will be useful to consider the difference between the longest and shortest paths for particular mazes. When considering this, he continues to restrict himself to mazes in which the entrance and exit are in rooms at diagonally opposite corners of the maze.

e i) For a maze made up from no more than 18 rooms, what is the maximum difference between the longest and shortest paths? Draw an example.

ii) For a 16 × 21 maze, what is the maximum difference between the longest and shortest paths? You are not required to draw an example.

(Cambridge AS & A Level Thinking Skills 9694, Paper 33 Q3, November 2012)

To think about

How many dates are there in the year when it is ambiguous what the date is, if you don't know whether the calendar is American or English? (The American calendar lists dates as follows: Month/Day/Year. The English calendar lists dates: Day/Month/Year.)

4.4 Ways to check your answer

Problems involve pairing up the restrictions and requirements of the question with the correct answer. Some answers are very easy to check, and some are not. Some solutions can be checked with a method that is independent from that which you used to solve the problem (which gives a very strong confirmation that you are correct), and some can be checked only by going over the whole process again.

The process of checking answers can be divided into three categories:

1 jigsaw-piece checking methods
2 optimisation methods
3 overview checking methods

1 Jigsaw-piece checking methods

Consider the following problem.

Sample question

> Try this problem yourself, before reading the analysis!

When I go for a walk with my dog, there is a field where she likes to retrieve sticks. I throw a stick 25 m in front of my current position and she runs to collect it, immediately bringing it back. I then immediately throw it again. I do this 6 times, continuously walking in a straight line at my normal pace (1.5 m/s). My dog runs at 4.5 m/s.

How far do I walk between throwing the stick the first time and my dog returning it the sixth time?

(Adapted from Cambridge AS & A Level Thinking Skills 9694, Paper 3 Q18, June 2009)

You may be able to solve the problem by framing the relationship between the distance that the protagonist walks and the distance that the dog travels, or by trial and improvement.

Now consider how your approach to the question changes if you are offered some choices:

A 50 m   **D 225 m**

B 75 m   **E 450 m**

C 100 m

The easiest way is to take each of the five answers, divide by 6 (the number of throws), and see if that works.

For example, if 6 throws takes me 50 m (option A), then each time I throw it, I must walk $\frac{50}{6} = 8.3$ m approximately, before my dog brings it back.

While I walk 8.3 m, the dog must run 25 m (to the stick), and then $25 - 8.3 = 16.7$ m back. This requires the dog to run at more than three times my speed, meaning it is not the correct answer.

Repeating this approach with the other options reveals that 75 m is correct.

That involves me walking 12.5 m each time, and my dog running $25 + 12.5 = 37.5$ m, which is three times the distance. So option B, 75 m, is the correct answer.

This process, familiar to those who have practised multiple-choice tests, is a close cousin to what you should do when you wish to check an answer: take your answer and see if it works. This process does not tell you how to correct a wrong answer – but it does tell you when to stop looking.

The following questions will help improve your sense for this.

Practice questions

For each of the following questions, you should begin by reviewing the multiple-choice answers and eliminating the incorrect ones (by inserting them into the question) if possible. You should also identify for which problems the multiple-choice answers prove useful, and for which ones the answers are practically useless.

1 A vegetable garden is to be divided up into three spaces which are identical in shape and area, as shown in the diagram on the right (which is not to scale). What is the area of each space?

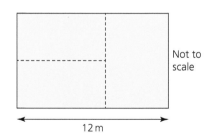

Not to scale

12 m

A 8 m²

B 16 m²

C 18 m²

D 32 m²

E 50 m²

2 A town council is deciding which bulbs to use for streetlighting in a new housing estate. They are faced with the following brands.

Bulb	Price in $	Lifespan in days
Glo	8	50
Shyne	10	75
Brite	20	120
Psun	60	200

The housing company has offered to pay for the **initial** installation of whichever bulbs the council recommends.

Each time a bulb needs replacing from then on, the cost of labour and fuel to the town is $20, on top of the cost of the bulb. There is no need to stay with one bulb type when it needs replacing.

What is the minimum cost for the first year of lighting?

A $60   C $80

B $68   D $140

3   Mr Hanson is organising a school trip to the local bowling alley and needs to calculate what to charge students. He offers the trip to all 30 students in his Maths class. The school requires one member of staff to accompany every 15 students, for safety reasons. The bowling alley offers a free ticket for a member of staff with every 7 students.

A ticket to get into the bowling alley and play games all day with plastic tokens costs $15.

The cost of the coach to the bowling alley (which can take up to 50 people) is $90.

Mr Hanson is unsure how many students will come, but wishes to divide the cost of the trip equally between the students – including the cost of any staff whose tickets are not free.

What is the difference between the smallest and largest amount that the students will be asked to pay?

A $87   C $102

B $90   D $105

4   Tiana is making alcohol-free cocktails, or 'mocktails', at a restaurant. The restaurant has two specialities called a 'Delice' and a 'Felice'. She is very methodical, and always takes the same amount of time to make a 'Delice' and the same amount of time to make a 'Felice'. She times herself making two orders:

Felice, Delice, Felice, Delice, Felice, Delice, Felice: 16 minutes

Felice, Delice, Delice, Delice, Felice: 14 minutes

How long does it take her to make a 'Delice'?

A 1 minute   C 3 minutes

B 2.5 minutes   D 4 minutes

For which of the practice questions were the multiple-choice answers useful?

What you should have found is that it was possible to eliminate the incorrect answers from the multiple-choice list for some of the problems (1 and 4), but that the multiple-choice answers were of no use for others (2 and 3); in those cases you just had to work through the question and see if your answer happened to be the same as any of those given.

The first type could be defined as jigsaw-piece type problems: once you have found/created the correct jigsaw piece, you do not need an expert to confirm that it is the right one. You simply push it into place by its neighbours, and if it fits, it fits! In problem-solving terms, once you have carefully constructed a correct answer (created the jigsaw piece), it is easy to check it is correct by inserting it back into the right place in the question.

The second type could be defined as phone-number type problems: the only way to check that you have correctly remembered a phone number is to go back and read through the numbers one by one. In problem-solving terms, it is only really possible to check an answer by re-running the calculation from the beginning.

Problems 1 and 4 are classic jigsaw-type problems.

For both problems it is easier to consider the solutions on offer and establish whether they agree with the original question, than it is to tackle the question 'from the ground up'.

For instance, in question 1, if the area of each of the three spaces was 8 m² then they would each have to have dimensions of 2 m × 4 m (since the gardens must be twice as long as they are wide, and these are the only numbers that satisfy this and give 8 m²). Clearly 2 m + 4 m does not give a length of 12 m – the complete length of available garden space – so the area cannot be 8 m².

Repeating this approach with the other possible answers reveals that 32 m² is the correct answer: the gardens can each be 4m × 8m and these, added together, also give the correct complete length of 12 m.

Similarly, in question 4, does Tiana take one minute to make a Delice? If yes, then three Delices require three minutes, meaning the four Felices take 13 minutes in the first order, and two Felices take 11 minutes in the second. This does not fit with the information about Tiana's methodical mocktail-making methods!

Working through the cases reveals that Tiana must take 4 minutes to make a Delice: this leaves her with 4 minutes for the four Felices in the first order, and 2 minutes for the two Felices in the second order. Without having to go near any algebra, it is easy to see that this conforms to the requirements of the situation.

As a rule, if you find that working backwards to check whether an answer is correct is far easier than working the problem forwards, then it is a jigsaw-type problem. The key skill is to recognise these when no multiple-choice answers are given.

In questions 2 and 3, after a moment's study, you will see that the alternative answers are of no apparent use at all. You cannot work backwards from them. They are phone-number type problems.

Question 2 requires you to select values from the table and combine them in a delicate series of tasks, according to the restrictions of the problem. A possible answer, such as $80, cannot be 'fitted back into the structure of the problem' or used as a source of further inferences, as can be done with questions 1 and 4. The right answer can be found only by completing the task 'forwards' and there is almost no easy way to cross-check.

Question 3 also defies checking – you cannot take one of the answers, such as $87, and insert it back into the original structure. Both of these problems involve optimisation, and this rarely allows for jigsaw-type verification techniques – see the next section for discussion of how to tackle optimisation problems.

All of the practice questions that follow are jigsaw-type problems, and you should stop to consider how the answer can be checked when you reach it.

Practice questions

1   Amy and Bahula are sharing out some sweets. They take a handful each and there is none left in the box. Amy has the most so she gives Bahula as many as Bahula already has. Bahula then gives Amy as many as Amy now has. They now have the same number.

What is the smallest number of sweets there could have been in the box originally?

(Adapted from Cambridge AS & A Level Thinking Skills 9694, Paper 13 Q22, June 2011)

2   The hose on a foot pump is only long enough to reach the tyre valve on each of a motorbike's wheels when the valve is precisely at its lowest point.

Prior to starting work, the motorbike is positioned such that both valves are at their lowest point. The circumferences of the front and rear wheels are 2.1 m and 2.4 m respectively.

Rolling the bike forwards, how many times must the front wheel revolve before both valves are simultaneously at their lowest point again?

(Adapted from Cambridge AS & A Level Thinking Skills 9694, Paper 11 Q3, Nov 2010)

3   George is making his will. He has a collection of 50 silver boxes. He intends to leave 6 boxes to each of his children and 5 boxes to each of his grandchildren. This will make up the 50 exactly.

How many children does he have?

(Adapted from Cambridge AS & A Level Thinking Skills 8436, Paper 1 Q49, Nov 2004)

4   A construction toy contains various square pieces which need to be packaged by laying them flat into a rectangular tray. The tray has a handle on one edge. For this question, only consider squares with sides parallel to the sides of the tray at all times.

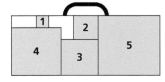

It is possible to place squares with sides of length 1 unit to 5 units in a 5 × 12 rectangular tray as shown on page 164, but they do not fill the tray and so the pieces can slide during shipping.

a   i)   Which of these squares might be found in a different position after shipping?

   ii)   Draw a rearrangement of these pieces inside a 5 × 12 rectangle which would result in fewer pieces being able to move.

Carrie manages to fit all the squares with sides from 1 unit to 11 units into a 19 × 27 rectangular tray.

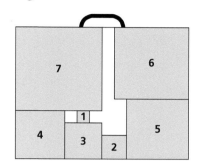

b   How many unit squares would be needed to fill all the gaps?

Squares of side 1 to 7 can be placed in an 11 × 14 rectangular tray as shown on the right.

c   Which one of these seven squares can never move, no matter how many of the others do?

Having the contents move during transport is often undesirable. It may be worth adding one or more extra pieces to stop them doing so.

By moving just the smallest square in the configuration above, it would be possible to insert into the tray a single 'filler' piece made up from no more than 6 unit squares, so that no pieces can move.

d   Design such a 'filler' piece and show where the smallest square should be placed relative to it.

e   Draw another arrangement of the seven squares, without any extra pieces, within this 11 × 14 rectangle, so that none of the squares bigger than 3 × 3 can move.

(Cambridge AS & A Level Thinking Skills 9694, Paper 32 Q1, November 2014)

2 Optimisation methods

Problems where you are asked to find a maximum or minimum value very rarely conform to the jigsaw-piece type model, because there is always a variety of possible answers which fit the basic requirements. The difficult thing is finding the biggest one.

These problems were introduced in Section 1.3 and highlighted as noteworthy because they require the problem solver to find a unique solution, on the threshold of the impossible. As already mentioned, you need to be sure both that (a) your solution is possible, and (b) no solutions greater than yours are possible. Normally this can be done by considering the possibilities in rank order and considering 'the next one up'.

An example of this in action follows.

Sample question

> Try this problem yourself, before reading the analysis!

When I want to use my computer:

◆ loading my email programme takes 1 minute

◆ loading my word-processing software takes 2 minutes

◆ loading my music programme takes 3 minutes

◆ initialising the virus protection takes 3 minutes

◆ checking the hard disk takes 4 minutes.

My computer can do up to three things at a time, but once it has begun doing something it carries on until it has finished it.

What is the shortest possible time before all of these tasks are completed?

(Adapted from Cambridge AS & A Level Thinking Skills 9694, Paper 12 Q19, June 2014)

It is best to begin by finding some boundaries, so first find two values between which the answer MUST lie:

> **Is there a time which is clearly a lower bound, below which it is not possible for the computer to complete the process?**

One answer we can be confident of is 4 minutes: one of the processes takes 4 minutes so the computer could not complete them all in less than that.

> **Is there a time by which they could definitely all be completed – an upper bound?**

An answer we can be confident of is 13 minutes: even if the computer was able to do only one task at a time, it could still do them all in 13 minutes (1 + 2 + 3 + 3 + 4 = 13).

We can then try to improve on our boundaries. A diagram is useful in this, as shown here.

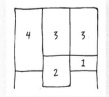

The computer can do three things simultaneously – shown in the diagram by the three columns. By placing the task time slots into the available spaces we have quickly been given a solution which shows that a five-minute maximum run time (three-minute task + two-minute task) is possible. At this point it is worth double-checking that this does conform to all the requirements in the question.

It does.

We now need to improve upon this solution (if possible), or confirm to ourselves that this is the optimal solution (if not). This does look like it cannot be improved. But just feeling that it 'really looks the best solution' is not a strong response here. We may well be trapped within a blinkered perception of the question.

Ideally we should look for an independent justification.

If we add up the timings and divide by three, we find the fastest they could run concurrently, without any gaps. The total time is 13 minutes, and $\frac{13}{3} = 4.33$ minutes. Given that the tasks all take a whole number of minutes, we can be sure that it is not possible to complete all of them in less than five minutes.

This is a classic demonstration that the answer is optimal.

You should aim to follow this general process when solving and checking optimisation problems.

Finding a maximum	Finding a minimum
Find a lower bound: anything that is possible will do	Find an upper bound: anything that is possible will do
Find an upper bound: something that is definitely impossible	Find a lower bound: something that is definitely impossible
Narrow your interval of possibility, trying to find higher and higher values that are still possible	Narrow your interval of possibility, trying to find lower and lower values that are still possible
When you think you have reached the edge, try to find an independent means of checking that the 'next case' is impossible	When you think you have reached the edge, try to find an independent means of checking that the 'next case' is impossible

Practice questions

1   Amy's mother sent her to the post office to buy stamps for a letter. By the time she got there, she had forgotten how much the letter would be to post, but she was sure it was between 8¢ and 12¢ inclusive. The post office sells stamps in every single cent denomination from 3¢ to 10¢, and then the next is 15¢.

What is the least amount that Amy could spend on stamps and still be able to cover any postage value from 8¢ to 12¢?

(Adapted from Cambridge AS & A Level Thinking Skills 9694, Paper 12 Q22, June 2014)

2   Kevin sells chocolates in his shop. He sells the chocolates in boxes of three sizes:

A small box will hold 10 chocolates and costs $4.

A medium box will hold 20 chocolates and costs $7.

A large box will hold 50 chocolates and costs $15.

Customers are allowed to choose any combination of the chocolates available when purchasing any size box of chocolates. When he closed the shop yesterday, Kevin had sold chocolates for a total of $783. Exactly 100 boxes had been sold during the day.

a   What is the greatest number of large boxes that he could have sold?

b   What is the least number of chocolates that he could have sold?

(Adapted from Cambridge AS & A Level Thinking Skills 9694, Paper 12 Q28, June 2014)

3   Richard is buying new carpet for his office. The carpet comes in tiles which are 50 cm by 50 cm.

The office is 820 cm long and 520 cm wide. Since there is no pattern on the tiles, any piece of a given size can be used and orientation is not important.

Richard wants to make sure that the whole tiles or pieces always meet in fours at their corners and that the smallest total number of pieces is used. How many tiles does Richard need to buy?

(Adapted from Cambridge AS & A Level Thinking Skills 9694, Paper 12 Q26, June 2012)

Taking it further

4   A newspaper report said that the average oarsman in a winning Olympic 'coxed four' (a rowing crew which involves five athletes) had altered dramatically between 1968 and 1988. In particular it said,

> *…the average weight had increased from 64 kg in 1968 to 72 kg in 1988, and the range of weights in a crew had exactly doubled over those years.*

Another report, by a different newspaper, said,
> *…the average weight remained at 64 kg from 1968 to 1988, but the range of weights exactly doubled over those years.*

You can assume that both newspapers had the same raw data (the weights of the athletes involved in 1968 and in 1988).

The apparent disagreement in the reports came about because of the different meanings of the word 'average': the first newspaper calculated the means of the weights, while the second calculated the medians.

The rules of the competition state that no participant may be less than 55 kg. For the purposes of this investigation, you should only consider weights which are whole numbers of kilograms, and you should not consider weights greater than 100 kg.

a   Give an example of five weights which have a **mean** of 64 kg.

b   What is the largest range that the weights from 1968 could have had, given that the claims made by the first newspaper are correct (and assuming that it used the mean in its calculation of the average)?

c   Give an example of five weights which have a mean of 72 kg and a median of 64 kg.

d   Give an example of five weights for the year 1968 and five weights for the year 1988 which could have supported the claims by both of the newspapers (assuming the first newspaper had used the mean in its calculations and the second had used the median).

A third newspaper gave the following response to the two newspaper reports above:
> *The conflicting reports of the weight differences in the Olympic rowing crews were meaningless, because they treated all five*

*athletes as equals; they are not. One is a coxswain who steers the
boat, and is always as light as possible (within the rules of the
competition), while the other four are the oarsmen who power the
boat. It is the weights of these four oarsmen which might reveal a
trend in the way athletes prepare for the sport. The average weight
of the four oarsmen actually increased by more than 11 kg from
1968 to 1988, and the range of their weights more than tripled.*

e   Show that the third newspaper could **not** have been referring to the
    mean, when it refers to the 'average'.

f   Find five weights for the year 1968 and five weights for the year 1988
    which are consistent with all three newspaper reports.

(Cambridge AS & A Level Thinking Skills 9694, Paper 31 Q3, November 2011)

3 Overview checking methods

Some problems allow you to check your answer by a completely
separate approach, such as considering:

» the symmetry of what you have been given

» the total number of options

» an extreme case

» the problem tackled in reverse

» a totally separate approach to the problem.

These approaches are difficult to classify, but practice and sharing
successful cases with your peers will help you get better at spotting
them.

A few examples are given below.

Sample question

A painter is given the task of painting numbers on the doors in a street. There
are one hundred houses.

How many times does he need to paint the number 7?

*(Adapted from Cambridge AS & A Level Thinking Skills 9694,
Paper 11 Q1, Nov 2009)*

Try this
problem
yourself,
before
reading the
analysis!

**If you gave the answer 10, then you probably forgot all the
'seventies': 70, 71, 72, ...**

**If you gave the answer 19, then you probably forgot the second
seven in 77.**

If you gave the answer 20, then you probably got them all.

**If you gave a different answer, then you either took an
unwarranted shortcut, or you added them up wrong!**

But how can you confirm your answer of 20 is right?

Apart from listing all the numbers from 1–100, and recounting every time the number 7 appears, you can instead step back from the problem and consider whether you would expect the answer 20. It is a nice number, with attractive factors (for instance 10) and multiples (100). Is there anything about the nature of the problem which should make us expect such a 'nice' number?

One aspect of the problem, which might loosely be called its symmetry, is that it doesn't matter whether the question is about 7s or 6s or 8s – it feels like the answer should remain the same regardless of which digit we choose. This line of thought leads to the question: how many digits would be used in total? Well there are 100 houses: some have one digit house numbers, some have two digit house numbers, and one has a three digit house number (100). This seems more complex than expected.

We can simplify the problem however, since it is about 7s (and not zeros). Imagine we had 100 houses numbered 00 to 99, with every house having a two digit house number (00, 01, 02, ..., 98, 99).

This would require 200 digits – and if each numeral was equally used, we would need 20 of each.

This sample question demonstrates a checking mechanism which is entirely separate from the original solution. Such mechanisms are gold-dust in the world of problem solving. They allow you to move on with absolute confidence that you have understood the problem fully, solved the problem, and avoided any unforced errors.

A second type of checking can occur when a problem can be tackled 'from two directions'.

Sample question

Try this problem yourself, before reading the analysis!

A child leaves home at 8 a.m. and walks to school. When she arrives at school, 15 minutes is spent having breakfast and then she has 20 minutes to catch up with friends before Lesson 1 begins. There are 6 lessons a day of 50 minutes' duration and a break after every 2 lessons. Morning break after Lesson 2 is 15 minutes, and lunch break after Lesson 4 is 1 hour long. At the end of the day it takes 25 minutes to walk home, which is 5 minutes longer than walking to school.

What time does Lesson 5 start?

(Adapted from Cambridge AS & A Level Thinking Skills 9694, Paper 11 Q2, Nov 2012)

This problem can be tackled 'from the ground up' by carefully tracking the checkpoint timings during the day, up to the point we are interested in:

Time	Activity
08:00	Leave home
08:20	Breakfast at school
08:35	Friends
08:55	Lesson 1
09:45	Lesson 2
10:35	Break
10:50	Lesson 3
11:40	Lesson 4
12:30	Break
13:30	Lesson 5

Can we be sure that the chain of timings has been connected without error?

The trick here is to realise that it is fairly easy to see how long the child's day at school is, and then check that this fits once the last two sections of the day (Lesson 6 and the walk home) are taken into account. This amounts to an independent check on the process.

The total timings for the day are:

Activities	Time (mins)
Walking to and from school	25 + 20
Breakfast and chat	15 + 20
Lessons	6 × 50
Breaks	15 + 60
TOTAL time	455 minutes 7 hours 35 mins
Arriving home	15:35

It is easy to check that Lesson 5 starting at 13:30 supports this arrival time at home: Lesson 6 would start 50 minutes later, at 14:20, and finish at 15:10. Her 25-minute walk home would enable her to arrive back at 15:35.

Answer checked!

For each of the following questions, there is a cumulative method for finding the answer, and an alternative method which allows you to confirm it.

1 In the words of Ford Prefect in Douglas Adams' *The Hitchhiker's Guide to the Galaxy*:

'Time is an illusion. Lunchtime doubly so.'

Arnold is fed up: his watch always seems to be lying to him. When he is at work, his watch seems to run very slowly, but when he is at home in the evening it seems to run much more quickly. He has, therefore, invented a new watch which shows apparent time rather than actual time. It is correct every day at 9 a.m. but:

From 6 a.m. to 9 a.m., it runs at $1\frac{1}{2}$ times the normal speed. From 9 a.m. to 1 p.m. and 2 p.m. to 5 p.m., it runs at twice the normal speed. From 1 p.m. to 2 p.m. (lunchtime), it runs at $\frac{1}{2}$ the normal speed. From 5 p.m. to 10 p.m., it runs at the normal speed. From 10 p.m. to 6 a.m. it stops completely.

What does the watch show at 10 p.m.?

(Adapted from Cambridge AS & A Level Thinking Skills 9694, Paper 1 Q47, Nov 2005)

2 A charity is selling tickets which may win prizes. The tickets all have three digits, from 001 to 999. A prizewinning ticket has the first two numbers adding to give the third, for example, 246.

How many winning tickets are there?

(Adapted from Cambridge AS & A Level Thinking Skills 9694, Paper 11 Q11, Nov 2016)

3 Four friends have just returned from a holiday and wish to balance their finances to ensure that the communal costs are split equally between them. The total communal costs paid by each of them so far are:

Steven paid for all the flights, which cost $120 per person.

Dean paid for the hotel for all of them, which cost $300 in total.

Tom paid for all the meals, which cost $48 in total.

Gus paid for their entry to the local museum, which cost $12 in total.

Who should pay whom, and how much, to ensure that everyone pays the same total, using the fewest transactions possible?

4 The Gatwick Express is a high-speed railway service between Gatwick Airport and central London. Journey time is 30 minutes. When a train arrives at its destination, there is a minimum 20-minute wait before it makes the return journey. This is to allow the driver and guard to have a rest and to walk from one end of the train to the other. The schedule is set out below.

London to Gatwick	Gatwick to London
First train 03:30	First train 03:45
04:30	05:20
Every 15 minutes from 05:00	Every 15 minutes from 05:50
Until 00:00	Until 00:00
Last train 00:32	Last train 01:35

How many trains are needed to run this service?

(Adapted from Cambridge AS & A Level Thinking Skills 9694,
Paper 11 Q17, June 2015)

Taking it further

5   The results in a sailing regatta are decided by adding up the positions each
crew achieves in each race. It is not possible to finish at exactly the same
time as another crew in a race, so each race position is always awarded to
only one crew.

Your rank in the regatta is determined by the number of crews ahead
of you. The crew with the lowest total score in the regatta is ranked 1st
overall, the second-lowest is ranked 2nd, etc. If two or more crews tie for
a particular rank, then subsequent rankings are adjusted accordingly. For
example, if two crews are both ranked 6th in the regatta then the next
rank awarded is 8th (since there are seven crews ahead). The rankings are
recalculated after each race. There are 10 crews competing in the regatta,
and they all finish every race.

a   Show that it is possible to finish 3rd in each of the first three races
and yet be ranked 4th so far, by listing possible positions for the crews
ahead of you.

b   What is the best ranking you could have after two races, if you finished
6th in both of them?

c   If you finish 4th in every race in a five-race regatta, what is the worst
final ranking you can have? Suggest positions for the crews who beat
you.

d   What is the lowest position you could finish in the first three races if
you finished in the same position each time (e.g. 2nd, 2nd, 2nd) and
still be able to be ranked 1st before the fourth race? Justify your answer.

(Cambridge AS & A Level Thinking Skills 9694,
Paper 32 Q1, November 2013)

5 Processing skills and problem solving

By the end of this chapter you will be able to engage and practise each of the following eight key areas of problem solving:

★ proportional reasoning
★ compound units
★ finding averages
★ finding lengths, areas and volumes
★ rounding
★ parsing relationships algebraically
★ finding the nth term of a sequence
★ bases and binary.

To be an expert problem solver you need to be able to work on a number of different levels: the development of a personal heuristic is at the heart of this, requiring intellectual honesty, courage and self-scrutiny. The strategies that are discussed in Chapters 2 and 3 will help only if you adopt such a reflective approach.

But you will be held back as a problem solver if your processing skills are weak: precision, speed and confidence in wielding these skills will give you more time to experiment when you are problem solving under timed conditions. They are not strictly *necessary* for success, but they will enhance your chances, and the misuse of each of these skills will almost definitely diminish your chances of success. If they are an area of weakness for you, it is worth knowing that they are, and treading carefully. None of these are likely to be new to you – but all of them involve processes which are easy to misjudge or apply wrongly.

As you progress through the course, combining the active 'heuristic-developing' methods of Chapter 1, the strategies of Chapters 2 and 3, the meta-tasks of Chapter 4 and the requisite numeracy skills which are briefly discussed in Chapter 5, you must track your weaknesses and your priorities. Success in problem solving depends upon a 'bespoke' approach, in which you know which areas need time and input, and which are dependable. A problem-solving 'diary' is the most appropriate tool for this – which you use to complete your workings for all the multiple problems you tackle, but also to record the insights you have, and track your strengths and weaknesses. Begin with a page at the front entitled 'Areas to develop'.

The following exercise can inform what you have on that first page.

Begin with sample questions on each of the key areas. Three questions in each area will enable you to gauge whether you need to delve further. If you find that you are weak in any of these eight areas, you *must* practise them – the training exercises for this are beyond the scope of this textbook.

Can you do it?

Attempt the following three questions for each of the key areas.

» The first question requires basic competence in processing skills.
» The second question is more challenging and involves avoiding common misconceptions.
» The third question is more challenging still and requires confidence as well as competence.

5.1 Proportional reasoning

Sample questions

Try this problem yourself, before reading the analysis!

1 What is $150 increased by 20%?
2 If 75 squibs are worth $30, what are 60 squibs worth?
3 The price of a coat is reduced by 20%, then increased by 20%, then reduced by 20% and then increased by 20%. What percentage of the original price is the final price?

1 **This can be done by finding the appropriate fraction $\left(\frac{20}{100}\right)$ of $150 and then adding it on:**

Alternatively, you can combine the operations (of finding 20% and adding it to the original) in one multiplier operation:

Start

100% + 20% = 120%

$\downarrow \div 100$

$\times 1.20$ multiplier

Finish

$150 \times 1.20 = $180

The answer: $180

If you struggled to get this answer, admit it! And arrange your own proportional reasoning boot camp. It is a vital processing skill.

2 **This requires you to find an appropriate multiplier, which converts 75 squibs into 60 squibs:**

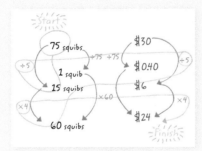

The answer: $24

If your answer to the first question was correct but you struggled to reach this answer, admit it! And go in search of some proportional reasoning problem-solving practice.

3 **This requires applying the multipliers for increasing and reducing, successively:**

reduce by 20% : ×0.8
increase by 20% : ×1.2

$100 \times 0.8 \times 1.2 \times 0.8 \times 1.2$
$= 92.16\%$

The answer: 92.16%

If you managed the first two correctly but struggled with this then mark your problem-solving diary. You probably don't need skills practice – but you do need to gain confidence in wielding these skills.

5.2 Compound units

Sample questions

Try this problem yourself, before reading the analysis!

1   How long does it take a fly travelling at 5 metres/second to cover a distance of 32 metres?

2   Does someone travelling at 10 metres/second break a 30 kilometres/hour speed limit?

3   If a book costs 2¢ per page to print, and it contains 100 words per page, and our press prints 1000 words per minute, how much does it cost to print non-stop for an hour?

1   **The compound unit (metres/second) can be used to derive the key relationship here. You need to check the units are consistent: metres/second, metres and seconds.**

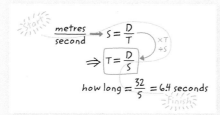

The answer: 6.4 seconds

If you struggled to get this answer, admit it! And arrange your own compound units boot camp. It is a vital processing skill.

2   **Compound units calculations become fiddly when the units are not consistent: you need to convert the two speeds into the same unit in order to compare them.**

The answer: 10 metres/second is the same as 36 kilometres/hour, so YES they are breaking the speed limit.

If your answer to the first question was correct but you struggled to reach this answer, admit it! And go in search of some compound units problem-solving practice.

3 **You need to creatively combine these rates in order to reach one which involves 'cents per hour'.**

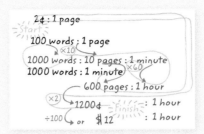

The answer: 1200¢ or $12

If you managed the first two correctly but struggled with this then mark your problem-solving diary. You probably don't need skills practice – but you do need to gain confidence in wielding these skills.

5.3 Finding averages

Sample questions

1 What is the mean and median age of this family: 40 years old, 42 years old, 3 years old, 10 years old and 15 years old?

2 The 8 people in a lift have a mean weight of 80 kg. Then a person gets in, and the mean weight reduces to 75 kg. What did the extra person weigh?

3 My five beansprouts have a mean height of 30 cm, a median height of 25 cm, and two of them are exactly 20 cm tall. What is the tallest that the tallest one could be?

> Try this problem yourself, before reading the analysis!

1 **The two standard measures of central tendency (or 'average') in data are the mean and the median. For the mean, you need to remember to add the pieces of data, as well as add up how many there are; for the median, remember to put them in order first.**

$$\text{mean} = \frac{\text{sum of data}}{\text{number of data points}}$$

$$= \frac{40 + 42 + 3 + 10 + 15}{5}$$

$$= 110 \div 5 = 21 \text{ years old}$$

median : middle value when in order

in order : 3, 10, 15, 40, 42

median = 15 years old

The answer: 15 years old

If you struggled to get this answer, admit it! And arrange your own averages boot camp. It is a vital processing skill.

2   **The total of all the data can be found by multiplying the mean and the number of data points. It's the 'hidden relationship' behind the mean, and can be very useful to know.**

$$\text{mean} = \frac{\text{TOTAL}}{\text{NUMBER}} \quad \text{so TOTAL} = \frac{\text{MEAN} \times \text{NUMBER}}{}$$

before

total Weight = 80 × 8 = 640 kg

after

total Weight = 75 × 9 = 675 kg

extra person = 675 − 640 = 35 kg

The answer: 35 kg

If your answer to the first question was correct but you struggled to reach this answer, admit it! And go in search of some averages problem-solving practice.

3   **The restrictions placed by the mean, the median and the given data allow for some choices for the missing beansprouts:**

5 beansprouts
mean height = 30 cm } total 150 cm height

20, 20, 25, ?, ?

65 + 85 = 150

two missing heights = 85 cm

min height = 25

⇒ max height = 60 cm

The answer: 60 cm

If you managed the first two correctly but struggled with this then mark your problem-solving diary. You probably don't need skills practice – but you do need to gain confidence in wielding these skills.

5.4 Finding lengths, areas and volumes

Sample questions

Try this problem yourself, before reading the analysis!

1 What is the perimeter and area of this shape (if the units are all in cm)?

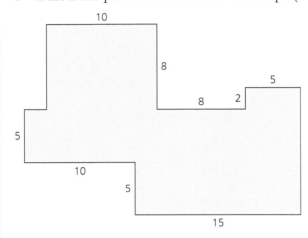

2 Which of these three triangles has the greatest perimeter? Which has the greatest area?

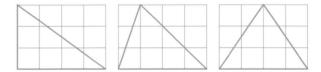

3 Find dimensions for a cuboid, such that its surface area (in cm²) is less than its volume (cm³).

1 The 'opposite sides' in a shape full of rectangles can be deduced – and therefore allow for the perimeter to be calculated. Calculation of the area can always be done by breaking the shape into 'familiar shapes' (in this case rectangles).

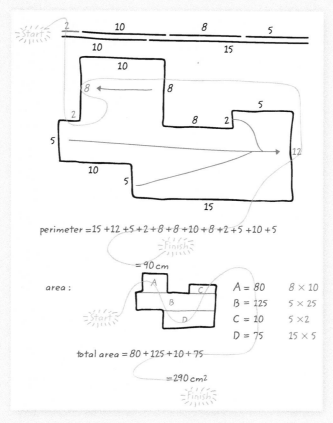

perimeter = 15 + 12 + 5 + 2 + 8 + 8 + 10 + 8 + 2 + 5 + 10 + 5

= 90 cm

area:

$A = 80 \quad 8 \times 10$
$B = 125 \quad 5 \times 25$
$C = 10 \quad 5 \times 2$
$D = 75 \quad 15 \times 5$

total area = 80 + 125 + 10 + 75

= 290 cm²

The answer: perimeter = 90 cm and area 290 cm²

If you struggled to get this answer, admit it! And arrange your own lengths, areas and volumes boot camp. It is a vital processing skill.

2   The area of a triangle is found by multiplying the base and the perpendicular height, and halving the answer. We are often fairly poor at estimating the areas of shapes which are not made out of rectangles, and it is tempting to just reach for the lengths of two sides when trying to calculate it: it is a subtle and slightly counter-intuitive formula, and should be used with care. It means that all these triangles have the same area. The perimeter can only be found by measurement, or by applying Pythagoras' Theorem.

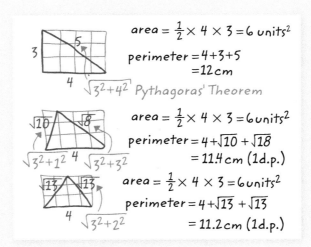

The answer: the left-hand triangle has the largest perimeter and the areas are all the same.

If your answer to the first question was correct but you struggled to reach this answer, admit it! And go in search of some lengths, areas and volumes problem-solving practice.

3   Calculation of the surface area requires considering the areas of each of the six faces and adding them together. The volume is found by calculating the product of the length, width and height (that is, multiplying them together). The comparison of the area and the volume is not meaningful!

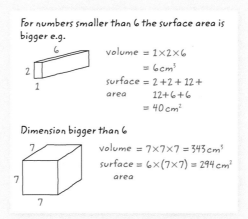

The answer: an example of a cuboid which satisfies this requirement is a cube of length 7 cm.

If you managed the first two correctly but struggled with this then mark your problem-solving diary. You probably don't need skills practice – but you do need to gain confidence in wielding these skills.

5.5 Rounding

Sample questions

1 What is the length 119.354 metres rounded (a) to 1 decimal place, (b) to the nearest metre, and (c) to 1 significant figure?

2 What is the length 119.354 metres rounded to the nearest 2 cm?

3 Two animals are weighed at the zoo, their weights rounded to 1 significant figure, then added: if the resulting (rounded) number is 200 kg, what is the largest that they could actually weigh together?

Try this problem yourself, before reading the analysis!

1 **The only robust way to choose what a number rounds to is to write out the two options that are possible given the level of accuracy (to 1 decimal place means the scale goes up in tenths), and decide which it is closer to.**

The answer: (a) 119.4 m   (b) 119 m   (c) 100 m

If you struggled to get this answer, admit it! And arrange your own rounding boot camp. It is a vital processing skill.

2 **Rounding to the nearest 2 cm means envisaging a scale which escalates in 2 cm gradations: 2 cm, 4 cm, 6 cm, … You can then work out which point on the scale it is closer to.**

The answer: 119.36 m or 11 936 cm

If your answer to the first question was correct but you struggled to reach this answer, admit it! And go in search of some rounding problem-solving practice.

3 **The largest intervals are available if the weights are bigger than 100 kg.**

For example, all the weights that are greater than or equal to 85 kg and less than 95 kg round to 90 kg, whereas all the weights that are greater than or equal to 95 kg and less than 150 kg round to 100 kg.

So two animals weighing just less than 150 kg would both round to 100 kg and satisfy the requirements of the question. They would have a total weight of just less than 300 kg.

The answer: just less than 300 kg

If you managed the first two correctly but struggled with this then mark your problem-solving diary. You probably don't need skills practice – but you do need to gain confidence in wielding these skills.

5.6 Parsing relationships algebraically

Sample questions

Try this problem yourself, before reading the analysis!

1   Write an expression for the number of shoes in the room, if there are 'k' people in the room each wearing 2 shoes, all but three people are carrying a pair of ballet shoes in their hands, and there is a pile of 13 'spare' ballet shoes in the corner.

2   Write down an expression for the percentage of this rectangle that is shaded blue in terms of lengths a, b, c and d:

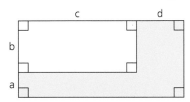

3   Write down inequalities which summarise the following information: The showroom contains Bugattis (B), Ferraris (F) and Lamborghinis (L). The total number of cars in the showroom cannot exceed 15.

At least one-third of the cars must be Bugattis.

There cannot be more of any one make of car than the other two makes added together.

1   **If construction of algebraic expressions leaves you cold, you can always replace the missing value with a number to shed light on the logic of the problem: for example, imagine $k = 10$.**

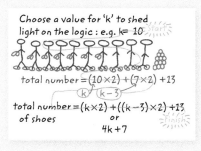

Choose a value for 'k' to shed light on the logic : e.g. $k = 10$ start

total number $= (10 \times 2) + (7 \times 2) + 13$

k $(k-3)$

total number of shoes $= (k \times 2) + ((k-3) \times 2) + 13$

or

$4k + 7$ finish

The answer: $(k \times 2) + ((k - 3) \times 2) + 13$

If you struggled to get this answer, admit it! And arrange your own parsing algebra boot camp. It is a vital processing skill.

2

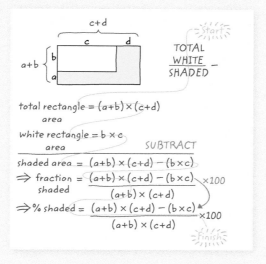

total rectangle area = $(a+b) \times (c+d)$

white rectangle area = $b \times c$

SUBTRACT

shaded area = $(a+b) \times (c+d) - (b \times c)$

$\Rightarrow$ fraction shaded = $\dfrac{(a+b) \times (c+d) - (b \times c)}{(a+b) \times (c+d)} \times 100$

$\Rightarrow$ % shaded = $\dfrac{(a+b) \times (c+d) - (b \times c)}{(a+b) \times (c+d)} \times 100$

The answer: $\dfrac{((a + b) \times (c + d)) - (b \times c)}{(a + b) \times (c + d)} \times 100$

If your answer to the first question was correct but you struggled to reach this answer, admit it! And go in search of some algebraic problem-solving practice.

3 **As with problem 1, the logic of these statements is easier to see if simple numbers are used:**

Choose values for B, F and L to shed light on the logic

eg B = 2 F = 3 L = 5

'TOTAL CARS CANNOT EXCEED 15'

$2 + 3 + 5 = 10$ — does total exceed 15?

$10 \leq 15$ ✓

$B + F + L \leq 15$

'AT LEAST $\frac{1}{3}$ ARE BUGATTIS'

$\dfrac{2}{2+3+5} = \dfrac{2}{10} \overset{?}{\geq} \dfrac{1}{3}$ — are at least $\frac{1}{3}$ Bugattis?

$\dfrac{B}{B+F+L} \geq \dfrac{1}{3}$

'NO MORE OF ANY ONE MAKE THAN THE OTHER TWO'

$2 \overset{?}{\leq} 3 + 5 \quad 3 \overset{?}{\leq} 2 + 5 \quad 5 \overset{?}{\leq} 3 + 2$

$B \leq F + L \quad F \leq B + L \quad L \leq B + F$

The answers: $B + F + L \leq 16$, $B \geq \frac{1}{3}(B + F + L)$, $B \leq F + L$, $L \geq B + F$, $B \leq F + L$

If you managed the first two correctly but struggled with this then mark your problem-solving diary. You probably don't need skills practice – but you do need to gain confidence in wielding these skills.

5.7 Finding the nth term of a sequence

Sample questions

Try this problem yourself, before reading the analysis!

1   What is the 100th term in the linear sequence beginning 11, 14, 17, 20, ... ?

2   If the 20th, 21st and 22nd terms of a linear sequence are 30, 26 and 22 (respectively), what was the first term?

3   A year on Jupiter lasts 10 475.8 Jupiter days. If the first day of the year on Jupiter is a Monday, what day of the week is the last day of the year? How many Mondays are there in a year on Jupiter?

(You will need to pretend that Jupiter follows a seven-day Earth week for this question to have any effect on you.)

1   **Finding the terms of a linear sequence involve linking it to the appropriate times table:**

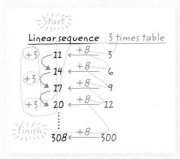

The answer: 308

If you struggled to get this answer, admit it! And arrange your own linear sequences boot camp. It is a vital processing skill.

2   Once you have identified the right times table, you need to identify which term you want:

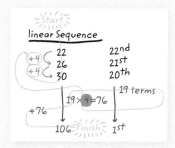

The answer: 106

If your answer to the first question was correct but you struggled to reach this answer, admit it! And go in search of some linear sequences problem-solving practice.

3   It is useful to begin the list 'long-hand' in order to check that the number patterns are what you expect: in this case, the days on which the Sundays fall are all multiples of 7. This enables you to reach deep into the sequence and check that happens at the end of a year on Jupiter.

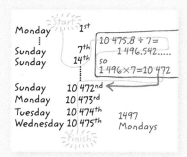

The answers: the 10 475th day is a Wednesday. There will have been 1497 Mondays.

If you managed the first two correctly, but struggled with this then mark your problem-solving diary. You probably don't need skills practice – but you do need to gain confidence in wielding these skills.

5.8 Bases and binary

Sample questions

1 What is the binary number 11011 written as a decimal number?

2 What is the decimal number 38 written in base 4?

3 If you are buying an object worth $26, but the seller has not specified which base he is working in, what is the least it could cost? Give your answer as a decimal number.

Try this problem yourself, before reading the analysis!

1 **Base 2 (or binary) requires numbers to be expressed as powers of 2:**

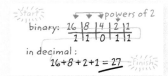

The answer: 27

If you struggled to get this answer, admit it! And arrange your own bases boot camp. It is a vital processing skill.

2 **Base 4 has column headings which are powers of 4: 1, 4, 16, 64 and so on. If you are to write the decimal number '38' in base 4, you need to consider how you build it out of those building blocks, without using any digits bigger than 4.**

base 4:   64 | 16 | 4 | 1
            | 2 | 1 | 2
38 = (16×2) + (1×4) + (1×2)

The answer: 212

If your answer to the first question was correct but you struggled to reach this answer, admit it! And go in search of some base-related problem-solving practice.

3 **A base tells you what the column headings are, and how many digits or symbols you need to express all numbers. For instance, base 10 has column headings which are powers of ten and uses ten symbols (0123456789). These two separate facts are closely linked.**

In this question you must use the fact that the number includes the digit '6', to conclude that it must be written in base 7 or above. The least it could cost is indeed its value in base 7.

Start

Lowest base using digit '6' is
    base 7

base 7: 49 | 7 | 1
             | 2 | 6

in decimal:
    $(2 \times 7) + (6 \times 1) = \$20$ finish

The answer: in base 7 it is worth $20.

If you managed the first two correctly, but struggled with this then mark your problem-solving diary. You probably don't need skills practice – but you do need to gain confidence in wielding these skills.

Evaluating evidence

Key terms

The credibility of evidence consists of the aspects which might make a wise person more or less likely to believe it to be true. Credibility includes the reliability of the source, the plausibility of the content of the evidence and corroboration or consistency with other evidence.

The reliability of sources consists of qualities which make them more or less worthy of trust.

By the end of this chapter you will be able to:

★ assess the credibility of evidence
★ assess the representativeness of evidence
★ assess the presentation of evidence.

'Evaluating' means judging the worth of something. If you plan on using evidence to support a decision you are making, you should first evaluate it. This means determining whether the evidence is strong enough to justify using it in the way you are considering. Aspects which may make evidence strong or weak for the purpose include how **credible** (believable) it is, how **representative** the data are of the people or things about which a claim is being made, and whether the **visual representation** of data is fair or distorted.

6.1 Credibility: reliability

If you are wise, your willingness to believe any evidence which is presented to you will be influenced by the **reliability** of the source (the person, institution or publication presenting the evidence).

Within Critical Thinking, it is customary to identify five factors which might make a source more or less reliable: reputation, ability to see, vested interest, expertise and neutrality/bias.

An easy way of remembering these factors is that their initial letters spell the word 'raven' (the bird *Corvus Corax*).

Vested interest

Ability to see (hear, etc.)

Expertise

Reputation

Neutrality/Bias

▲ **The five factors in a source's reliability**

Reputation

Some sources of evidence have a **reputation** for being trustworthy or for being likely to make false claims. In the case of personal sources, this reputation may refer to the individuals personally or to some category to which they belong, such as their occupation. Opinions may vary. For example, some people would say, 'He is a government minister, and so he would not lie,' whereas others might comment, 'He is a politician, and so you cannot trust a word he says.'

Similarly, citizens of many countries have learned that some newspapers and television stations can be trusted, whereas others tend to present news from the perspective of a particular political party or proprietor. For example, in the UK, the BBC (British Broadcasting Corporation) has a very good reputation for presenting news and opinion accurately and fairly, but some countries (and some groups within the UK) regard the BBC as the servant and spokesman of Western secular capitalist imperialism.

Examples

- Betty believes that maintaining good relationships has the highest priority. Her friends and relatives know that if they ask her opinion, she tells them what she thinks will please them most. This reputation *reduces* the reliability of her stated opinions.
- The Orange Rat Company has been convicted on many occasions for making false claims in its advertising. This reputation *reduces* the reliability of the claims the company makes about its products.
- Stephen believes in encouraging his students. So he always tells them their work is good, even when it is not. But the students know this. His reputation *reduces* the reliability of his comments on the students' work, although probably not of anything he might say in other contexts.
- Ajab is a devoutly religious young man, who is renowned for always speaking the exact truth, even when it is in his interests to lie. His reputation *increases* his reliability.

Ability to see (hear and so on)

Eye-witnesses of events have greater reliability than someone who has only been told about them, but this reliability may be reduced if their view was obstructed or from a distance, if they do not have good eyesight, if they were not paying attention or if they did not see the whole incident.

'Ability to see' might, in other situations, refer to a different sense, or to a combination of sense and other personal experiences (for example, in the case of a character witness). It could also refer to access to relevant evidence (for example, a government department has good ability to see official records).

Vested interest

'**Vested interest**' means a motive to give evidence which will benefit oneself in some way. An explanation of vested interest includes identifying what the person is motivated to do, and how doing so will benefit them. You might correctly state that someone has a vested interest but in order to explain the vested interest fully you need to state explicitly what this person is motivated to do and how they will benefit.

Examples

- People who have committed a crime have a vested interest to lie or to conceal part of the truth, in order to avoid being punished.

- People applying for a job have a vested interest to exaggerate their achievements and conceal their failures, in order to maximise their chances of being appointed.

- Employees who have made a mistake or acted dishonestly have a vested interest to conceal the truth, in order to avoid being disciplined or dismissed.

- Suspects being tortured have a vested interest to tell the torturers whatever they want to hear (whether it is true or not), in order to avoid further pain.

- Companies have a vested interest to exaggerate the benefits of their products, in order to increase sales.

- Newspapers have a vested interest to sensationalise stories, in order to increase sales.

 To think about

Why might academic researchers have a vested interest to misreport the results of their research? How many reasons can you think of?

Respondents to surveys sometimes have a vested interest to give dishonest answers, which affects the reliability of the survey results. Many young people are likely to give false answers to questions about their lifestyle and experiences, either because they want to appear wilder than they really are or because they do not want to admit that they have gone against their moral or religious principles. One reason why political opinion polls are so unreliable as a guide to election results could be that some respondents try to impress the pollster by claiming they intend to vote for a political party which is perceived to have a high status; when the time comes to vote, however, they instead vote for a party with a lower status.

 To think about

If teenagers lie about their lifestyle, do you think they are more likely to say they have had experiences when they have not, or to deny having experiences which they have had? Is there a difference between boys and girls?

Although most cases of vested interest refer to concealing or misrepresenting the truth, people sometimes have a vested interest to be truthful and honest. This, of course, strengthens their reliability. Both kinds of vested interest quite often compete with one another. For example, politicians sometimes have a vested interest to conceal the truth in order to avoid admitting they have made mistakes or committed misconduct, but if they think there is any chance that the truth will come out, they also have a vested interest to tell the truth, in order to avoid being revealed as dishonest and untrustworthy.

Another way in which the reliability of witnesses can be strengthened is when they have a vested interest to misrepresent the truth but do not do so. For example, if police officers giving evidence in a criminal trial admit that, because their attention wandered at the crucial moment, they did not actually see the crime being committed, they increase the reliability of their evidence. The police officers have a vested interest to say they saw the crime happen but, by resisting the temptation to do so, they prove themselves trustworthy. Similarly, a suspect who admits a crime is more reliable than one who denies it, even though many suspects are innocent and their denials are truthful.

Expertise

Another aspect of evidence which should influence how much we rely on it is how expert the source is on the subject concerned.

Evidence from professionals is more credible in relation to their own area of expertise than evidence from amateurs or from professionals in different fields. They would not have been appointed to their job if they did not have the necessary skills and qualifications.

Neutrality/Bias

Both people and documents can be either neutral or biased. People in certain jobs, such as judges, the police and sport referees, are expected to be impartial (neutral), while bystanders who are present but not involved are disinterested, and so have little reason to distort the truth. Conversely, if you are closely related or connected to someone – such as a family member, friend, colleague or team member – then you are likely to be motivated to support them, and you could be described as biased. Other forms of bias include racism and sexism.

Like people, documents can also be either neutral or biased. A report is considered to be neutral if it presents all sides of a case equally. If it presents only one side of a case, then it is biased.

However, the mere fact that people who have studied the evidence come down on one side or the other does not make them biased. Refusing to make up your mind on all issues is not a virtue.

Key terms

The expertise of a source is its specialist knowledge or skills related to the subject.

Bias is a motive or tendency to give greater weight or prominence to one point of view rather than another.

Neutrality is the absence of bias.

To think about

Bob is not interested in politics. He does not watch the television news or read a newspaper and he does not vote in elections. Hanna is very interested in politics. She has strong political opinions, but she does not belong to any political party or pressure group. Anton's strong political views have motivated him to a join a political party and to spend time volunteering for it. Whose political views do you think would be of greatest value – Bob, Hanna or Anton?

Surveys can be biased if the questions are designed to encourage certain answers. Questions like this are known as **leading questions**. For example, respondents are more likely to reply 'Yes' to a question if it begins 'Do you agree that …?' Another way in which questions can be designed to produce misleading responses is to limit the range of answers available (for example, to 'Yes' or 'No'), thereby ruling out moderate opinions. Some people – perhaps even a majority – might have chosen a moderate opinion if it had been available as an option.

Assessing reliability

The fact that someone's reliability is weak does not mean that their evidence is necessarily untrue, but it does mean that we should be rather sceptical towards it.

For example, unsavoury rumours might emerge about a particular celebrity, which they then quickly deny. We may judge that the rumours are unlikely to be true, but we should also not put much faith in the denial if we suspect that the celebrity would have denied the rumours whether they were true or not. Rumours can damage a celebrity's image, lose them endorsements, or prevent them getting more work, all of which give the celebrity a strong vested interest to deny any allegations.

Because of this vested interest, the general public has become very suspicious of denials from figures such as celebrities and politicians. People who wish to harm the reputation of such public figures are aware of this and, unfortunately, are able to make up any wildly inaccurate allegations, knowing that the victims' denials are not likely to be believed.

In many cases, two or more credibility criteria apply to a single source. In order to evaluate the source fully, it is necessary to identify both or all of these factors. For example, researchers employed by commercial companies are almost certain to have expertise in the subject of their research, but they also have a vested interest to make exaggerated claims on behalf of products made by their employers. Sources with good ability to see often also have good expertise and/or bias.

From a set of sources suggesting that Kovinad (a fictitious medication used to reduce cholesterol) might cause heart disease.

Expert evidence

My name is Dr John Aihara. I am Consultant in Cardiac Medicine at Westtown University Hospital. I am also a paid adviser to the company which manufactures Kovinad. Kovinad has been proved to reduce cholesterol, and I am certain that it has saved the lives of many people. I prescribe Kovinad to all of my patients.

a   Suggest one factor which **strengthens** the reliability of Dr Aihara's evidence. Briefly explain your answer.

b   Suggest one factor which **weakens** the reliability of Dr Aihara's evidence. Briefly explain your answer.

a   • **As a consultant in cardiac medicine at a university hospital, he has expertise in heart disease.**

    • **As a consultant in cardiac medicine, he cares for many patients with heart disease and therefore has very good ability to see.**

    • **As a consultant in a university hospital, he has a good reputation, which he would not want to lose by giving false evidence.**

b   • **As a paid adviser to the manufacturer of Kovinad, he has a vested interest to make favourable comments about it.**

    • **As a paid adviser to the manufacturer of Kovinad, he is biased in favour of it.**

Source A

Press release reproduced in several newspapers

Some Britons have knees, elbows and other joints that appear to be more than a decade older than their actual age, according to research. Younger people are also affected – with around one in five of those aged 25 to 34 having a 'joint age' over 50. Some under-35s have even older joints than their parents and in some cases their grandparents, according to the statistics.

The findings are based on data from 13 000 people who submitted information about themselves to the online Joint Age Calculating Tool,

➤

run by a company producing dietary supplements. They answered a series of questions about their lifestyles, including their occupation, weight, how much exercise they do, of what type and how often. They noted any strenuous activities and included information on their diet, such as how much dairy produce and oily fish they eat, as well as noting any pains in their joints. People were also asked to complete a series of exercises, including touching their toes and crossing one leg to see how far their knee could bend towards the floor.

The findings suggested that being overweight was a significant factor in joint age, with those who were overweight or obese adding five years to their joint age on average.

Source D

Email from dietary supplement company

Thank you for completing the first stage of the online Joint Age project. You should now enrol for Stage 2. Take our fish oil capsules daily for three months and then complete the online questionnaire again. Compare the two sets of results.

Although Source A was published as a news report, it consisted of a press release from manufacturers of dietary supplements. How reliable is this report?

(Cambridge AS & A Level Thinking Skills 9694, Paper 23 Q2 (a), sources A & D, November 2013)

6.2 Credibility: plausibility

Key term

The plausibility of a claim is the likelihood of it being true, based on the content of the claim in the light of existing knowledge, irrespective of the reliability of its source.

In addition to the reliability of the source, the credibility of evidence is influenced by the **plausibility** of what is being claimed. Plausibility refers to the intrinsic likelihood of a claim, irrespective of the reliability of its source. A claim which could easily be true, and does not really raise any doubts, is more plausible and hence more credible than something which seems unlikely to be true.

In many cases, the plausibility of the evidence and the reliability of the source compete with one another. Miracles are a good example of this. The philosopher David Hume claimed that although it was theoretically possible for miracles to occur, it would always be more likely that the witnesses were lying or mistaken. If someone were to tell you that he had personally seen a miracle occur, your assessment of the credibility of his claim would be based on balancing the implausibility of the claim against the reliability of the witness.

To think about

If a trusted friend were to tell you (not as a joke) that she had met an alien visitor from another planet, how likely is it that you would believe her? What (if anything) could convince you she was telling the truth?

Practice question

Source A

Advertising leaflet

The dangers of drinking coffee

Why would you drink something that is so hot it would burn you if you spilled it? If it burns your skin, what do you think it does inside your body? Hot beverages destroy your cells, and could lead to cancer!

Coffee contains caffeine, a central nervous system stimulant that is followed by a depressed phase resulting in exhaustion, nervousness, irritability, fatigue and often headaches. Caffeine constricts the blood vessels of the brain and causes decreased flow of blood, which cuts the oxygen supply to the brain, resulting in gradual brain damage.

Caffeol is the volatile oil in caffeine, an irritant to the lining of the stomach which causes poor digestion. Another chemical in this liquid drug is caffeo-tannic acid. This is an irritating astringent to the cells that line the stomach and intestines, which also destroys the pepsin in the gastric (stomach) juice needed to digest protein.

Our herbal drink is an excellent alternative to drinking coffee. Made of roasted carob, barley, chicory root, figs, dates, orange peel and almonds, it is delicious and has the same taste as coffee. Many people think it is even better.

Source B

Magazine article

The health benefits of drinking coffee

All of the following research findings were published in professional medical journals. All comparisons are with those who drink no coffee.

- Drinking 6 cups of coffee per day reduced risk of advanced prostate cancer (study of 50 000 men over 20 years).
- Drinking 5 cups of coffee per day reduced risk of Alzheimer's Disease by 65 per cent (study of 1400 middle-aged Finns).
- Drinking 4 cups of coffee per day reduced risk of stroke by 43 per cent (study of 83 000 nurses who had never smoked).

- Drinking 3 cups of coffee per day reduced risk of gallstones by 20 per cent (study of 127 000 health professionals).
- Drinking 2 cups of coffee per day reduced risk of suicide by 60 per cent (study of 86 000 women over a period of 10 years).
- Drinking 1 cup of coffee per day reduced risk of Type 2 diabetes by 7 per cent (literature review of 18 studies).

Suggest two reasons why Source B is more credible than Source A.

6.3 Credibility: corroboration and consistency

When two pieces of evidence are presented on a topic, they may **corroborate** one another (each piece of evidence makes the other more likely to be true), be **consistent** with one another (both pieces of evidence may be true), or be **inconsistent** with one another (the two pieces of evidence cannot both be true).

An example of corroboration is when two people independently claim to have witnessed the same event and the key details of both accounts are the same. However, the sources do not corroborate one another if they are not independent, for example, because one has copied or been influenced by the testimony of the other, or has a motive to support the other.

To think about

If you read two accounts of an event in two newspapers, what might lead you to suspect that they are not independent and therefore do not corroborate one another?

The results of two experiments corroborate one another if the experiments were conducted by different researchers, on different test subjects, under different conditions and achieved similar results.

Example

The birthdate effect
Source A

There is solid evidence from around the globe that, on average, the youngest children in their year group at school don't perform as well as their older classmates. This is called the 'birthdate effect'. In the UK, where the school year starts on 1st September, the disadvantage is greatest for those born in the summer months (June, July, August). The effect of being the youngest in the year group also happens in other countries where the school year begins at different times in the calendar year.

The birthdate effect is most evident during infant and primary school but it still occurs in the proportions of students who go to university.

The most likely explanation for this phenomenon is that the youngest children in a year group tend to be less mature than their older classmates, leading to unequal competition that puts the younger children at a disadvantage.

Source B
Research report

A high school in the UK analysed the birth dates of players selected for sports teams at the school. A high proportion of selected players were born in the autumn, making them the oldest within their year groups. Children born in the summer (the youngest in each year group) were under-represented. It seems likely that children born in the autumn are favoured because they are more physically mature than younger children in the same year group.

Source B focuses on a specific type of achievement (sport), whereas Source A is more general. Nevertheless, Source B corroborates the claim in Source A that the oldest students in a school year tend to perform better than the youngest.

6.4 Representativeness

Some research can investigate every member of the group which is being studied, either because it is a relatively small and narrowly defined category or because the information is available through official records, such as censuses or registrations of births and deaths. For example, if a school wished to assess the success or failure of its new A Level teaching policy, it could compare the exam results of every student in the year before and the year after the change in policy; however, this procedure relies on the two years being comparable in every other respect. If smoking was abolished in Westland, and the government wanted to see whether and to what extent the number of deaths from lung disease was reduced following this change in the law, it could analyse all the death certificates for as many years as it chose.

However, much research is undertaken by means of samples. A sample can be criticised for being unrepresentative if its members share a characteristic which does not apply to other members of the population, and if that characteristic could plausibly influence the results. For example, if all the members of a sample were of the same sex, it could not necessarily be assumed that the findings also applied to the other sex. Similarly, a sample would be unrepresentative if it was limited to one age group or one occupation, unless the findings and conclusions had the same restriction.

News report

A survey of doctors in the UK has revealed that 1 in 10 of them admit to having given a placebo to at least one of their patients. About 10 per cent of the doctors in the study said that at least once in their career they had given a patient a sugar pill or an injection of salty water rather than a real medicine. One in 100 of them said they did this regularly. Almost all of the doctors said they had provided patients with treatments such as vitamins, complementary medicines or medication intended for other illnesses. Three quarters of the doctors said they offered treatments of those kinds on a daily or weekly basis.

A placebo is medical treatment which is not expected to have any physical effect, but may improve symptoms simply because patients believe it will do so. The fact that the study was limited to doctors in one country (the UK) does not invalidate the conclusion, since the stated conclusion is also limited to that country. If a broader conclusion had been drawn, referring to doctors in general, the restriction of the survey would have constituted a weakness only if there was some reason to suggest that the UK might be untypical in some way. If you wanted to claim that the survey was unrepresentative, you would need to specify in what way the UK might be untypical of other nationalities or locations. It is highly unlikely that there are relevant physiological differences between UK residents and other nationalities, but doctors in different countries may have different cultures and working practices, which would be relevant in this case.

Number

Samples are by definition smaller than the whole group about which a claim is being made, but some samples are too small to be the basis for a valid conclusion. So a sample can be criticised for its size only if it is unreasonably small.

Selectivity

The method of selection of a sample may influence results in various ways. People often select data which support the claim they are making. This practice is sometimes referred to as 'cherry-picking', because it is like eating the cherries from a fruit cake and leaving the rest of the cake.

Since the Cloudy Lemon Company introduced new management systems in 2014, its profits have increased significantly. In 2009, the annual profit was $5.5 million, but in 2017 it had increased to $7.8 million. This shows how successful the new systems have been.

Anyone reading the Cloudy Lemon Company report should suspect that the years have been chosen to make the increase appear as large as possible. 2009 was probably less successful than the other years before the introduction of the new management systems, and 2017 was probably the most successful year following the changes, because there is no other obvious reason for choosing those two years. If they had compared 2013 (the last full year before the changes were introduced) with 2015 (the first full year after they had been introduced), no suspicion would be aroused.

Even if data are provided for a continuous period, the starting point may give a wrong impression. For example, the following graph records the number of divorces in the fictitious country of Westland following the introduction of the Divorce Law Reform Act in 2000:

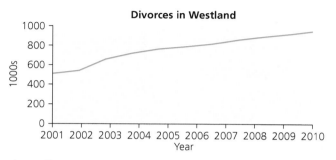

Divorces in Westland

These figures appear to support the claim that the new divorce law has caused the number of divorces to rise significantly. However, if the graph is extended backwards, to begin a few years before the passing of the law, it becomes clear that the rise in numbers began before the passing of the Divorce Law Reform Act, and that the change in the law was therefore probably not the main cause of the increase in the number of divorces:

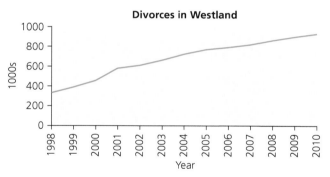

Divorces in Westland

Surveys of public opinion can easily be distorted by taking the sample from a particular group of people. For example, if the people surveyed were all students, they might be more in favour of making university education free of charge than the general public. If the organisation conducting or sponsoring the survey wanted to use the results to support a campaign for making university education free of charge, they would have a motive for limiting the respondents in this way, but not admitting they had done so.

If the sample for a survey of public opinion is self-selected (that is, if it is made up of those who choose to respond to a general invitation), it is likely to consist only of people who feel relatively strongly about the subject. Those whose opinions are not so strong (probably the majority) are not counted.

▲ Survey of public opinion

If the selection is random, it may be unintentionally limited. For example, if a survey is conducted in a shopping centre or by house calls during the daytime, retired and unemployed people are likely to be over-represented. If the survey is conducted via the internet, the respondents will be limited to people who have internet access.

Practice question

News report

Research finds links between coffee and depression

A study has found that having a cup of coffee several times a day could help to prevent female depression. When compared with drinking one cup per week or less, four or more cups of caffeinated coffee decrease the possibility of clinical depression by 20 per cent. The researchers from the US note that they can't be certain that drinking coffee actually prevents depression. Nonetheless, they calibrated their results to allow for many other risk aspects, for example marital status, activity levels, smoking and medical conditions. They also found no comparable correlation with other sources of caffeine or decaffeinated coffee.

The research concerned 50 739 women who took part in the Nurses' Health Study. This study was a large-scale US investigation examining links between lifestyle and health. The women had an average age of 63; none of them had depression at the outset of the 10-year study. Data from this study come from the Archives of Internal Medicine.

Do you think the sample used for this research was representative? Briefly explain your answer.

Proxy measurement and extrapolation

A graph similar to the one shown was published in several media articles around 2010–11.

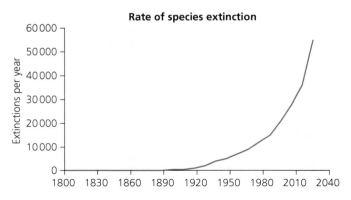

Key term

A proxy measurement or indicator is a statistic which is believed to be closely correlated to a measurement of interest which is not directly accessible.

The text accompanying the graph predicted that 'By 2022, 22 per cent of all species will be extinct if no action is taken' and added, 'Moreover, some species even disappear before we know that they existed.'

There are two major problems with this graph, both of which are frequently encountered in statistical claims.

The first problem is proxy measurement. A proxy is a stand-in. In some research, it is impossible to measure the thing you are investigating. In such cases, researchers often measure something else, which they think is closely related to what they are really studying and will give them a good idea of what they want to know. This is known as proxy measurement.

If some species become extinct before their existence is known, then obviously they cannot be counted directly. These statistics of extinctions are derived from a mathematical model which calculates the number of species becoming extinct by measuring the loss of habitats. The reader has no way of checking the accuracy of this model, and is expected simply to believe its findings, however implausible they may seem to be. Statistics which make claims about one phenomenon on the basis of measuring something else are inherently incredible, and they are typically put forward by people, organisations or companies with a clear vested interest to make the statistics support a case which they are making.

The second problem with the graph is extrapolation.

The graph assumes that a current rapid increase in the rate of growth will continue in the future. This extrapolation of trends is also a frequent feature of dubious claims, especially when inviting people to invest large sums of money. Extrapolation is least credible when it is based on a small amount of data and there is reason to suspect that some of those data are unusual.

Key term

Extrapolation consists of estimating a value by extending a known sequence of data beyond those currently available.

6.5 Presentation of data

If data are presented in the form of a graph or table, various aspects of the mode of presentation may misrepresent the statistics.

Point zero

The range of values on the y-axis of a graph should be chosen in order to represent the data fairly. Normally, the lowest value should be 0 (zero), unless that would hide a small but significant change.

Irregular intervals

Another way of giving a misleading impression of a trend is to have irregular intervals between the points on the x- and/or y-axes of a graph.

Symbols

The use of symbols to represent data can be eye-catching, but it can also be misleading. In particular, the relative size of the symbols may not be proportionate to the data. If the height of a two-dimensional or three-dimensional image is in proportion to the statistics, but the width (and perhaps the depth) of the image is also in proportion, then the image itself will be bigger than the statistics justify.

Example

The following table records trends in income and taxation in Westland between 1986 and 2015. These are 'real terms' figures, that is, they have been adjusted for inflation, based on the 1986 value of the dollar. Both sets of figures show a slow and fairly regular rise.

Year	Average income per head ($000)	Average tax per head ($000)	Year	Average income per head ($000)	Average tax per head ($000)
1986	37.1	8.6	2001	38.9	10.2
1987	37.3	8.6	2002	38.9	10.3
1988	37.5	8.8	2003	39.1	10.5
1989	37.6	8.9	2004	39.2	10.6
1990	37.8	9.1	2005	39.2	10.6
1991	37.9	9.3	2006	39.3	10.7
1992	38.0	9.4	2007	39.4	10.8
1993	38.2	9.4	2008	39.6	10.8
1994	38.3	9.5	2009	39.6	10.9
1995	38.4	9.6	2010	39.7	10.9
1996	38.4	9.6	2011	39.8	11.0
1997	38.6	9.7	2012	39.9	11.0
1998	38.7	9.8	2013	39.9	11.1
1999	38.7	9.9	2014	40.0	11.2
2000	38.8	10.1	2015	40.2	11.3

The government of Westland would have a motive for exaggerating the increase in income since they came to power in 2011 (in order to suggest that people have become more prosperous under their rule) and understating the increase in taxation (in order to suggest that the government has been frugal in its spending and its demands).

Graph 1 sets out all the figures from a neutral perspective.

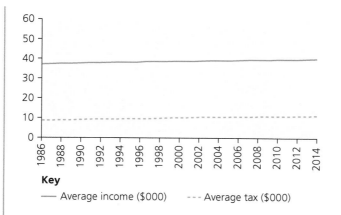

Key

—— Average income ($000)   - - - Average tax ($000)

Graph 2 makes the growth in income appear greater than it is, because the *y*-axis does not begin at zero. Yet a graph which did begin at zero would show barely any variation at all over that period, which would not be of much use. By ignoring the period before the present government came to power, Graph 2 distracts attention from the fact that the rise in income has been roughly consistent under successive governments.

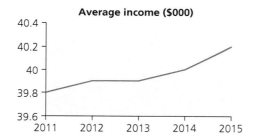

Graph 3 appears to overstate even further the growth in income between 2011 and 2015, because it uses a two-dimensional image to express a one-dimensional increase; furthermore, the image may be mentally interpreted as three-dimensional. It is also not very easy to see exactly what values are being expressed by the symbols.

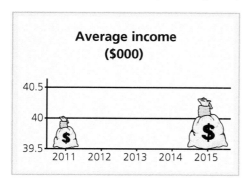

Graph 4 appears to show that taxation is rising at a lower rate under the present government, by using irregular points on the *x*-axis (years).

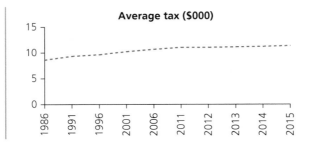

▶ EXTENSION ACTIVITY

Find in a newspaper or on the internet an example of a graph used to present data. Has the method of presentation been manipulated in order to give a false impression?

6.6 Applying the skills of evaluating evidence

AS Level

The first part of a Critical Thinking paper usually provides several pieces of evidence related to a single topic, and some parts of the first question test the evaluation of that evidence. The sample question and practice question located at the end of Chapter 7 test the skills which you have studied in Chapter 6 together with those you will study in Chapter 7.

The second question is usually about using the evidence. If you are asked to draw on various pieces of evidence in order to argue a simple case (for example, in the second question of the AS Level exam), your use of the evidence should include some recognition of how credible or incredible it is.

A Level

The third question of an Applied Reasoning exam normally tests the evaluation of the evidence supplied in one of the documents. This question may focus on the skills developed in this chapter and/or those explained in Chapter 7; so a sample question and a practice question are included at the end of Chapter 7.

Evaluation of evidence is also part of the fourth question, because you should take a critical approach to the sources.

7 Using evidence

Academic research, policy-making and popular journalism are among the many activities which make use of evidence. The many ways in which evidence is used can be broadly divided into two categories: explaining and drawing inferences. When people explain evidence, they make suggestions of what happened *before* the evidence, in order to bring it about. Astrophysicists, for example, try to come up with explanations for their observations of the birth, life and death of stars, planets, galaxies, nebulae and other objects in the universe. Inferences, by contrast, move *forward*, beyond the evidence, to predict future occurrences or to recommend policies or courses of action.

You may be asked to assess an explanation or inference which has been stated either in a source or in the question itself; alternatively, you may be asked to suggest an explanation or inference of your own.

There is a connection between assessing explanations or inferences supplied by others and suggesting your own explanations or inferences. If you are able to suggest alternative explanations or inferences, then this constitutes a weakness in the explanation or inference you have been given.

7.1 Explanations

Assess explanation for evidence

Explanations may be weak if:

» they fail to account for the whole of the evidence they claim to explain
» they rely on speculative additional information or unstated assumptions
» other explanations are at least equally plausible.

Key term

A confounding variable is a factor which was not the one being studied but may have influenced the results of an experiment.

The last of these is particularly relevant in cases where two situations or groups are compared but there is more than one difference between them. Social scientists refer to these as 'confounding variables'; in other words, a difference between the situations or groups which is not the one being studied, but may have influenced the results.

Example

A class of high school pupils took an intelligence test. Their mean score was 47 per cent. They then took vitamin tablets every day for a year. Their mean score on an intelligence test at the end of that period was 53 per cent.

This fictitious experiment certainly does not prove that taking vitamin tablets improves intelligence – or even the ability to score well on intelligence tests. The students were a year older on the second occasion. They had at least one previous experience of taking such a test. And the second test may have been of a different level of difficulty (or, if it was the same test, they may have remembered some of the answers from the previous year).

When more than one explanation is offered, you may be asked whether the explanations are consistent with one another or contradict one another. In other words, do you have to choose between them or could they both be true?

Sample question

Source A
News Report 2006 – Southland National News

The hidden cost of economic success

The current economic boom is good news for most people, but there is another side. The number of cases of depression, as measured by the number of prescriptions issued for antidepressant medication, has been rising steadily over the last few years.

High-achievers in business are currently receiving high rewards and a luxurious lifestyle which most other people envy. What they don't see is the stress and insecurity caused by the fear of losing this material prosperity.

'Money doesn't buy happiness' is an old cliché, but we now have the evidence which proves it.

Source B
News Report 2012 – Southland National News

The cost of the recession

Figures released today reveal the psychological cost of the current economic recession. Rising unemployment and reductions in public expenditure have created a rise in mental health problems, especially depression. This is shown by the number of prescriptions for antidepressant medication, which rose last year by comparison with the previous twelve months.

Source A claims that economic prosperity causes depression, while Source B claims that economic hardship has the same effect. Do these claims contradict one another? Briefly explain your answer.

(Cambridge AS & A Level Thinking Skills 9694, Paper 21 Q2 (b), sources A & B, June 2013)

No, these claims do not contradict one another. Prosperity can cause stress because of pressure of work, competitiveness and/or the fear of losing what one has, whereas under conditions of hardship, people fear being unable to pay their bills or meet their basic needs. Both are departures from moderation/the norm. The explanations in Sources A and B do not claim to be the only causes.

Correlation

Key term

Correlation is a statistical relationship between sets of data, or the tendency for phenomena to occur together.

Claims made by serious researchers, popularisers of science and journalists looking for a striking headline are often based on a **correlation** between sets of statistics.

For example, if heart disease occurs more frequently among people who eat large quantities of processed meat than in the population as a whole, it is tempting to claim that eating processed meat causes heart disease. Some newspapers have published so many claims of this kind concerning diet and health that commentators and comedians have suggested that everything either causes cancer or is a potential cure for cancer – and sometimes both. But there are other ways of explaining such correlations.

A correlation between two sets of data may be due to coincidence. Billions of sets of data are now available, and there is a limited number of patterns which they can display. So it is inevitable that many sets of data will resemble one another, despite being unconnected. The website www. tylervigen.com has collected many of these 'spurious correlations'. For example, this website shows a close correlation between US spending on science, space and technology and the number of suicides by hanging, strangulation and suffocation. The number of films featuring the actor Nicolas

Cage between 1999 and 2009 correlates closely with the number of people who drowned by falling into a pool over the same period. And the *per capita* consumption of mozzarella cheese between 2000 and 2009 correlates closely with the number of doctorates awarded in Civil Engineering. It is virtually certain that none of these correlations has any causal basis whatsoever.

If there is a causal basis for the correlation between two sets of data, it may be that A causes B, or B may cause A, or perhaps C (some other factor) causes both A and B.

The relationship may be quite complex. For example, if the Divorce Law Reform Act in Westland made it easier to obtain a divorce, and if the number of divorces in the country rose significantly following the introduction of the Act, it is likely that the change in the law was partly responsible for the rise in the number of divorces. But the change in the law was probably in part a response to a change in public opinion, which made divorce more acceptable. In addition, people who knew the new law was likely to be introduced may have delayed applying for a divorce until it became easier, following the introduction of the new Act.

To think about

There is a strong statistical correlation between being overweight and having Type 2 diabetes. It is frequently alleged that excess weight causes diabetes, and some countries have developed public health policies on the basis of this claim.

How many *other* possible explanations can you think of for the correlation between excess weight and Type 2 diabetes?

▶ EXTENSION ACTIVITY

Look in newspapers or on news websites for examples of claims based on statistical correlation. Share them in a small group and discuss what you think is the basis for the correlation (for example, cause, coincidence, and so on).

Suggest explanation for evidence

Explanations for evidence are likely to refer to **motivation** (why someone or a group of people acted in a particular way), or the basis for a **correlation**. As explained on page 208, alternative explanations are often the result of the unintentional inclusion of a confounding variable in an experiment.

Suggesting explanations for evidence is a task which relies less on your understanding of the sources provided, and more on your own imagination. Try to avoid the following three common mistakes:

» When suggesting 'alternative' or 'other' explanations, there is no value in re-stating the explanation already given in the source.

» 'Alternative' explanations have to explain the facts or evidence as they are, not in some alternative reality where the facts or circumstances are different.

» If you are trying to suggest more than one explanation, they must be distinct. Splitting one explanation into two halves or expressing it again in different words does not constitute suggesting two explanations.

Sample question

Source B

Research report

An analysis of the birth dates of players selected for school representative sports teams was carried out at a high school in England. Autumn-born children, the oldest within their year groups, were found to be over-represented and summer-born pupils under-represented. In the selection of players for school sports teams, the autumn-born on average may be favoured due to initial advantages related to increased physical maturity.

Source C

Participation rates in English football leagues by dates of birth

	Sept–Nov	Dec–Feb	Mar–Jun	July–Aug	TOTAL
Premier	288	190	147	136	761
Division 1	264	169	154	147	734
Division 2	251	168	123	131	673
Division 3	217	169	121	102	609
TOTAL	1020	696	545	516	2777

Source B explains why the birthdate effect might occur in school sport, but this explanation does not apply to adult footballers, because they are not competing only against people from the same school year. Yet Source C shows that the birthdate effect does still influence players' chances of becoming a professional footballer.

Suggest two possible explanations for why the effect of birthdate on sporting ability seems not to disappear in adulthood.

(Adapted from Cambridge AS & A Level Thinking Skills 9694, Paper 21 Q2 (b), sources B & C, June 2014)

➤

As stated in the question, the birthdate effect cannot apply directly to adults, in relation to either academic or sporting achievement, since it refers only to advantages over people from the same age-cohort, which does not apply once people have left school. So the question is asking you to think of reasons why being advantaged early in one's life may have continuing indirect benefits.

Suitable answers include:

➤ Players who show promise at school are likely to be selected for extra training and competition, which improves their skills.

➤ Players who show promise at school are likely to develop confidence in their own abilities, which continues into later life.

➤ Players who are selected for representative teams while at school are likely to come to the notice of scouts looking for talent on behalf of professional clubs.

➤ People who do not show sporting promise at school are likely to develop different interests.

Practice question

Sources A and B, on pages 208 and 209, claim that a rise in the number of prescriptions of antidepressant drugs indicates an increase in the number of patients with depression. Suggest **two** possible alternative explanations of your own for the rise in the number of prescriptions.

(Adapted from Cambridge AS & A Level Thinking Skills 9694, Paper 21 Q2 (a), June 2013)

7.2 Inferences

The motive for gathering evidence or doing research is usually in order to draw useful inferences from it. These inferences usually consist of either **predictions** of other data or **recommendations** of actions or policies which should be taken in light of the evidence.

Drawing inferences

You may be asked to do any of the following:

» draw a logical inference from a piece of reasoning
» predict what is likely to happen on the basis of the evidence provided
» identify a recommendation which would be supported by the evidence provided.

Key term

An inference is a conclusion which can be drawn from one or more reasons or from evidence.

Research report

Research has found that overweight people travel farther in their seats before their seat belts engage in the pelvic area during a car crash, compared to normal-weight people. The delay in seat-belt activation is due to an excess of soft tissue in the abdomen, which prevents the belt from gripping the pelvis firmly. The upper body is held firmly, but the lower body is not. This can put intolerable strain on vital organs, leading to an increased risk of serious injury or death.

From the evidence in this report, it is possible to conclude that overweight people who travel in cars should lose weight. Suggest an **alternative** conclusion which could be drawn from the same evidence.

(Adapted from Cambridge AS & A Level Thinking Skills 9694, Paper 21 Q2 (c), source D, June 2016)

Car designers should re-design safety features, especially seat belts, in order to make them suitable for a wider range of body sizes/overweight people.

Report in medical journal

Not enough therapists for talking cure

Most psychiatrists agree that the most effective way of treating depression is Cognitive Behavioural Therapy (CBT), which involves many hours of talking to a trained therapist. Although CBT has produced impressive results, it is labour-intensive and time-consuming. As CBT has become the treatment of choice for people suffering from depression, waiting lists have grown. Training more therapists cannot be achieved quickly. Unfortunately, many doctors who know that CBT would offer the best hope for their patients are currently unable to offer it immediately. In many cases, the condition deteriorates before the 'talking cure' can begin. This creates a vicious circle, whereby the severity of the condition causes the treatment to take longer, which in turn makes another patient have to wait even longer for a therapist to become available.

How are the facts in this report likely to affect the amount of antidepressant medication sold?

(Adapted from Cambridge AS & A Level Thinking Skills 9694, Paper 21 Q2 (c), source C, June 2013)

Assess inference from evidence

Several different tasks relate to assessing inferences which other people have drawn or might draw from evidence. For example, you may be given some data from a research study (perhaps in the form of a table or a graph) and also a report of the claims made by the researchers. You may then be asked either how well the data support the reported claims or how well a claim expresses the findings of the research.

Source A
News report

Driving safely and wearing seat belts are two ways to reduce the chances of dying in a car accident. Losing weight might be another one. A recent study, led by Dr Thomas R Rice, of the Division of Environmental Health Sciences at the University of California at Berkeley, looked at whether there was any link between being overweight and the likelihood of dying from injuries suffered in car accidents.

'Findings from this study suggest that overweight people are more likely to die from traffic collision-related injuries than people of normal weight involved in the same sorts of collision,' the researchers wrote.

Source B
Research data

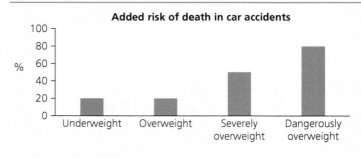

Findings from the University of California at Berkeley study

Source A claims that losing weight may be a good way 'to reduce the chances of dying in a car accident'. How well does the graph in Source B support this claim?

(Adapted from Cambridge AS & A Level Thinking Skills 9694, Paper 21 Q2 (b), sources B & C, June 2016)

It supports the claim partially (neither well nor badly). It does support the claim in the case of overweight people (and even more so if they are severely or dangerously overweight), but not in the case of people whose weight is considered normal. Since underweight people also have an increased risk, they should certainly not lose weight.

In order to answer this question, it is necessary to interpret the graph correctly. As stated in the title of the graph, the percentage figures refer to *added* risk of death, that is, compared to people of normal weight.

The skill of evaluating an inference is what you need to answer the question, 'Can you reliably draw the conclusion ...?' or to explain why you cannot draw the conclusion ... You may be able to find the answer to such questions by looking only at what is said in the source, or you may need to add some thinking of your own.

Sample question

Dr Asif

As a doctor for more than forty years and a homoeopath for the last twenty, I know that homoeopathy is a most valuable tool and nine times out of ten my treatment of choice. One only has to see its dramatic effect in treatment of fevers, depression, anxiety and pain, to become a convert. It does work! Furthermore, no homoeopathic remedy has ever been withdrawn or banned because it was dangerous.

'Homoeopathy should be used for all patients.' Can this be reliably concluded from Dr Asif's statement? Explain your answer.

(Cambridge AS & A Level Thinking Skills 9694, Paper 21, Q2 (a), source B, June 2011)

No. This statement is too strong to be concluded from Dr Asif's statement. Dr Asif admits that he chooses it in only nine cases out of ten, which means he does not use it for all patients, and the list of conditions for which he claims it has a 'dramatic effect' is limited, which suggests it is less effective for other conditions/patients.

Sample question

Mrs Courtney

My daughter was diagnosed with a thyroid complaint that would have meant a lifetime on medicine, with all sorts of possible side effects and at goodness knows what expense. This medicine would never have been a cure – it would just have made her less ill. After 6 months of homoeopathic treatment, her blood tests were completely normal and she was bouncing around like she never had before. Hers is not an isolated case, and certainly not due to the placebo effect, since she was dragged most unwillingly to see the homoeopath, and proclaimed that she didn't believe in any of it!

Dr Branchflower

Unfortunately you don't say what the condition was, nor who made the diagnosis, nor what other medication was being taken, nor what other medical conditions had been diagnosed … and a whole host of other important complicating factors. Not all thyroid 'complaints' require lifetime treatments. Many illnesses eventually come to a natural end without being treated, and this was probably one of them. It is certain that the homoeopathic treatment did absolutely nothing, since it contained no active medical ingredient.

How effectively does Dr Branchflower reply to Mrs Courtney's claims? Explain your answer.

(Cambridge AS & A Level Thinking Skills 9694, Paper 21 Q2 (b), Source B, June 2011)

Dr Branchflower answers Mrs Courtney's arguments well, by pointing out the important information missing from her account of her daughter's illness and by suggesting alternative explanations for the improvement in her daughter's condition, but he is unlikely to persuade her, because he is unable to prove that the improvement did not happen as a result of homoeopathy.

The **placebo effect**, mentioned by Mrs Courtney, can sometimes be an explanation for apparent benefits of unorthodox medical treatment. Repeated research has shown that to some extent the belief that a treatment will produce a cure is sufficient to improve symptoms.

Practice question

Source A

Conclusion of research report

This study did not establish a cause-and-effect relationship between oral health and heart disease. However, even when adjustments are made for other contributory factors, there is a clear increase in the risk of developing heart disease for those people that brush their teeth only rarely or never.

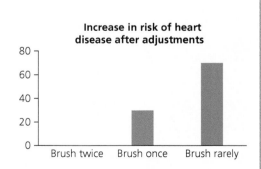

Increase in risk of heart disease after adjustments

Source B

Press release

One in three adults in the UK does not brush their teeth for the recommended full two minutes, experts believe. The Chief Executive of the British Dental Health Foundation said, 'Your dentist can remove any build-up of plaque and tartar on your teeth, but everyday care is vital and is down to the individual. Your toothbrush is one of the best weapons against gum disease.' He said many studies over the years had shown that the average time for brushing teeth is only around 45 seconds, less than half of that necessary to do a good job. 'Yet our study shows people think they are doing considerably better than this,' he said. 'Gum disease is the largest cause of tooth loss in adults, and poor mouth health is being linked to more and more serious illnesses such as heart disease, strokes and diabetes, but it is a preventable condition, and a good mouth health routine at home is key to preventing it.'

Does the information in Source B support or challenge the conclusion in Source A? Justify your answer.

(Adapted from Cambridge AS & A Level Thinking Skills 9694, Paper 23 Q2 (c), sources C & D, November 2012)

A question may add a further fact concerning the evidence supplied and ask you to draw an inference from it or to evaluate an inference which someone else has drawn, for example, stating 'A student who read this source commented ...'

Practice question

Doctors have warned that tourists are risking their lives by relying on homoeopathy to protect them against malaria. This warning follows an undercover investigation which revealed that alternative medicine clinics willingly sell travellers homoeopathic protection against malaria despite official advice that there is no evidence that these treatments work. It also comes after a study published in a medical journal claimed that, in some clinical trials, homoeopathic remedies performed no better than sugar pills.

According to this report, recent scientific research has suggested that homoeopathy is ineffective as a medical treatment. Can we reliably conclude that people will cease to use homoeopathic treatment as a result of this research?

(Cambridge AS & A Level Thinking Skills 9694, Paper 21, Q2 (c), source D, June 2011)

Assessing relevance and significance

If you are asked to explain the relevance or significance of some evidence, you are expected to draw an inference which strengthens, weakens or affects the interpretation of the claim, question or topic under discussion. Questions asking 'How relevant?' or 'How significant?' are asking you to make a judgement based on drawing such an inference. If no relevant inference can be drawn, the judgement should be that the evidence is not relevant or significant.

A particularly dangerous type of heart attack is known as STEMI. Research based on over 11 000 patients in several countries has shown that people who had completed less than eight years of education were significantly less likely to receive certain treatments for a STEMI than patients who had spent more than sixteen years in education. About 17.5% of patients with less than eight years' education died within a year of suffering a STEMI, whereas only 3.5% of those whose education had lasted for more than sixteen years failed to survive a year after a STEMI.

Explain the relevance of this evidence to the claim that people's educational level affects their health and longevity.

This evidence supports the claim in relation to a particular illness. The finding that people with more education are more likely to receive certain treatments probably applies to other conditions as well, and suggests a plausible explanation for the increased longevity of people with more education. People who receive longer education often live in relatively wealthy countries, where better medical resources are available. They a lso tend to have better-paid jobs, which enable them to afford better health care.

Scientists in the US conducted an experiment to test the hypothesis that cold temperatures make people more likely to catch the cold virus. The experiment was conducted on mice and used a virus which affects mice similarly to the way the cold virus affects humans. At warmer temperatures, mice which had been infected with this virus activated natural defences against it, but they activated fewer antiviral defences at cooler temperatures, thereby enabling the infection to survive and grow more easily.

How significant is this evidence?

It is quite significant (neither very significant nor insignificant). It is not directly relevant, because the virus was not the human cold virus and the test subjects were mice, not humans, but the findings do provide a plausible link between cold temperatures and the cold virus, which should be tested directly.

Sample question

UK blogger

I don't agree with the birthdate effect research. I was born in July and I have two first-class honours degrees, but my son was born in November and he never went to college. In my view, it is not true that people who are born in the autumn or early winter are more intelligent than people born in the summer. The point about sport may be right, though, because I am no good at sport.

How significant is this evidence in relation to the claim that children born soon after the beginning of the school year tend to perform better than those born later?

Not significant. It does not support the claim, because in that family the person born towards the end of the school year performed better than someone born earlier. However, it also does not count against the claim, because the claim refers to greater probability, and does not imply that all children born early in the school year perform better than those born later.

Questions about the **usefulness** of evidence have potentially two aspects: credibility and significance. If the credibility of the evidence is weak or if you cannot draw a significant inference from it, then the source is not very useful.

A question which asks you how effectively one source responds to the evidence in another source tests your understanding of both sources.

The birthdate effect

There is strong evidence from around the world that, on average, the youngest children in their year group at school perform less well than their older classmates. This is known as the 'birthdate effect'. In the UK, where the school year starts on 1st September, the disadvantage is greatest for children born during the summer months (June, July, August). The effect of being the youngest in the year group also applies in other countries where the school year begins at other times in the calendar year. The birthdate effect is most pronounced during infant and primary school but it is still evident in the proportions of students who go to university. The most likely explanation for this phenomenon is that the youngest children in a year group are, on average, less mature than their older classmates, leading to unequal competition that disadvantages the younger group.

Can it be reliably concluded from this report that university students who were born early in the school year are likely to gain better degrees than those born at other times of the year? Briefly justify your answer.

(Adapted from Cambridge AS & A Level Thinking Skills 9694, Paper 21 Q2(a), source A, June 2014)

No, this cannot be reliably concluded. The reasons why this is so include two relatively straightforward points:

➤ **It is plausible that the birthdate effect could continue into university, but there is no evidence in the source to suggest that it does.**

➤ **Maturity levels are likely to be the same by the time individuals reach university age.**

And two points which require more thought:

➤ **Not all members of a year group attend university. University students compete against people who have gained the same entry requirements as themselves, rather than against the whole year group.**

➤ **If people born at other times of the year have to be slightly more talented in order to gain a place at university (compared to those born early in the school year), then they might be expected to perform better. In fact, this is the case, but if this question had been asked in an exam, you would not have been expected to know that, unless one of the sources gave that information.**

Any one of these answers would be sufficient to answer this question.

Other tasks which may occur when asked to assess inferences from evidence include:

» identifying factors which weaken the support the evidence gives to a stated claim

» judging to what extent further evidence succeeds in responding to a claim.

Inadequate information

Inferences sometimes go further than the evidence justifies. For example, evidence from a single year is insufficient as the basis for a claim about trends, and evidence about one country does not justify a claim comparing it with other countries, unless evidence is given about them too.

A claim that a product is 'more' effective is meaningless unless it clearly identifies what it is being compared against. For example, if the manufacturers of a product designed to help people stop smoking claim that users are 'seven times more likely to quit' using their product, the claim has no meaning and cannot be checked for accuracy. Even if they specify 'seven times more likely to quit than by willpower alone', although it is relatively easy to identify people who are using the product, it is quite unclear who qualifies as someone trying to stop smoking 'by willpower alone', and the company has a strong vested interest to interpret the category in their own favour. Perhaps they include all smokers who are not using their product, in which case many of them are probably not trying to stop at all.

> ### EXTENSION ACTIVITY
>
> From a newspaper, a poster, a flyer or the internet, find an advertisement promoting a product or a service. If necessary, make a copy of it. Carefully scrutinise its claims. Is any essential information missing? Are any misleading claims made? If possible, share these findings with two or three students and your teacher.

▲ This CEO of a large Eastlandish company earns more than any of the male workers in that company

Outliers and the 'fallacy of division'

In many cases, research discovers that members of one category have a greater probability of something than the members of another category. For example, economics or sociology researchers may have discovered that the average income of female citizens in the fictitious country Eastland is 87 per cent of the average income of men. That means that many women in Eastland earn less than many men. It does not mean that all men in Eastland earn more than all women, and the fact that a particular woman is highly paid does not disprove – or even constitute evidence against – the research finding concerning average earnings.

Individual cases which lie outside a trend are often termed 'outliers'. They are normal features of any investigation, and do not invalidate the findings of the research, provided there are not so many that they obscure the pattern.

The inference that a claim must be true of a particular member of a category because it is true of the category in general is an example of the 'fallacy of division', which claims that something that is true for the whole must also be true for the parts of the whole. Another way of explaining this point is that a claim made about 'most' or 'many' does not imply 'all'.

UK blogger

I don't agree with the birthdate effect research. I was born in July and I have a first-class degree and a doctorate, but my son was born in November and he never went to college. In my view, it is not true that people who are born in the autumn or early winter are more intelligent than people born in the summer.

This example is not a valid criticism of the birthdate effect research. The fact that *more* people born at the beginning of the academic year do well than people born later does not mean that *everyone* born in the autumn or early winter performs better than *everyone* born in the summer. So the family of the UK blogger does not give a reason for doubting the claim that people born in the early part of the school year tend to perform better than those born towards the end of the school year.

The claim in the headline of the following report is a more precise example of the fallacy of division:

Children as young as 11 admit buying alcohol underage
A survey of children between the ages of 11 and 17 has revealed that more than half of them admitted to buying alcohol from supermarkets before they were old enough to do so legally.

This example is taken from a jurisdiction in which 18 is the minimum age for legally buying alcohol. Quite apart from the likelihood that some of the respondents were boasting rather than telling the truth, the reference to 11-year-olds in the headline is not justified by a survey of people aged between 11 and 17, because it may be (in fact, it is likely) that all or nearly all of the people who admitted buying alcohol underage were at the top end of the age range surveyed, and that no 11-year-olds, or very few, gave this response. It is even possible that no 11-year-olds were interviewed, and the researchers may not have been aware of this, if instead of asking respondents their exact age they simply asked if they were between 11 and 17.

Suggesting additional evidence required

In many situations which require evaluating and using evidence, it becomes necessary to suggest additional evidence which would solve a problem in the evidence which has been presented. Investigators then know what to look for. There are two stages in this process: identifying a problem or weakness in the existing evidence; and thinking of what further information would resolve it.

- The reliability of Dr Aihara's evidence (on page 195) is weakened by his vested interest to promote the use of Kovinad. So his evidence will be strengthened if other consultant cardiologists, who are not paid by the manufacturers of Kovinad, prescribe the drug as much as he does.

- The claim made by the Cloudy Lemon Company (on page 200) about the success of its new management systems is weakened by the suspicion that the data have been cherry-picked to support the claim. So it will be strengthened if the profits in other years before and after the introduction of the new systems are similar to those from 2009 and 2017.

- The claim that 11-year-old children have been buying alcohol illegally (on page 222) is weakened because the report does not divide the 11-17-year-olds by years. So it will be strengthened if the respondents to the survey are asked their ages and a significant number claimed to be aged 11. It will be strengthened even more if there is some verification of their ages – for example, if the survey took place in a school or other institution which has reliable information about birthdates.

Answers to questions of this kind should not be counterfactual. For example, if you already know that a CCTV camera was not working, it is pointless to suggest as pertinent additional evidence the CCTV recording which might have been taken if the camera had been working properly.

Doctors have warned that tourists are risking their lives by relying on homoeopathy to protect them against malaria. This warning follows an undercover investigation which revealed that alternative medicine clinics willingly sell travellers homoeopathic protection against malaria despite official advice that there is no evidence that these treatments work. It also comes after a study published in a medical journal claimed that, in some clinical trials, homoeopathic remedies performed no better than sugar pills.

Suggest further evidence which would **weaken** the claim that 'tourists are risking their lives by relying on homoeopathy to protect them against malaria'.

If other clinical trials of homoeopathic medicine showed that they were effective, especially in protecting people from malaria.

Research has shown that the amount of education people have had is linked to their chances of suffering from various health problems, including heart conditions, emphysema, diabetes and asthma. Those who have been educated to a higher level are less likely to have high blood pressure and high levels of cholesterol; they tend to function better, both physically and mentally. The most plausible explanation for these health differences is that people with more education are less likely to smoke, to drink excessively and to be overweight or obese. They are also more likely to seek early treatment for high blood pressure and diabetes.

What *additional* evidence would *strengthen* the hypothesis that the link between education and health is caused by educated people making healthy lifestyle choices?

Ethical criticisms

Academic research is intended to be objective and publicly defensible. Readers might personally disapprove of the results of some academic research for their own ethical reasons, but this would not be a valid criticism of the research itself. For example, someone might criticise the research on the relationship between birthdate and academic achievement because it goes against the principle of equality of opportunity. This would not be a valid criticism, because the researchers were describing what they had found *was* the case, not recommending what *should be* so.

7.3 Applying skills of evaluating and using evidence

AS Level

One or more parts of the first question in the Critical Thinking paper usually relate to using evidence, while other parts concern the evaluation of evidence (the skills presented in Chapter 6). One part of the first question may ask whether one of the sources is an argument (see page 247).

Study the evidence and then answer the questions.

Source A

Extract from a History textbook

King Edward IV of England died suddenly in 1483. He had two sons, Edward, aged 12, and Richard, aged 9. Before the king died, he appointed his younger brother, Richard, Duke of Gloucester, to be Protector of the young princes. This meant that Richard would rule the country until his nephew, Prince Edward, became old enough to rule by himself.

If Richard could make people believe that the young princes had no right to the throne, he would be next in line and become king. He imprisoned the princes in the Tower of London. Then he declared that his brother, Edward IV, had never been legally married to the princes' mother and that the boys were therefore illegitimate. This meant that neither of them could inherit the throne. In July 1483, Richard, Duke of Gloucester, was crowned King Richard III. The two princes were never seen again, and Richard became very unpopular because it was widely believed that he had murdered them.

In 1485, Henry Tudor challenged Richard for the throne. Richard died in battle and Henry became King Henry VII. Like Richard, Henry had good reasons for wanting the princes dead (if they were not already), because their claim to the throne was stronger than his.

Source B

Life and Death of Sir James Tyrell

Sir James Tyrell was a trusted servant of Richard III. In 1501, Tyrell supported an unsuccessful rebellion against King Henry VII and was accused of treason. His jailers reported that before being executed, he confessed under torture that he had employed two men to murder the princes in the Tower, but he did not say who had ordered him to do it.

Source C

Extract from an English Literature textbook

Shakespeare's play, *The Tragedy of King Richard III*, cannot be rightly understood without reference to the political circumstances of the time when it was written. Theatres were tightly controlled by the government. If a particular play was thought to be politically dangerous, the theatre would be closed and the author might be punished. Queen Elizabeth I – the monarch at the time – was the granddaughter of Henry VII. Any play which showed that Henry had been justified in replacing Richard as king would have been very acceptable to the authorities. This is probably why Shakespeare portrays King Richard as deformed in both body and personality. In the play, Richard employs Sir James Tyrell to murder the princes in the Tower.

Source D

The Richard III Society

The Richard III Society was founded in 1924 by a group of amateur historians. The Society believes that the traditional accounts of the character and career of King Richard III are seriously unreliable and unfair. They aim to promote research into his life and times, and to reassess his place in English history. The Richard III Society denies that the princes in the Tower were murdered on the orders of Richard. They may have been killed by Henry VII or they may have survived.

a   State **two** reasons why the evidence reported from Sir James Tyrell (Source B) is unreliable.

b   How useful are the views of the Richard III Society in Source D in discovering whether Richard ordered the murder of the princes in the Tower of London?

c   In 1674, builders repairing the Tower of London discovered the skeletons of two children under a staircase. On the orders of King Charles II, the skeletons were reburied with royal ceremonies in Westminster Abbey. How significant is this discovery in deciding whether the princes were murdered?

*(Adapted from Cambridge AS & A Level Thinking Skills 9694,
Paper 21 Q1 (a) – (c), June 2012)*

Source E

After studying the reigns of Richard III and Henry VII, students at a high school were asked what they thought happened to the princes in the Tower. Here are the results of the survey:

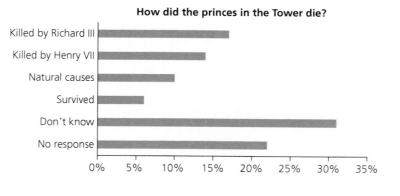

How did the princes in the Tower die?

d   Suggest **three** reasons why the survey results in Source E are **not** useful in deciding what happened to the princes in the Tower.

A Level

As stated at the end of Chapter 6, the third question in the A Level paper covers the skills identified in Chapters 6 and 7. Because the assessment at A Level is holistic, questions may relate not only to any of the issues raised in Chapters 6 and 7 but also to flaws and weaknesses in reasoning, such as those discussed in Chapter 9.

Sample question

Table 1

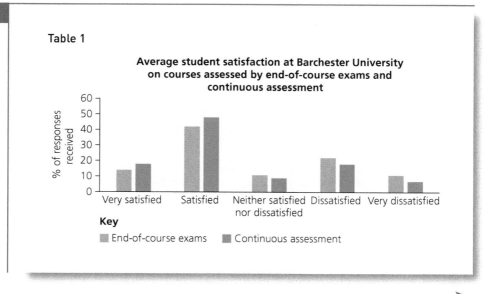

Average student satisfaction at Barchester University on courses assessed by end-of-course exams and continuous assessment

Key
- End-of-course exams
- Continuous assessment

Table 2

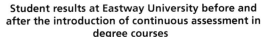

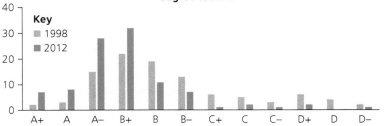

Student results at Eastway University before and after the introduction of continuous assessment in degree courses

All courses ending in 2007 and earlier were assessed by end-of-course examinations only. All courses ending from 2008 onwards were assessed by continuous assessment only.

a   Table 1 was used by students at Barchester University to support their claim that students prefer continuous assessment to end–of–course exams. Identify **three** weaknesses in the support given to the claim by this evidence.

b   Table 2 was used by students at Barchester University to support their claim that the use of continuous assessment improves student performance. Identify **three** weaknesses in the support given to the claim by this evidence.

a   • **There may have been other, more significant differences between the two types of courses and/or students. For example, continuous assessment may have been used on courses aimed at mature students, and they may be more appreciative of the opportunity to gain a university education than school-leavers.**

   • **The results are based only on the students who returned the forms. Most students may not have bothered, in which case the differences may be insignificant.**

   • **The fact that students on courses assessed continuously are more satisfied with their university experience than (different) students on courses assessed by end-of-course exams is not the same as saying that students prefer continuous assessment to end-of-course exams. They were not asked that question.**

b   • **Eastway University may have been chosen because it was the only (or most striking) example of this improvement.**

   • **There is no obvious reason why 1998 and 2012 were chosen to represent respectively the years up to 2007 and 2008** onwards, other than being cherry-picked as the worst and best results respectively.

- **The claim relies on the dubious assumption that degree results either constitute or accurately reflect 'performance'. The change in mode of assessment may have made it easier to gain the higher grades.**

This graph illustrates the outcome of an exit poll in a general election in a country in Europe. As they left polling stations after voting, voters were asked who they had voted for. Those polling stations that were surveyed were typical of the demographic of the entire country.

The electoral register was compared with the total number of votes in order to establish the proportion of those in each age group that did not vote.

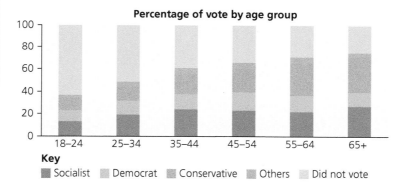

a   Suggest two reasons why this graph may not accurately reflect the votes cast in the election.
b   On seeing this graph, one voter commented, 'There is no point in giving the vote to 16-year-olds, because this graph shows that most of them would not bother voting, anyway.' How well does the graph support this comment?
c   Another voter said, 'As you grow older, you behave more responsibly, and are more likely to vote.' How well does the graph support this comment?

8 Analysing reasoning

By the end of this chapter you will be able to:

★ recognise an argument
★ identify key elements of an argument and explain their function
★ identify unstated assumptions in an argument.

8.1 Arguments

In everyday language, the word argument refers to a disagreement. In Critical Thinking this word has a different, specialised meaning, and you will be expected to understand and use the word in this sense.

Conclusions of arguments often include words like 'should' or 'must'.

Describing the conclusion as 'persuasive' is not a value judgement. It means that the apparent *intention* of the reasoning is to persuade the reader to do something or to believe something. It may not necessarily *succeed* in achieving this intention, but that does appear to be the purpose of the reasoning.

Example

Smoking is expensive and causes many serious illnesses. So people who smoke should try to give up.

Example

It is not fair to expect Majid to look after his grandchildren. He has no experience of caring for children and he cannot hear very well.

Other kinds of speaking or writing are sometimes confused with arguments.

An **opinion** is not supported by reasons. It may be quite an extended piece of speech or writing, but the content consists entirely of what the author believes, and gives no reasons to persuade the reader to agree.

Example

Schools should not tell their students what they may and may not wear. School uniform should be abolished, and students should be free to wear whatever clothes they choose.

At first sight, this may look like an argument, but in fact it consists of an opinion expressed three times, in slightly different ways.

A **description** states what is the case, but it does not explain why, and it does not try to persuade the reader to do anything or to believe anything.

Example

The government of Eastland consists of congress, which is elected by constituencies, a senate, which is appointed, and the president, who is directly elected. In order to become law, any proposal has to be accepted by all three branches of government.

A **narrative** tells what happened.

Example

Sara really enjoyed the weekend. Her cousins came to visit, and on Saturday evening they watched a film and ate a takeaway.

An **explanation** does not seek to persuade. It gives reasons why a situation is as it is.

Example

Emily's grandmother loves her dearly. So she has given her money to help her go to university.

The first sentence in this example explains why Emily's grandmother *has* given her money, not why she *should*. So it is an explanation, not an argument.

Example

- Without education, the fundamental human rights of liberty and pursuit of happiness are very limited. Therefore most countries have recognised education as a human right.
- Without education, the fundamental human rights of liberty and pursuit of happiness are very limited. Therefore education should be recognised as a human right.

This pair of examples illustrates the similarities, and the crucial difference, between an explanation and an argument. The first example explains why a state of affairs has come to pass, whereas the second tries to persuade the reader to agree with a claim. So the first is an explanation, whereas the second is an argument.

It is sometimes difficult to decide whether a particular passage is an argument or an explanation. It may depend on the context, whether the conclusion is taken as agreed by all parties or the author is trying to persuade their audience to agree with it.

▲ This is not an argument

Extended arguments quite often begin with a description or narrative, which sets the context for the argument itself.

To think about

A question quoted a short passage and asked, 'Is this an argument?'

Tara answered, 'It is not an argument, because the author is not disagreeing with anything.'

Dan answered, 'It is not an argument, because it includes only one opinion.'

What mistake had these students made?

Practice questions

Which of the following short passages are arguments, and which are not? You do not necessarily have to know what the passage is, if it is not an argument, merely whether it is an argument or not.

1   The train is due to leave at 8 a.m. but it is sometimes early. So we had better aim to reach the station by 7:50 a.m.

2   The government should take action to reduce the number of road accidents in our country.

3   Lena forgot to make a note of her homework and so she failed to hand it in on time.

4   Healthcare should be provided free of charge. The right to health is a basic human right.

5   Children today behave badly compared to when I was young. Modern parents are not strict enough with their children, and there is not enough discipline in schools.

6   University education should be provided free of charge. Every country needs a constant supply of people capable of filling important jobs like doctors, engineers and teachers, and so the population as a whole should meet the cost of training them.

7   I'm sorry my homework is late. My computer crashed last night just when I had finished writing the essay. So I couldn't print it off.

8   It's not my fault I am late. An accident on the main road caused a long traffic jam.

9   We will have to put up the prices of our products, because our costs have recently increased.

10   In the past, local parents tended to look out for children in a community, deciding what behaviour was appropriate, how it should be dealt with, and supporting each other in doing so. These days, however, adults tend to ignore problems rather than intervene in the discipline of another person's child, often because they fear they might be attacked.

8.2 Conclusions

The conclusion of an argument consists of what the author is trying to persuade a reader to do or to believe. The reasons express *why* they should accept the conclusion.

When an argument includes more than one reason, they may support the conclusion either **separately** or **together**. If two reasons act separately, the second strengthens the first, because two reasons are better than one, but either of the reasons would support the conclusion without the other. The same is true if there are more than two reasons. If the reasons act together, each of them is essential, since none of them would support the conclusion without the other(s).

Example	It is not fair to expect Majid to look after his grandchildren. He has no experience of caring for children and he cannot hear very well.

These two reasons support the conclusion separately.

Example	Ben will have to rethink his plans for higher education. The university he hoped to go to requires high grades, but his exam results were lower than he had expected.

These two reasons support the conclusion together, but not separately.

'Therefore' and 'because'

The relationship between reasons and a conclusion is often expressed using the words 'therefore' or 'because'.

[reason] **therefore** [conclusion]

or [conclusion] **because** [reason]

For example:

Liv should work hard at school, **because** she wants to go to university.

or Liv wants to go to university; **therefore** she should work hard at school.

Some other words mean roughly the same as 'therefore' or 'because' and can be used in the same way to indicate the structure of an argument. 'So' is the equivalent of 'therefore', and 'as' and 'since' can be used in the same way as 'because'. However, these words also have other meanings, and so 'therefore' and 'because' most clearly identify reasons and conclusions.

If those connecting words are not used, it is usually possible to insert them in order to work out which is the reason and which is the conclusion.

For example:

Liv should work hard at school. She wants to go to university.

It makes sense to say:

Liv should work hard at school, **because** she wants to go to university.

or Liv wants to go to university; **therefore** she should work hard at school.

But it does not make sense to say:

Liv should work hard at school; **therefore** she wants to go to university.

or Liv wants to go to university, **because** she should work hard at school.

In that way, you can tell that 'Liv wants to go to university' **is the reason, and** 'she should work hard at school' **is the conclusion.**

Practice questions

Here are some short arguments. Identify the conclusion of each argument.

1   The college car park is overcrowded. So we need to introduce a system of parking permits.

2   The DNA of all citizens should be recorded on a national database, because this will help the police to identify criminals.

3   Parents should never shout at their children or tell them they are 'naughty'. Treating children in those ways lowers their self-esteem. This encourages them to behave badly.

4   To force all children to attend schools provided by the state would be an offence against human rights, because everyone should be free to spend their own money in whatever way they choose and this includes buying a superior education for their children if they can afford to do so.

5   Education is a human right. It is wrong to allow wealthy parents to buy for their children an education superior to that experienced by other children. All children should be required by law to attend schools provided by the state.

6   Recent research has revealed that structured activities, such as sports, scouts or martial arts, are better for young people than unstructured youth clubs. At the age of 30, people who have attended structured activities at the age of 16 are less likely to be depressed, to live in social housing, to have no qualifications and to be single, separated or divorced. Those who have attended youth clubs are slightly more likely than average to smoke, be single parents, commit crimes or have a low income. Every secondary school pupil should therefore be required to take part in two hours of structured extracurricular activities a week.

7   Some teachers have been accused of helping their students by writing for them some of the work which will be assessed as part of their course. But helping students to gain higher grades is precisely what teachers are supposed to do. So teachers who write work for their students are simply doing their job.

8   Night clubs in one town have installed electronic fingerprint readers at their doors as a way of denying access to troublemakers. This is the latest in a series of measures taken by businesses to collect and store personal information about their customers. 'If you have nothing to hide, then you have nothing to fear' was the reported reaction of one young person to this news. But this view is naïve. We all have things to hide, which is why the right to privacy has been universally recognised as a basic human right. What about the young man who has told his girlfriend he has to work late, when he is actually spending the evening at a club with his mates? Or the representative who is videoed doing personal shopping when her employer thinks she is visiting clients? Neither of them is doing anything illegal, but someone will know where they were, and there is no guarantee that they will keep this knowledge to themselves. The potential for this information to be used for blackmail is so great that sooner or later some underpaid security officer will find a way of utilising it.

9   Women's boxing has been included in recent Olympic Games, but the decision to introduce it was a mistake. Some feminists have welcomed it as another step towards achieving equality between women and men, but it is of no benefit to women to allow them to hurt and harm one another. True equality between the sexes includes recognising their physical and cultural differences.

10 Most people assume that all university degrees are of equal value, but recent research has revealed that the time spent in classes and on directed study by undergraduates varies widely between universities, especially in different countries. The reason for this is that universities set their own syllabuses, courses and assessments. This inequality of effort is unfair to students and to employers, who naturally imagine that all degrees represent the same kind of effort and achievement. An international agreement is urgently needed to lay down universal expectations for university courses.

Intermediate conclusions

Most arguments are more complex than consisting simply of reasons and a conclusion. They are made up of several sub-arguments, each consisting of a conclusion supported by one or more reasons. In turn, these conclusions support the conclusion of the whole argument. They are known as **intermediate conclusions (ICs)**, because they occupy an intermediate position between the reasons and the main conclusion, or in some cases a further IC. ICs may appear even in quite short arguments, for example consisting of a reason supporting an IC supporting the main conclusion.

Example	University education should be provided free of charge. Every country needs a constant supply of people capable of filling important jobs like doctors, engineers and teachers, and so the country as a whole should meet the cost of training them.

The words 'and so' identify the final clause of this argument as a conclusion, but if you follow the line of reasoning carefully, you will see that it is not the main conclusion of the argument. It is an intermediate conclusion, and the first sentence is the main conclusion.

1   Many people believe it is a bad use of money for companies and institutions to pay people to work in advertising and public relations. On the contrary, spending money on public relations and advertising should be the top priority for organisations of every kind.

2   If manufacturers want to boost sales, they should put their money into advertising. The biggest influence on sales is not how good a product actually is, but how good potential purchasers think it is, and this opinion is affected mainly by advertising. While spending money on improving a product might at best produce a minimal increase in sales, companies can achieve far better results by investing the money in advertising.

3   Similarly, when members of the public need to employ a builder, a mechanic, or even a beauty therapist, they generally choose one they have heard of, and usually have no idea how good they are at their job. Such workers should spend money on advertising. It would be a waste of time and effort for them to try to develop a good reputation for the quality of their work.

4   Politicians sometimes claim that their first aim is to improve the quality of life in their country or their local area. But even well-intentioned political parties and individual politicians will never achieve any of their goals without being elected. Since the main factor in winning elections is publicity, this must be the first priority of all politicians. Once they have gained power, their focus moves to winning the next election, and then the one after that.

5   It may seem obvious that deploying more police officers in the community would be the best way of improving public safety. However, public safety is a state of mind, which has little relation to the actual prevalence of crime. So police forces should cut back the number of police officers and devote more of their resources to public relations. Sending one extra police officer onto the streets might make a few people feel a little more confident about their own safety, but by spreading the word about low crime and high conviction rates, one additional public relations officer would make a community feel much safer.

Main conclusion

(On the contrary,) spending money on public relations and advertising should be the top priority for organisations of every kind.

Intermediate conclusions

» If manufacturers want to boost sales, they should put their money into advertising.

» Such workers (builders, motor mechanics, beauty therapists) should spend money on advertising.

» This (publicity) must be the first priority of all politicians.

» (So) police forces should cut back the number of police officers and devote more of their resources to public relations.

a Using the exact words from the passage as far as possible, identify the main conclusion.

b Using the exact words from the passage as far as possible, identify **three** intermediate conclusions.

1 Many scientists believe that the universe is infinite. They infer that a very large number of planets have the conditions in which life could develop. One estimate is that over a hundred thousand billion potentially life-bearing planets exist. It is very likely that there are many alien species which have both the desire to explore the universe and the ability to do so.

2 Since 1984, astronomers from the Search for Extraterrestrial Intelligence (SETI) have been scanning the airwaves looking for radio signals from outer space. They believe they were successful on one occasion. In 2003, they detected signals from an area in space where there are no planets or stars. Since we know of no way in which these signals could have occurred naturally, we can only conclude that someone was deliberately transmitting them from a distant planet in the hope that someone from elsewhere in the universe would reply.

3 Many people have reported seeing unidentified flying objects (UFOs). Some of the reports may have been practical jokes, and others based on genuine mistakes, but the people who have made the reports include airline pilots, military personnel and police officers – people who know what a weather balloon looks like and would not mistake one for a UFO. By far the most likely explanation of these observations is that the UFOs are vehicles containing visitors from other planets.

4 There is also a lot of persuasive evidence that people have been abducted by aliens. Although some of the witnesses may be delusional, most of them seem normal, rational and credible. Since many of those experiences occurred in the daytime, they cannot be explained away as vivid dreams, and the similarities in the accounts of these experiences cannot be mere coincidence.

5 The cumulative evidence is overwhelming that members of other species from distant planets have contacted the Earth on many occasions. Those idiots who refuse to believe this must be motivated solely by prejudice. Their only argument is circular: aliens do not exist; so anyone who claims to have encountered them is either mistaken or lying; therefore there is no evidence that aliens exist.

(Cambridge AS & A Level Thinking Skills 9694,
Paper 21 Q3 (a) & (b), June 2016)

Find an 'opinion' article from a newspaper from your country or locality. Does the article have a main conclusion?

→ If it does, does the whole of the passage support that conclusion?

→ If the article does not state a main conclusion, is it obvious what the main conclusion would be, if it were stated, and is the reasoning strengthened or weakened by the absence of the main conclusion?

→ If possible, share the article with two or three other students. Do they agree with your answers?

Keep the article for use in the next Extension Activity.

8.3 Additional argument elements

Evidence and examples

Reasoning can be strengthened by the use of **evidence** or **examples**.

Authors and speakers sometimes fail to make it clear whether they intend something to be understood as evidence or as an example. This is especially common in speeches and conversation. Statistics and the results of surveys are most likely to be used as evidence, whereas several items introduced by 'such as' or a similar expression are probably examples. Also, it is sometimes difficult or impossible to decide whether a piece of information is being used as evidence to support a reason, or as a reason to support an intermediate conclusion.

Key terms

Evidence consists of facts or data which *support* a reason.

An example is a specific instance which makes reasoning clearer by *illustrating* it.

Sample question

The following is an extract from an argument in favour of war.

Wars bring numerous economic advantages to the countries which participate. In 1944, at the height of World War II, expenditure on the war added 60–70 per cent to the Gross Domestic Product of the United States. Enrolment into the armed services solves issues of unemployment, while factories no longer stand doing nothing when supplies of tanks, planes, guns and ammunition are urgently needed. The work of reconstruction employs many people after the war.

Identify the function of the following element in this paragraph:

'In 1944, at the height of World War II, expenditure on the war added 60–70 per cent to the Gross Domestic Product of the United States.'

Evidence supporting the claim that 'wars bring numerous economic advantages to the countries which participate'.

Sample question

The following is an extract from an argument in favour of the introduction of an international language.

> The only reason why some people might not want to learn this international language is that it will be of limited use to them at first, because very few people will understand it. These objectors are persuaded by their own comfort and ease rather than long-term advantages to everyone. Additionally, the small number of users is a very feeble objection, because all new methods of communication – such as telephones, cars and the internet – are of little use until enough people have adopted them, but once some brave people have made the commitment they become necessary parts of everyday life.

Identify the function of the following element in this paragraph: 'telephones, cars and the internet.'

Examples of new methods of communication.

Sample question

The following paragraph is an extract from an argument in favour of developing new methods of punishment, other than sending criminals to prison.

> Depriving criminals of their freedom fails to repay victims or society. Instead of adding an extra burden to public spending, as they do under the current system, criminals should be made to compensate society for the harm they have done. They could do the types of socially valuable work which people cannot afford to pay for, such as collecting litter or sweeping the streets. If they had to wear a distinctive uniform (such as a bright pink jacket with the word 'offender' written on it in large letters) while undertaking this community work, they would be exposed to contempt and rude comments from members of the public who saw them, which in many instances might help them to understand the consequences of their crimes and persuade them to obey the law in future.

Identify an example in this paragraph, and state what it is an example of.

Any one of the following:

➤ **Collecting litter: an example of socially valuable work which people cannot afford to pay for.**

➤ **Sweeping the streets: an example of socially valuable work which people cannot afford to pay for.**

➤ **A bright pink jacket with the word 'offender' in large letters: an example of a distinctive uniform which could be worn by offenders undertaking community work as a punishment.**

The following is an extract from an argument challenging the view that a right to health is one of the fundamental human rights.

The United Nations International Covenant on Economic, Social and Cultural Rights (UNIC), which has since been followed by several other international documents, asserts that we have a human right to 'the highest attainable standard of physical and mental health', which it specifies as the standard a state can achieve 'to the maximum of its available resources'. That is absurd, since no government provides, or even tries to provide, the highest attainable standard of physical and mental health; nor do they allocate the maximum of their available resources to healthcare. Governments have many other priorities for those resources, such as defence, law and order, education and the environment, and they do not breach anyone's rights when they restrict their spending on health.

Identify an example in this paragraph, and state what it is an example of.

Counter assertions and counterarguments

Counter assertions and counterarguments are 'counter' in two senses: they express a different opinion from the remainder of the argument and they are introduced in order to be countered. The difference between a counter assertion and a counterargument is that a counter assertion is an unsupported claim, whereas a counterargument consists of reason(s) supporting a counter conclusion.

Counters are quite often used at the beginning of an argument, in order to set the context. In such cases, the whole of the argument is the response to the counter. Counters may also be introduced in the course of the reasoning, in order to forestall a possible objection. However, this can be a risky strategy because, if the counter is not convincingly rejected, it may weaken the author's argument.

Key term

A counter assertion or counterargument expresses an alternative opinion which an author introduces in order to explain why it is wrong. If the counter consists of a simple claim, it is a **counter assertion**, but if the claim is supported by reasoning, it is a **counter-argument**.

A common point made against this argument is that there are some who do not disclose their identity and do good in secret, but even these unknown deeds are inspired by selfishness. The pay off in these instances is not the respect of other people, but the internal good feelings gained from the knowledge of having been kind.

The first half of the first sentence is a counter assertion. The second half of that sentence is not only the intermediate conclusion of the paragraph (because it is supported by a reason in the following sentence), but it is also a response to the counter.

The college car park is overcrowded. Some students have suggested that we should extend the car park, because not being able to park on site causes serious inconvenience to students and staff. However, no land is available for that purpose. So we need to introduce a system of parking permits.

The second sentence of this argument is a counterargument. The conclusion, 'we should extend the car park', is supported by the reason, 'not being able to park on site causes serious inconvenience to students and staff'. 'No land is available for that purpose' is the author's response to the counter.

Sample question

The following is an extract from an argument in favour of the introduction of an international language.

> The only reason why some people might not want to learn this international language is that it will be of limited use to them at first, because very few people will understand it. These objectors are persuaded by their own comfort and ease rather than long-term advantages to everyone. Additionally, the small number of users is a very feeble objection, because all new methods of communication – such as telephones, cars and the internet – are of little use until enough people have adopted them, but once some brave people have made the commitment they become necessary parts of everyday life.

Identify a **counterargument** in this paragraph.

'it will be of limited use to them at first, because very few people will understand it.'

Sample question

The following is the final paragraph of an argument. The final sentence is the main conclusion of the whole argument.

> Admittedly, some changes do ultimately turn out to have been for the better, but the problem is that we cannot tell beforehand which ones they will be. It is always more likely that any particular proposal will lead to catastrophe than that it will result in an improvement. So the best practice is to be safe, by resisting all change.

Identify the function of the following element: 'Admittedly, some changes do ultimately turn out to have been for the better.'

Counter assertion.

Look again at the newspaper article which you kept from the previous Extension Activity. Does it include any counter assertions or counterargument?

→ If so, are they accompanied by an effective response? Do they strengthen or weaken the argument overall?

→ If the argument does not include any counters, suggest some which could be used. Don't forget to include responses. Does this new material strengthen or weaken the argument?

Keep the article for the next Extension Activity.

8.4 Detailed analysis

You may be asked to give a complete analysis of an extract from a longer passage. If you are, the task will have two parts: to label the elements and to explain how they relate to one another. You may explain the relationships between the elements either in words or by means of a diagram.

First, it is necessary to identify the main conclusion of the paragraph(s), which probably serves as an intermediate conclusion for the whole passage. Then look at the support. Is the conclusion supported by a single strand of reasoning, or more than one? Look at the strands of reasoning one by one. Do they consist of reasons supporting an intermediate conclusion (which in turn supports the conclusion of the paragraph), or do they support the conclusion directly? Do the reasons support their conclusion separately or jointly? Is there a counter? If so, is it a counter assertion (simple claim), or a counterargument (claim supported by reasoning)? Is there a response to the counter and – if so – is it supported by one or more reasons (i.e., is it an intermediate conclusion)? Does the paragraph contain any evidence or any examples and – if so – which part of the reasoning do they support or illustrate?

Examples

The following short pieces of reasoning are excerpts from an argument of which the main conclusion is 'The right to freedom of expression should not be acknowledged as a human right.'

The first step which led to the Nazi persecution of the Jews and other minority groups was the unrestricted expression of offensive opinions about certain categories of person. The intention behind the Universal Declaration of Human Rights was to prevent anything like that persecution from occurring again. So the alleged right to freedom of expression is less important than the right to security of person and protection from discrimination. Since the expression of offensive opinions threatens those rights, it should be prohibited.

R1 The first stage in the Nazi persecution of the Jews and other minorities was the unrestricted expression of offensive opinions about certain categories of person.

R2 The intention behind the Universal Declaration of Human Rights was to prevent anything like that persecution from occurring again.

IC (So) the alleged right to freedom of expression is less important than the right to security of person and protection from discrimination.

R3 Since the expression of offensive opinions threatens those rights,

MC it should be prohibited.

R1 and R2 jointly support IC. IC and R3 jointly support MC.

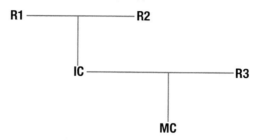

A number of people who had access to government secrets have recently claimed that they had a moral duty to expose such secrets, because they contained evidence of corruption in high places. But people in positions of trust like these cannot be allowed the same rights of freedom of expression as ordinary members of the public. The defence of national security is part of the role of governments, and so they must have the power to prevent people with access to state secrets from risking public safety by betraying them.

CA(C) A number of people who had access to government secrets have recently claimed that they had a moral duty to expose such secrets,

CA(R) because they contained evidence of corruption in high places.

RCA = MC But people in positions of trust like these cannot be allowed the same rights of freedom of expression as ordinary members of the public.

R The defence of national security is part of the role of governments,

IC (and so) they must have the power to prevent people with access to state secrets from risking public safety by betraying them.

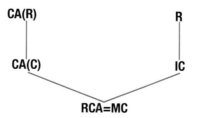

8.5 Unstated assumptions

Like 'argument', the word 'assumption' has a specialised meaning in Critical Thinking, which is different from its everyday sense. In order to remind you of this specialised meaning, the Thinking Skills course will always use the compound expression 'unstated assumption'. Despite this assistance, the most common mistake made by students is to misinterpret the expression 'unstated assumption' as if it meant 'unsupported statement'.

An unstated assumption is a step in a piece of reasoning which is *required* in order for the conclusion to be validly drawn, but is *not stated* explicitly. Another way of putting it is to say that an unstated assumption is a missing link between reasons and a conclusion.

For example, think about the simple argument which we considered earlier:

Liv wants to go to university; therefore she should work hard at school.

You probably did not think that this argument was incomplete, because the missing step is so obvious, but if you think about it more deeply, you will realise that the complete argument is:

Liv wants to go to university; in order to gain a place at university it is necessary to work hard at school; therefore Liv should work hard at school.

Actually, the unstated assumption in this example does not need to be quite as definite as this. Any of the following alternatives would support the conclusion 'Liv should work hard at school' in conjunction with the statement 'Liv wants to go to university':

» It greatly improves your chances of going to university if you work hard at school.

» Anyone who works hard at school is more likely to go to university than someone who does not work hard.

» Most people who gain a place at university have worked hard at school.

If a claim is stated in the argument, it cannot, of course, be an *un*stated assumption.

If something is not stated, a method for checking whether it is an assumption or not is the **reverse test**. If the opposite of the claim would prevent the conclusion from being drawn, then the claim itself is being assumed. For example, if working hard at school did *not* greatly improve your chances of going to university, then the conclusion 'Liv should work hard at school' would not follow from the reason 'Liv wants to go to university'. So the argument *does* rely on the unstated assumption that it greatly improves your chances of going to university if you work hard at school.

Example

A large proportion of prisoners experience mental illness. They should therefore be treated instead of punished.

This brief argument relies on one or both of two assumptions:

» that people who are mentally ill should not be held responsible for their behaviour (because if that is not assumed, the first sentence does not support the claim that these prisoners should not be punished)

» that punishment and treatment are mutually exclusive (because if that is not assumed, the treatment could be in addition to punishment, rather than an alternative to it).

Authors sometimes unintentionally make unstated assumptions when they consider part of the support for their conclusion to be so obvious, trivial or uncontroversial that it does not need to be stated. In other cases, they may not realise that there is a significant gap in their reasoning. But authors sometimes try to conceal a significant weakness in the reasoning by failing to state it explicitly. That is why the skill of identifying unstated assumptions is worth developing and is included in the Thinking Skills syllabus.

A useful way of identifying assumptions may be to ask yourself how you would argue *against* the reasoning. It is likely that the *opposite* of your counterargument is being assumed.

The following paragraph is an extract from an argument in favour of abolishing the police force. Some of the arguments you encounter (in the exam and elsewhere) may have conclusions which you are likely to disagree with, like this one. In order to analyse or evaluate such arguments, you need to put your feelings aside and think clearly about the actual reasoning used.

Example

Membership of a police force gives frequent opportunities for corruption, and it is these opportunities which motivate some people to join the police. In some countries, there are actually worse crooks inside the police force than outside. By taking away many opportunities for criminal activity, the abolition of police would make the world a less dangerous place.

The obvious objection to this reasoning is that abolishing the police force would create more opportunities for criminals than it would remove. So this section of the argument relies on the implausible assumption that the abolition of the police force would *not* create more opportunities for criminals than it would remove. Since that is a significant weakness in the case for abolishing the police, it is highly likely that the author has deliberately left it unstated, in the hope that some readers would not notice.

The following are extracts from arguments. In each case, identify an unstated assumption required by the reasoning.

It has often been suggested that an international language should be used alongside national languages, to facilitate communication between different countries. Since wars are provoked by misunderstanding, the introduction of a single language would achieve world peace.

There is also a lot of credible evidence that people have been abducted by extraterrestrials. Although some of the witnesses may be confused, most seem normal, rational and reliable. Since many of those events happened in the daytime, they cannot be discredited as vivid dreams, and the resemblances between the accounts of these experiences cannot be only coincidence.

To think about

Students were asked to identify an unstated assumption in the following extract.

Since 1984, astronomers from the Search for Extraterrestrial Intelligence (SETI) have been scanning the airwaves, looking for radio signals from outer space. They believe they were successful on one occasion. In 2003, they detected signals from an area in space where there are no planets or stars. Since we know of no way in which these signals could have occurred naturally, we can only conclude that someone was deliberately transmitting them from a distant planet in the hope that someone from elsewhere in the Universe would reply.

Arianna's answer was: 'The fourth sentence assumes that if we do not know how the radio signals could have occurred naturally, they did not occur naturally.'

Lola's answer was: 'The fourth sentence assumes that the cause of the signals must be alien life.'

Pietro's answer was: 'The fourth sentence assumes that anyone transmitting from a distant planet would not be "natural".'

Who do you think gave the best answer?

> **EXTENSION ACTIVITY**
>
> Look carefully and in detail at the Opinion article which you used for the previous two Extension Activities. Can you identify any 'missing links' in the argument? How badly do they weaken the reasoning and the support for the conclusion? If possible, work initially on your own and then compare answers with two or three fellow students.

8.6 Applying the skills of analysing reasoning

AS Level

You may be asked (for example, as part of question 1 in the AS Level exam) whether a particular short passage of reasoning is or is not an argument.

If a passage includes a conclusion supported by one or more reasons, then you should state that it is an argument, and identify the conclusion and supporting reasons. If a passage does not include a conclusion supported by one or more reasons, then you should state that it is not an argument and explain why. In each case, you should refer to the specific content of the passage.

Sample question

For over thirty years I have been a doctor, and I've been a homoeopath for the last fifteen, so I know that homoeopathy is very effective. The vast majority of the time it is my preferred treatment. I became an advocate for its benefits as soon as I witnessed its startling effect in treating issues ranging from pain and fevers to depression and anxiety. Homoeopathy works! Medical health professionals should prescribe homoeopathic treatments to all patients who might benefit from it.

Is this an argument?

This is an argument. The conclusion, 'Medical health professionals should prescribe homoeopathic treatments to all patients who might benefit from it' is supported by the reason 'Homoeopathy works!', which in turn is supported by evidence drawn from the author's clinical experience.

The birthdate effect

There is solid evidence from around the globe that, on average, the youngest children in their year group at school don't perform as well as their older classmates. This is called the 'birthdate effect'. In the UK, where the school year starts on 1st September, the disadvantage is greatest for those born in the summer months (June, July, August). The effect of being the youngest in the year group also happens in other countries where the school year begins at different times in the calendar year.

The birthdate effect is most evident during infant and primary school but it still occurs in the proportions of students who go to university.

The most likely explanation for this phenomenon is that the youngest children in a year group tend to be less mature than their older classmates, leading to unequal competition that puts the younger children at a disadvantage.

Is this an argument?

This is not an argument. It makes a detailed claim, that younger children in an age group tend to perform less well at school than their older classmates, explains how this applies in practice and offers a possible explanation for the phenomenon, but it does not draw a persuasive conclusion.

Read the following extracts and for each one state whether it is or is not an argument. Briefly justify your answer in each case.

1   If you have a big task to perform at work today, you should drink more water. In an experiment, students who drank water during an exam performed 10 per cent better than those who did not. Although this study tested only students in a specific context, the researchers believe that the results also apply to other stressful situations, like job interviews and presentations. Improving hydration could reduce anxiety, and anxiety has been shown to have a negative effect on performance in exams.

2   Research has shown that the amount of education people have had is linked to their chances of suffering from various health problems, including heart conditions, emphysema, diabetes and asthma. Those who have been educated to a higher level are less likely to have high blood pressure and high levels of cholesterol; they tend to function better, both physically and mentally. The most plausible explanation for these health differences is that people with more education are less likely to smoke, to drink excessively and to be overweight or obese. They are also more likely to seek early treatment for high blood pressure and diabetes.

3 Economics is a major influence on the significant life choices which individuals make in developed countries like the United States. Investing money in college education is a good decision, because people who have been to college earn consistently higher incomes throughout their lifetimes than people who have had less education. There is also a link between education and improved health and longevity. People who have had a college education are less likely to suffer from various diseases which would reduce the quality and length of their lives.

If you wish to analyse an argument (such as the passage supplied in Section B of the AS Level exam), the first task is to identify the main conclusion. In a well-constructed argument, the main conclusion is supported by several mini-arguments, each of which leads to an intermediate conclusion. Identifying these intermediate conclusions is the second step in analysing an argument.

Each of these two analytical tasks has two aspects: first, to identify the correct part of the passage and, second, to recognise where the element begins and ends. For example, a sentence may contain both an intermediate conclusion and a reason supporting it. In order to identify the intermediate conclusion successfully, you would need not only to select the correct sentence but also to avoid including the reason in your answer.

Other elements you may need to identify are evidence, example, counter assertion and counterargument. Tasks of this kind may either name an element and ask you to find it or quote a sentence, clause or phrase from the passage and ask you to name it and explain its function.

The final aspect of analysis which is included at AS Level is identifying unstated assumptions. This is a rather different task, simply because – being unstated – assumptions are not visible in the argument as presented. The task involves looking for a significant gap in the reasoning and expressing a reason which would fill that gap.

To think about

Most of the questions in the third question will instruct you to use the exact words from the passage in your answer. Why will you *not* be told to do that in a question asking you to identify an unstated assumption?

Read the passage and answer the questions below.

1 One of the most widely held convictions in modern Western society is that individuals are all entitled to their own opinions. Many people think they can say anything, however ill-considered, and if they are challenged reply, 'Well, that's my opinion and I'm entitled to it.' But if that opinion is wrong, or if they hold it for no good reason, then they are not entitled to it.

2 The claim to be entitled to one's opinion is a poor excuse for intellectual laziness. It should matter to us that our opinions are not misguided and when someone disagrees with us, we should want to explore the issue and find out who is right.

3 Even worse, the unsupported assertion of an opinion should be recognised as an attack on rationality. The alleged entitlement to one's own opinion apparently applies even if the opinion being expressed is immoral, offensive, contradicted by powerful evidence or nonsensical. Yet humans were defined by the sixth-century philosopher Boethius as 'beings of a rational nature'. So if we voice an opinion without having thought about the issue, weighed the evidence and considered alternative views, we are being less than human.

4 Anyone who thinks that all opinions are equally acceptable is a fool. Some opinions are based on persuasive reasoning, whereas others are merely asserted. Some political opinions create huge social problems, whereas others promote prosperity and national unity. So of course they are not equally acceptable.

5 Admittedly, some judgements do vary between individuals, because of differing personal values and tastes. For example, in a particular situation one person may think it is important to tell the truth, whereas another may prefer to maintain smooth relationships by telling a 'white lie'. Some people like spicy food, whereas others don't. No one has the right to say that any of those preferences is right or wrong.

6 Other opinions, however, are matters of fact rather than taste, and in these cases it is possible for an opinion to be right or wrong. To take an extreme example, anyone who disagrees with the judgement that torturing babies is wrong is a moral imbecile, whose opinion does not deserve to be taken seriously. Anyone can prefer the music of The Beatles to that of J S Bach if that is their taste, but if they go further and claim that John Lennon was a greater musician than Bach, then they are simply wrong. No one is entitled to hold an opinion which is evidently wrong.

a Using the exact words from the passage as far as possible, identify the main conclusion.

b Using the exact words from the passage as far as possible, identify **three** intermediate conclusions.

(Adapted from Cambridge AS & A Level Thinking Skills 9694, Paper 23 Q3 (a) & (b), November 2012)

c Identify the function of the following element in paragraph 5:
'Some people like spicy food, whereas others don't.'

d State an **unstated assumption** required in the reasoning of
paragraph 3.

a **If that opinion is wrong, or if they hold it for no good reason,
then they are not entitled to it.**

b • **'The claim to be entitled to one's opinion is a poor excuse
for intellectual laziness.'**

   • **'If we voice an opinion without having thought about the
issue, weighed the issue and considered alternative views, we
are being less than human.'**

   • **'Anyone who thinks that all opinions are equally acceptable
is a fool.'**

   • **'No one is entitled to hold an opinion which is evidently
wrong.'**

c **Examples of preferences which cannot be considered right or
wrong.**

d **Opinions which are not based on thinking about the issue,
weighing the evidence and considering alternative views are
not rational.**

Practice question

Read the following passage and then answer the questions below.

1 Whom would you prefer as your teacher? Someone who just managed
to pass a degree examination thirty years ago and has never opened a
book since, or someone who is fascinated by his subject and has read
widely in it, but left university without taking a degree because the
teaching and the course were boring and he wanted to be free to pursue
topics that interested him? This shows that possession of a university
degree is no guarantee that someone will be a good teacher.

2 The rapid changes in knowledge mean that a university education quickly
becomes out of date. Furthermore, most graduates will readily admit that
they have forgotten nearly everything they learned at university. The only
way a degree could be a reliable indication of competence in a subject
would be if degrees had a time limit built into them and needed to be
updated every five years in order to remain valid. Under the present system,
they mean nothing.

➤

3   In addition, experts are often bad teachers, because they think that their task is to pass on their knowledge to their students. That approach to education belongs firmly in the past. Education is about learning, not teaching, and the knowledge required to pass an exam is more reliably available from textbooks specially written for the exam and from the internet than from the fallible memory of the teacher.

4   Some people may suggest that teachers need paper qualifications in order to show that they have been taught how to teach, but any teacher knows that is not true. Either you can teach or you cannot. If you can, you do not need anyone to show you how to do it, and if you cannot, then no amount of guidance or instruction will turn you into an effective teacher.

5   The only qualification required to be a teacher should, therefore, be the ability to enable students to pass their exams. Such a change from paper qualifications to a focus on skills would be consistent with current trends, since most employers are now far more interested in the abilities which potential recruits have to offer rather than their academic qualifications.

a   Using the exact words from the passage as far as possible, identify the main conclusion.

b   Using the exact words from the passage as far as possible, identify **three** intermediate conclusions.

(Cambridge AS & A Level Thinking Skills 9694, Paper 23 Q3 (a) & (b), November 2014)

c   Identify the function of the following element in paragraph 4: 'Teachers need paper qualifications in order to show that they have been taught how to teach.'

d   State an **unstated assumption** required if the reasoning in paragraph 3 is to support the main conclusion.

A Level

The first question in the Applied Reasoning paper normally consists of questions about analysis, and refers to Document 1. As in the Critical Thinking paper, you are likely to be asked to identify the main and intermediate conclusions, though the passage is likely to be a little harder at this higher level. Regardless of the level, you should ensure you continue to use the actual words from the passage, rather than putting the ideas into your own words.

Response by the Student Union of Barchester University to the draft proposals for a new degree of Bachelor of Humanities

1. We are disappointed that, under the draft proposals, degrees will be awarded solely on the basis of written examinations taken at the end of the course. Since the panel which produced the proposals was chaired by the former Dean of Humanities, now retired, it is not surprising that the proposals are so old-fashioned and backward-looking.

2. We recommend that the new degree should be assessed solely by essays and projects written during the course. This will put our university in the forefront of innovation. Instead of remaining in the third rank of universities, implementing our suggestion will make us be seen as trendsetters.

3. Some students perform badly in examinations because they are nervous under stress, have poor memories or find it difficult to think quickly. It is unfair that they should be penalised for these difficulties, because they are not their fault. These problems are especially relevant to this course, because it is aimed at mature students, many of whom are likely to have a history of academic failure.

4. Traditional written examinations assess short-term memory, superficial thinking and the ability to write quickly. These are not the skills which Higher Education should be developing. The purpose of universities is to enable students to explore subjects at depth, to develop their own informed opinions on matters of universal importance, and to ponder unhurriedly on the mysteries of the Universe.

5. The former Dean has argued that unseen written examinations produce a wider range of marks than assessment by essays, but that is not a valid reason for relying on them. You could obtain an even greater spread by listing the candidates according to their birthdays, but it would not be measuring anything significant.

6. There is also no merit in the superficial criticism that students might 'cheat' by obtaining their essays from the internet. The ability to answer problems by researching on the internet is, in fact, one of the most valuable skills in the modern workplace.

7. Writing an essay forces students to engage with the material they have been taught or can discover for themselves and to apply it to a specific issue. These are the skills which employers are looking for. Group projects are especially valuable, since they develop and assess teamwork in addition to other skills. So anyone who passes a degree assessed in these ways should be in a very strong position for gaining a job.

Student President

a Identify the main conclusion of this argument.

b Identify the intermediate conclusions in paragraphs 1–5 of this argument.

(Adapted from Cambridge AS & A Level Thinking Skills 9694, Paper 42 Q2, June 2015)

c Give a detailed analysis of the final paragraph of this argument.

d Paragraph 5 in this argument contains the element,

'unseen written examinations produce a wider range of marks than assessment by essays'.

Name this element and describe its function in the reasoning in paragraph 5.

e Identify an **unstated assumption** that underlies the reasoning in paragraph 5 of this argument.

a **MC We recommend that the new degree should be assessed by essays and projects written during the course.**

b • **'It is not surprising that the proposals are so old-fashioned and backward-looking.'**

   • **'It is unfair that they [students] should be penalised for these difficulties [performing badly in examinations because they are nervous under stress, have poor memories or find it difficult to think quickly].'**

   • **'These [short-term memory, superficial thinking and the ability to write quickly] are not the skills which Higher Education should be developing.'**

   • **'(But) that [that unseen written examinations produce a wider range of marks than assessment by essays] is not a valid reason for relying on them [unseen written examinations].'**

c **Either**

The principal intermediate conclusion, which directly supports the main conclusion of the argument, is the last sentence. The first two sentences jointly support this IC. The third sentence consists of a subsidiary IC supported by a reason. This IC supports the principal IC of the paragraph.

Or

R1 Writing an essay forces students to engage with the material they have been taught or can discover for themselves and to apply it to a specific issue.

R2 These are the skills which employers are looking for.

IC1 Group projects are especially valuable,

R3 since they develop and assess teamwork in addition to other skills.

IC2 So anyone who passes a degree assessed in these ways should be in a very strong position for gaining a job.

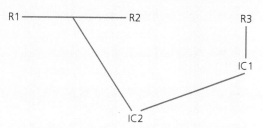

d **This is a counter assertion to the overall conclusion of the argument. The remainder of paragraph 5 is a response to this counter assertion.**

e **The response to the counter assertion relies on the assumption that the range of marks produced by written exams does not measure 'anything significant'.**

Practice questions

Read the following passage and then answer the questions.

Who should vote?

1 Depending on which country you live in, your 16th, 17th, 18th or 21st birthday could be the age at which you can drive, get married, or buy alcohol – at least legally. We have these laws for a reason, but age should not be used as a criterion in deciding who should select the next government.

2 Voting is far too important to be based on such an arbitrary measure as a person's age. Drinking, relationships and driving are personal matters, but voting affects other people. In deciding who should govern us we need to take into account politics, economics, science and human nature. We do not suddenly develop a full understanding of these things when we wake up on our 18th birthday.

3 Many politicians have advocated lowering the voting age in an attempt to show that they are 'in touch with young people', but young people care less about voting and more about fashion and music. In the town of Middlesbrough in the north of England, most of the local schools entered a candidate to be Youth Mayor of Middlesbrough. Unsurprisingly, the candidate from the school that cast the most votes won the election. This just shows that teenagers will vote for the candidate they perceive to be on their team, rather than considering the policies on offer.

4 In terms of deciding anything, age is largely meaningless anyway. We might as well separate people based on height. Everyone knows people of the same age with wildly differing abilities, or people of different ages with the same ability. There is no upper age limit for voting: nobody says 'Sorry, granddad, take your opinion elsewhere'. So there should not be a lower age limit.

5 There has to be some way of deciding who votes, and age is at least easy to apply. Alternative systems are practical, though. A basic questionnaire, similar to an IQ test, would be straightforward to administer. People registering to vote could complete the test, which would include questions on general knowledge as well as cognitive ability. Those who got above a certain score would be registered to vote; those who did not could try again next time. That way the people who had the privilege of voting would be those who deserved it.

Trib

(Adapted from Cambridge AS & A Level Thinking Skills 9694, Paper 42 Document 1, November 2016)

a Identify the main conclusion of Trib's argument.

b Give a detailed analysis of paragraph 2.

c Identify the intermediate conclusions in paragraphs 3, 4 and 5.

9 Evaluating reasoning

By the end of this chapter you will be able to identify and evaluate:

★ logical fallacies
★ flaws in reasoning
★ use of appeals
★ weaknesses in reasoning.

The way to evaluate an argument is to identify **flaws** and **weaknesses** in the reasoning. Flaws (sometimes known as **fallacies**) are tricks or mistakes in reasoning which have long been recognised and in most cases have been given names. The Thinking Skills syllabus and exam use the word 'weaknesses' to refer to more general problems in reasoning.

If you study certain other subjects, such as English Literature, alongside Thinking Skills, you may be confused to find that some features of writing which you are accustomed to identifying as strengths are considered to be weaknesses in Thinking Skills. This is because there are significant differences between studying texts from literary and Thinking Skills perspectives. For example, an appeal to emotion may be an effective literary device, but from the perspective of Thinking Skills it may be seen as a flaw if it is used instead of a reason or to divert attention from a weakness in the reasoning.

If you are assessing the impact of a particular flaw or weakness on an argument, ask yourself:

» Does this weakness/flaw affect the argument as a whole or just one strand of reasoning?

» Does the weakness fatally undermine the claim it supports, or does it merely weaken the support?

» Does the weakness completely invalidate the part of the argument which it affects, or would a partial or weakened version of the claim remain tenable?

9.1 Logical fallacies

Logic is the branch of philosophy concerned with analysing reasoning. You might guess that there would be much overlap between logic and Thinking Skills, but in fact this small section of the syllabus contains the only part of logic which you will be expected to know. Rather like algebra, logic frequently uses letters to represent argument elements, in order to focus on the structure of reasoning, rather than the specifics of its content.

The following short arguments all have the same simple structure:

» If Emma is a student at Sunny Coast College, she has the right to borrow books from the college library. Emma is a student at Sunny Coast College. So she has the right to borrow books from the college library.

» If a grandmother loves her grandchild, she will give him a present on his birthday. Amir's grandmother loves him. So she will give him a present on his birthday.

» If a compound is acidic, it will turn the litmus paper red. This compound is acidic. So it will turn the litmus paper red.

This structure is often expressed as follows:

If p, then q; p; therefore q.

More fully, if the statement *p* is true, then the conclusion *q* must also be true. The statement *p* is true. So the conclusion *q* is also true.

This structure is **valid**. In other words, if the reasons are true, then the conclusion must also be true.

However, if at least one of the reasons is not true, then the conclusion may or may not be true. For example, the following argument is valid, but none of it is true (or of any use whatsoever).

> *If a person is three metres tall, he can touch the moon. My friend is three metres tall. So my friend can touch the moon.*

A negative version of this structure is also valid:

If p, then q; not q; therefore not p.

For example:

» If Emma is a student at Sunny Coast College, she has the right to borrow books from the college library. Emma does not have the right to borrow books from the college library. So she cannot be a student at Sunny Coast College.

» If a grandmother loves her grandchild, she will give him a present on his birthday. Amir's grandmother has not given him a present on his birthday. So she cannot love him.

» If this compound is acidic, it will turn the litmus paper red. The compound has not turned the litmus paper red. So it is not acidic.

Either deliberately or by mistake, speakers and writers sometimes use arguments which look rather like one or other of these two valid argument structures, but are invalid. Both of the following structures are invalid:

If p, then q; q; therefore p.

If p, then q; not p; therefore not q.

Key term

Validity is a quality of the structure of an argument, irrespective of its relation to truth or fact. If the structure of an argument is valid, it means that *if* the reasons happened to be true, the conclusion would *have to* be true.

For example:

» If Sofia is a student at Sunny Coast College, she has the right to borrow books from the college library. Sofia does have the right to borrow books from the college library. So she must be a student at Sunny Coast College.

» If Petra is a student at Sunny Coast College, she has the right to borrow books from the college library. Petra is not a student at Sunny Coast College. So she does not have the right to borrow books from the college library.

Neither of these conclusions is reliable, because there may be other ways of qualifying to borrow books from the college library. For example, Sofia and Petra may be teachers at the college or members of the public who have paid a fee to join the library.

In the Thinking Skills exam, you will not be expected to know the technical names of these types of invalid deduction, but if you are interested, the invalid structure *'If p, then q; q; therefore p'* is known as 'affirming the consequent', while *'If p, then q; not p; therefore not q'* is called 'denying the antecedent'.

In some cases, 'if' is used in the sense of 'if and only if'. This makes a difference to the conclusions that can be validly drawn. For example, the claim 'If a compound is acidic, it will turn the litmus paper red' probably means 'if and only if'. In other words, if the compound is not acidic, it will not turn the litmus paper red. In that case, it is valid to claim 'This compound has turned the litmus paper red; so it is acidic' or 'This compound is not acidic; therefore it will not turn the litmus paper red.'

> ### ► EXTENSION ACTIVITY
>
> In a small group, invent some examples of arguments using the structure *'If p then q; q; therefore p'*. Choose at least one where the reasons are both true, and guarantee that the conclusion is also true. Choose at least one where the reasons and the conclusion are all untrue and another where the reasons are untrue but the conclusion happens to be true.

Another way of expressing the same range of valid and invalid logical structures is based on the word 'all' instead of 'if'. For example:

All students at Sunny Coast College have the right to borrow books from the college library. Emma is a student at Sunny Coast College. So she has the right to borrow books from the college library.

The following two structures are valid:

All As are B; C is A; therefore C is B.

All As are B; C is not B; therefore C is not A.

And the following are not valid:

All As are B; C is B; therefore C is A.

All As are B; C is not A; therefore C is not B.

> ### ▶ EXTENSION ACTIVITY
>
> In the same small group as in the previous Extension Activity, revisit the brief arguments you devised in the *'If p then q ...'* formats. Express the same arguments in terms of *'All As are B ...'*

Necessary and sufficient conditions

Key terms

A necessary condition is something which must happen or be true in order for something else to happen or be true. If a sufficient condition happens or is true, then something else must also happen or be true.

Yet another way of expressing these valid arguments and fallacies is in terms of **necessary** and **sufficient conditions**. In a case where P cannot happen or be true unless N also happens or is true, then N is a necessary condition for P. In a case where P must happen or be true if S also happens or is true, then S is a sufficient condition for P.

The structures *'If p then q'* and *'All As are B'* can be used to express sufficient conditions. For example, being a student at Sunny Coast College is a sufficient condition for being able to borrow books from the college library. It is not a necessary condition, unless it is the only way of qualifying to borrow books from the library.

An example of an argument based on a necessary condition is:

> *In order to be accepted as a student at Greenfields Music College, you must be able to play a musical instrument to a high standard. James is a student at Greenfields Music College. So he must be able to play an instrument to a high standard.*

This is a valid argument. If the reasons are true, then the conclusion must also be true. This argument can be expressed as *'If p* (someone has been accepted as a student at Greenfields Music College)*, then q* (he or she must be able to play a musical instrument to a high standard)*; p* (James has been accepted at Greenfields Music College)*; therefore q* (James must be able to play an instrument to a high standard)'. Alternatively, *'All As* (students at Greenfields Music College) *are B* (able to play a musical instrument to a high standard)*; James is A* (a student at Greenfields Music College)*; therefore James is B* (able to play an instrument to a high standard)'.

However, it would not be correct to claim that because Chao can play a musical instrument to a high standard he must be a student at Greenfields Music College, because there are probably other entry requirements in addition to instrumental ability. Chao may have failed his A Level exams, or not impressed the tutors sufficiently at his interview. Or he may have chosen to attend a different college, or not to follow a musical career at all. Being able to play a musical instrument to a high standard is a necessary condition for admission to Greenfields Music College, but not a sufficient condition.

Some conditions are both sufficient and necessary, as in *'If and only if p, then q ...'*

A flaw which sometimes occurs in reasoning is a confusion of sufficient and necessary conditions. A necessary condition is interpreted as if it were sufficient, or a sufficient condition is interpreted as if it were necessary. In the example of Chao, a necessary condition is being interpreted as if it were sufficient, while the examples of Sofia and Petra wrongly interpret a sufficient condition as necessary.

Sample question

It has often been suggested that an international language should be used alongside national languages, to facilitate communication between different countries. Since wars are provoked by misunderstanding, the introduction of a single language would achieve world peace.

How is this reasoning weakened by a confusion of sufficient and necessary conditions?

From the claim that most wars are caused by misunderstanding, it is possible to infer that for countries to understand one another is a necessary condition for peace, but the claim that the introduction of a single language would bring about world peace relies on mutual understanding being a sufficient condition, which has not been established.

Practice question

Key terms

Equivocation consists of using ambiguous language to conceal a step in reasoning by shifting (without mentioning it) from one meaning of a word or expression to another.

Conflation consists of concealing a step in reasoning by treating two words or expressions as if they were interchangeable even though their meanings are different.

One of the arguments in favour of space exploration is that it has led to the invention of materials and equipment which have become very important in everyday life. In a similar way, war brings about major progress in science and technology. Radar, computers, satellites and even the internet were originally invented for military purposes, but we would find it difficult to be without them now.

To what extent is this reasoning weakened by a confusion of sufficient and necessary conditions?

9.2 Flaws in reasoning

The meaning of words

Some dishonest techniques in reasoning rely on manipulating the meaning of words. Both equivocation and conflation involve concealing a step in reasoning. This may happen accidentally or be a deliberate attempt to distract attention from a weak or controversial step in the reasoning.

If these steps in reasoning were made explicit, they would not be flawed, because readers or listeners would know that they were part of the argument, and would be free to disagree with them if they wished to do so. If used deliberately, equivocation and conflation are unfair attempts to avoid this scrutiny.

Any biologist will tell you that a human foetus is biologically human. It is physically impossible for the offspring of human parents to be of any other species. According to the law and morality, the deliberate killing of a human being is murder. So abortion is murder.

This example of equivocation is a version of an argument which occurred quite widely in several countries as part of the debates about abortion during the 1960s, 70s and 80s. It moves from a biological definition of 'human' (of the species *homo sapiens*) to an ethical or legal sense, meaning an entity which qualifies as a 'person'. Many people believe that all entities which are biologically human should be counted as moral persons, and it is possible to argue in favour of that view, but seeking to establish it by using a word in two different senses is not such an argument.

Humanity has evolved to its current state of advanced civilisation by means of 'natural selection', by which only the finest of the species have succeeded in passing on their genes. Life is a kind of war, in which those who have the most innovative minds and the toughest and most agile bodies defeat their competitors in order to prosper and to reproduce. Thus war has been a crucial element in evolutionary progress.

One of the arguments in favour of space exploration is that it has led to the invention of materials and equipment which have become very important in everyday life. In a similar way, war brings about major progress in science and technology. Radar, computers, satellites and even the internet were originally invented for military purposes, but we would find it difficult to be without them now.

These are the first two paragraphs of an argument in support of the claim 'Politicians and religious people should be working and praying for war.' Each of those paragraphs includes an example of conflation. Paragraph 1 illegitimately moves from 'a kind of war' to 'war', as if the two expressions meant the same, while paragraph 2 conflates 'military purposes' and 'war', ignoring the fact that military purposes are a slightly broader category than war, since technologies may be developed in order to avoid wars.

It has often been suggested that an international language should be used alongside national languages, to facilitate communication between different countries. Since wars are provoked by misunderstanding, the introduction of a single language would achieve world peace.

To what extent is this reasoning weakened by the flaw of equivocation?

Practice question

The following paragraph is an extract from an argument in support of the claim, 'You should never believe what you read in newspapers'.

> A less evident form of commercial pressure originates from the desire to increase profits by bringing costs down. It is more economical to copy a report from another paper or even a press release from a commercial company or pressure group than to send a reporter to find out the facts in person. Companies and campaigns know this only too well, and they can afford to pay journalists to produce prefabricated stories for the use of editors who want to fill their pages as inexpensively as possible. Readers need to realise that what they imagine are news reports are in many cases disguised attempts to influence their political views or purchasing habits.

To what extent is this reasoning weakened by the flaw of conflation?

Difficulty in definition

▲ Is this man bald?

A flaw known variously as the argument of the 'heap', 'beard' or 'bald man' relies on the difficulty in identifying a precise point in a gradual sequence where a significant change occurs. For example: How many grains of sand constitute a heap? How many hairs are enough for a beard, or disqualify someone from being described as bald? The technical term for this flaw is *sorites* (Greek for 'heap'). It would be ridiculous to claim that (say) six grains are not a heap, but seven are (or any other pair of adjacent numbers). But you cannot infer from this that there is no difference between a heap and not a heap.

Each of these (numbers of grains or hairs) is a continuum, consisting of many very small differences. The continuum may consist of numbers (as in these examples), or it may be a process of change. For example, a different argument of the beard could ask how many days a man must refrain from shaving before he counts as having a beard.

It does not greatly matter whether there is a heap of sand or just a few grains, or whether a man is bald or bearded or not. There are other situations, however, where changes or differences of this gradual kind are significant.

Even if it is impossible to identify a precise point on the continuum where a significant change occurs, there is a real difference, and the law often has to choose a particular boundary in order to recognise this difference. For example, young children should not be allowed to marry, enter into a contract, vote or drive a car, whereas mature adults should be allowed to do all four. By choosing a specific age, somewhere around 16–18, at which people become allowed to do these things, governments are not suggesting that someone one day younger than that age is too immature, and a marvellous sudden change occurs on their birthday, but merely that a line has to be drawn somewhere. Similarly, a government which wished to control protest meetings might need to decide how many people count as a crowd.

Circular argument

A **circular argument** is one which relies on asserting or assuming the very point which it seeks to prove.

Example

> The survival of an individual is not assisted by benefiting other people: so unselfish people put themselves at a disadvantage in the fight for survival and they are less likely than other people to succeed in passing on their genes. Eventually, the genes which cause unselfish behaviour would disappear. Based on their belief that true unselfishness would not survive, evolutionary psychologists and philosophers have asserted that actions which appear to be unselfish must in reality have a selfish basis. From this they conclude that unselfishness does not exist.

The second half of this argument is a blatant example of circular reasoning. The author admits that the conclusion came first, and that the reasoning depends on it.

One form of circular reasoning which occurs quite often consists of rejecting counterexamples. This is sometimes referred to as the 'no true Scotsman' fallacy, illustrated by the following example:

> *No Scotsman puts sugar on his porridge.*
>
> *But Dougal is Scottish, and he puts sugar on his porridge.*
>
> *Then Dougal is not a true Scotsman, because no true Scotsman puts sugar on his porridge.*

The initial statement appears to be a factual observation, referring to a clearly defined category (consisting of people who live in Scotland and/or are born of Scottish parents), and that is doubtless how the speaker wants it to be understood. But when the statement is challenged by a counterexample, the speaker changes his ground and interprets the initial statement as a **criterion**, rather than a factual observation.

Some perfectly reasonable statements can be wrongly accused of committing the 'no true Scotsman' flaw. For example, the following statement is entirely reasonable, and is not flawed or fallacious:

> *No responsible parent would leave a young child alone in the house overnight.*

The crucial difference between this and the claim that 'no Scotsman puts sugar on his porridge' is that this is explicitly a value judgement (or criterion), and not a factual observation. In this case, the response,

'Denise leaves her young child alone in the house overnight' is not a counterexample, but an example or application of the criterion, showing that (according to the speaker, at least) Denise is not a responsible parent.

The 'no true Scotsman' flaw can occur when someone claims that all the best authorities agree with a claim, if it is clear that the criterion for judging these authorities to be best is based on whether or not they agree with the claim. In such cases the fact that someone disagreed with the claim would automatically disqualify them from being considered as one of the best authorities. What appears to be a justified appeal to authority is revealed actually to be a criterion and a form of circular argument.

Example	All competent educational psychologists now recognise that it is natural for children to want to learn. Any psychologists who do not admit that this is true are living in the past, and we should ignore their ill-judged opinions.

The author leaves no room for doubt that the views of any educational psychologist who disagrees with him should be rejected. So his appeal to the authority of these psychologists is circular and therefore worthless.

> **EXTENSION ACTIVITY**
>
> Invent your own example of the 'no true Scotsman' flaw.

Key term

Begging the question consists of focusing an argument on an uncontroversial aspect of an issue while stipulating or assuming the key point.

A flaw known rather obscurely as 'begging the question' is similar to a circular argument, and some books treat them as the same thing, although strictly there is a subtle difference between them.

For example, it would be begging the question to argue that people accused of violent crimes should not be entitled to a fair trial, because they did not act fairly towards the people they attacked. It is not until a fair trial has been held that one can know that the accused person did commit the assault and thereby (if one accepts the argument) forfeited the right to a fair trial.

Because this use of the expression 'begging the question' is so obscure, it is now often used in a different (technically incorrect) way, whereby 'begs the question' means 'raises' or 'suggests' a question.

There are also powerful economic arguments for abolishing police forces. In order to secure their loyalty in times of social turmoil, governments need to pay police officers more than they are worth. In addition, huge sums of money have to be spent on computing, communications and surveillance equipment in order to keep up with the increasingly sophisticated nature of crime. Without the police force, this money could be spent in much more productive ways.

To what extent is the reasoning in this paragraph weakened by begging the question?

This flaw occurs in the second half of the second sentence, and significantly weakens that part of the reasoning, although not the remainder of the paragraph. The claim that police officers are paid more than they are worth is valid only if one accepts that they are worth less than they are paid, and no evidence or reasoning is given to support this assumption. Arguably, the money it costs to ensure the loyalty of the police is by definition what they are worth.

Making changes involves a substantial waste of time and effort. Dedicating that time and effort to adapting the present system in order to make it work as well as possible would be more cost-effective.

To what extent is this reasoning weakened by begging the question?

Causal flaws

Key term

A causal flaw is an unjustified inference that phenomena which occur together must have a causal relationship.

The general expression 'causal flaw' refers to any argument which claims that just because one event or phenomenon follows another or is accompanied by another, it must be caused by the other. If two phenomena regularly occur together, there is a **correlation** between them, but this correlation is not necessarily based on **causation**. This point should seem fairly familiar to you, because a similar point occurred in Chapter 7, in relation to drawing inferences from evidence.

Claims that when one event *follows* another, it must have been *caused by* the other are often accused of committing the *post hoc* fallacy. This is a short form of the Latin phrase *post hoc ergo propter hoc* ('after this, therefore because of this'). The equivalent flaw relating to events which occur together is sometimes referred to as *cum hoc* (Latin for 'with this'). You are not required to recognise or use these Latin terms (the expression 'causal flaw' or a brief explanation in English is just as acceptable), but you may use them if you wish.

- Recent changes made to the benefit system have caused real problems to poor people. Since the changes were introduced, the number of people asking charities for help in feeding their families has increased. *(post hoc)*
- The current Prime Minister of Eastland has been in office twice before. In all three periods, relations with the neighbouring country Westland have been very tense, whereas relations have been much more peaceful when the other political party has been in power. Obviously, the current Prime Minister of Eastland is a warmonger. (*cum hoc*)

Generalisations

Generalisations occur frequently in reasoning, and they are not necessarily problematic or flawed.

For example, there is nothing wrong with saying, 'Nearly everyone enjoys sitting outdoors on warm summer evenings' or 'Most nurses feel that their pay should be increased, in order to reflect the additional responsibilities which they are now expected to undertake.' However, two types or uses of generalisation are recognised as flaws in reasoning.

A **rash generalisation** is one which is based on inadequate evidence. One or two instances are not enough to prove a generalisation to be true, although they are usually sufficient to illustrate its meaning. Authors sometimes cherry-pick evidence to support a claim, in which case identifying evidence to the contrary is an effective response. For example, someone might claim that artistic geniuses always die young, and might cite in support of this claim the musicians Mozart and Schubert and the poets Keats, Shelley and Byron. There is no shortage of counterexamples of poets (such as Wordsworth and Tennyson) and composers (such as Bach and Haydn) who lived to a ripe old age, to show that these examples have been cherry-picked to support a rash generalisation.

A **sweeping generalisation** is one which may well be true in many or most cases, but is expressed or applied in such a way as not to allow for exceptions. For example, someone might claim that because modern teenagers devote many hours each week to social media, Lisa must spend a lot of time on social media, since she is aged 16. She could be an exception to a generalisation which is true in nearly all cases. However, if the comment said 'probably', instead of 'must', it would not be flawed.

Speakers and writers sometimes overstate their generalisations for rhetorical effect in a way which does not constitute a flaw, because the fundamental point is valid and listeners or readers are unlikely to misunderstand the way it has been expressed.

Key terms

A rash generalisation is one based on a small quantity of evidence, selected to support the claim.

A sweeping generalisation is a claim which is generally true but applied in such a way as to exclude exceptions.

The most common first language in the world is Mandarin Chinese, which has more than a billion speakers. However, there is no point in introducing lessons on Mandarin into the school curriculum in Western countries, because Mandarin is not spoken by anyone who is not Chinese.

This claim is not literally true, because there must be a few non-Chinese people in the world who have for various reasons learned Mandarin, but it is true enough and does not weaken the reasoning. It would be unnecessarily pedantic to criticise the speaker for not adding 'with a very few exceptions'.

Colour television has been available in the UK and many other countries in the world since the late 1960s. No one ever complained about the reliability of the signal or the condition of the picture and sound. Then somebody announced that the existing system was out of date and that digital television needed to be introduced in its place. This change was referred to as an 'improvement'. Broadcasters ultimately stopped transmitting in the old system, meaning the public had to buy new televisions. The quality of picture and sound is no better now than it was before, while the reliability of the signal is worse. This example demonstrates that improvements are always worse than what they replace.

To what extent is this reasoning weakened by generalisation?

The claim that 'No one ever complained' is probably exaggerated, but it does not significantly weaken the reasoning, because most readers would interpret it as meaning that not many people had ever complained, and that would be sufficient to make the author's point. The final sentence of the paragraph is a rash generalisation, because a single example (if true) does establish that improvements *may* be worse than what they replace, but is inadequate as the basis for a claim that they are *always*, or even usually, worse. This seriously weakens the reasoning.

Restriction of options

Speakers and writers sometimes try to force their listeners or readers to accept their opinion by denying or ignoring the existence of alternatives. They typically claim that there is a choice between two extremes and that no intermediate positions are available. Since one of those extremes is obviously (or allegedly) unacceptable, the other must be accepted. This debating trick is known as **restricting the options**.

Key term

Restriction of options **consists of denying the possibility of certain opinions or actions in order to force or trick someone into accepting an option which they do not choose.**

An untrue claim that there are only two options available is often termed a 'false dichotomy'. The word 'dichotomy' means dividing something into two. In reasoning, it refers to claiming that there is a choice between two options. Such a claim is a false dichotomy if there are actually more or fewer than two options available.

For example, many people across the world have on occasions felt their conscience impelling them to disobey a law which they regarded as unjust. Someone who disagreed with their actions might say:

> You either obey the law whether you agree with it or not or you claim the right to decide every issue for yourself. If everyone decided every issue for themselves, without any reference to the law of the land, chaos would result. So you should obey the law even if you disagree with it.

The speaker has attempted to trick his opponent by denying that any intermediate positions exist, which is clearly false. It makes good sense for someone to say, 'I will obey the law even if I disagree with it, except in those few and exceptional cases where it causes a serious offence to my conscience.' Denying that anyone can take that position is a false dichotomy and a dishonest trick in reasoning.

Another form of restricting the options is to offer a choice of alternatives without admitting the possibility of choosing both. For example, a government which was being accused of harming the economy by imposing high taxes in order to pay for the armed forces and armaments might respond, 'The duty of a government is to protect the country, not to make it prosperous.' Most people probably think governments have both duties and should try to strike a fair balance between the demands of both of them.

Another kind of false dichotomy can be referred to as 'a distinction without a difference': that is, an apparent choice is offered, but in fact both alternatives are the same. This is not exactly a restriction of options, but would certainly qualify as a weakness in reasoning.

Example	
	Making changes involves a substantial waste of time and effort. Dedicating that time and effort to adapting the present system in order to make it work as well as possible would be more cost-effective.

Presumably, 'adapting the current system in order to make it work as well as possible' will involve making changes. So the author is drawing a distinction without a difference.

Many descriptions of unidentified flying objects (UFOs) have been provided by people who claim to have seen them. A few of the reports may have been jokes, and others based on honest mistakes, but those who have made the reports include military personnel, police officers and airline pilots – in other words, people who know what a weather balloon looks like and would not mistake one for a UFO. The most likely reason for these observations is that the UFOs are vehicles containing extraterrestrial visitors.

To what extent is the reasoning in this paragraph weakened by the flaw of restricting the options?

Slippery slope

The traditional form of a slippery slope argument consists of claiming that once one small step is taken, a succession of further small steps becomes inevitable, each of which is marginally worse than what preceded it. The culmination of this process is a situation which no one would have chosen, but none of the individual steps was in itself significant enough to be opposed. Such arguments may be realistic, but they are unfair if there is a natural boundary which would differentiate between good and bad cases.

For example, in the 1960s in the UK, there was a lot of discussion about legalising abortion. One of the arguments used by opponents of abortion was that if the killing of foetuses were to be permitted, the next proposal would be to allow the killing of handicapped babies. This did seem a natural progression, and many of those who used this argument to oppose the legalisation of abortion really did think that euthanasia of handicapped babies would follow. However, subsequent experience showed that after abortion was legalised, the feared extension to infants did not occur. Birth seemed to be regarded by most people as a natural and crucially important boundary, which few, if any, wished to cross.

Within Thinking Skills, the expression 'slippery slope' may be used more loosely, to refer to any claim that the consequences of an action or opinion will be far worse than may appear.

A particular form of slippery slope argument is often known as 'the thin end of the wedge'. This refers to the suspicion that someone is deliberately taking the first step on a slippery slope in order to achieve an outcome which, if identified from the outset, would have been rejected. Opponents may object to the initial proposal on the grounds that it is the thin end of the wedge, that is, that once the first, trivial and apparently unobjectionable concession has been granted, its proposer will proceed

▲ The thin end of the wedge

in further small steps, until eventually he will achieve the goal he had intended from the beginning. The strength of a thin end of the wedge argument depends on whether anyone really does or does not want to bring about a more radical change than the one being proposed.

The thin end of the wedge argument is sometimes referred to as a 'camel's nose' argument. This refers to the fable of the camel's nose, which is a clear illustration of this method of reasoning:

One cold night, as a traveller sat in his tent, his camel asked him, 'May I share your tent?'

'Certainly not,' replied the traveller. 'There is room for only one.'

'Then could I just put my nose in your tent?' asked the camel. 'My nose is very cold.'

The traveller thought that a nose would not take up much room, and so he gave permission.

After a little while, the camel nudged him, and asked, 'Now that my nose is warming up, my head is very cold. May I put my head into the tent?'

The traveller thought that the camel's head would not take up much more room than its nose, and so he gave permission.

After a little while, the camel nudged him again, and asked, 'My head is warm, but my forelegs are very cold. May I put my forelegs into the tent?'

The traveller thought that the camel's forelegs would not take up much more room than its head, and so he gave permission.

After a little while, the camel nudged him again, and asked, 'My forelegs are warm, but my back legs are very cold. May I put my back legs into the tent?'

The traveller thought that the camel's back legs would not take up much more room than its forelegs, and so he gave permission.

Some time later, the traveller woke up, feeling cold. He realised that he was outside, while the camel was sleeping in his tent.

Slippery slope and thin end of the wedge arguments are flawed because they oppose a proposal which may in itself be good, or at least acceptable, on the grounds that permitting it may make it more likely that someone in some future situation will do something unacceptable. But those circumstances may not arise, or the dreadful outcome may not happen, or perhaps it would have happened anyway. So a slippery slope argument is by its nature quite weak.

Voluntary euthanasia must not be legalised. Once one exception is made to the rule against killing, further exceptions will inevitably follow. There will be no reason not to legalise compulsory euthanasia. This might begin with the painless killing of all patients who are already terminally ill, but it will go on to include children with incurable genetic disorders. Next to be killed will be elderly people being cared for at public expense and the next step might be the killing of habitual criminals and other groups considered to be 'undesirable'. Before long every member of society will be at risk of being killed.

Explain the flaw in this reasoning.

This paragraph is seriously weakened by the flaw of slippery slope. It ignores the fact that the element of voluntariness in relation to euthanasia is considered crucial by almost everyone, and thereby forms a natural barrier on the alleged slippery slope. The last step in the argument is ridiculous, because there is no reason to imagine that anyone wants to kill 'every member of society'.

Treating an opponent unfairly

Three flaws can be grouped together as ways of treating an opponent unfairly. Two of these flaws are usually referred to by Latin names, but the Thinking Skills syllabus gives them English titles. The specialised meanings of these expressions are explained later in this section.

A straw man is literally a dummy, stuffed with straw, used as a scarecrow or in mockery of a politician or other notorious person. A straw man argument is a deliberately distorted version of an opponent's argument.

Example

Vegetarianism is illogical and self-contradictory. Vegetarians claim that all living things have the same rights as humans, but if that is so, then they should object to eating plants just as much as they do animals, with the result that they would starve.

This version of what vegetarians believe is inaccurate and unfair; the riposte in the second half of the sentence is not relevant to their actual beliefs.

Sample question

It is very widely acknowledged that a right to health is one of the essential human rights; however, this view is gravely mistaken. A right to health would ask too much. For example, common colds may be inconvenient and uncomfortable, but they do not threaten any basic human good. Consequently we should not expect to avoid them.

Explain the flaw in this reasoning.

This section of reasoning is flawed because it is based on a straw man. Those who claim that health is an essential human right do not mean we have a right to be exempt from minor illnesses such as a cold.

Key terms

A personal attack consists of criticising opponents personally instead of responding to their arguments.

A counter-attack consists of rejecting criticisms on the grounds that opponents or other people are guilty of the same or equally objectionable conduct.

A **personal attack** in reasoning is often referred to as an *ad hominem* argument. This is the Latin for 'to the person'. In other words, the attack is directed towards the person, instead of to their arguments. Cases sometimes occur in which the personal attack is *in addition* to addressing the argument, rather than *instead*. This is still a flaw, but not as serious. If you were evaluating an attack like this, a strong answer would include an explanation of why it is not a serious flaw.

Counter-attacks are sometimes referred to as *tu quoque* arguments, from the Latin for 'you too'. This form of counter-attack is very common in politics, where a government minister may respond to a criticism from the opposition by claiming that when the other party was in power they had done no better. This may be a fair comment, but it should not be used in order to avoid responding to the complaint.

Within Thinking Skills, counter-accusations are a broader category than replying 'you too' to an opponent. It includes the defence that 'everyone else is doing it, too.'

The amassed evidence is overwhelming that extraterrestrials from distant planets have contacted the Earth many times. The idiots who refuse to accept this must base their opinions solely on prejudice. Their only argument is circular: extraterrestrials are not real; so those who claim to have encountered them are either mistaken or lying; therefore there is no evidence that extraterrestrials are real.

Identify two flaws in the reasoning in this paragraph.

> **The second sentence makes a personal attack on the opponents instead of responding to their arguments.**
> **The third sentence is a straw man. The author uses a grossly inaccurate version of the arguments put forward by his opponents in order to avoid responding to their actual arguments.**

Politicians claim they are working for peace, and religious people ask for peace in their prayers, but they should work and pray for war instead. Peace-mongers are cowards. The only reason for their resistance to war is that they lack the bravery to stand against oppression and injustice.

Identify two flaws in the reasoning in this paragraph.

9.3 The use of appeals

Arguments frequently make appeals, for example to authority, popularity, experience, tradition, novelty or emotion. If such an appeal is **relevant** and **proportionate**, it does not constitute a weakness in reasoning. But an appeal which is **irrelevant** or **disproportionate** does constitute a weakness in reasoning.

Arguments are often strengthened by appeals to **authority**, such as the opinion of someone with relevant expertise and ability to see. There is nothing flawed or weak about claiming in support of an argument the opinion of a recognised authority on the topic being discussed. The opinion of a celebrity, however, or of a specialist in a different field, may not be worth much. In addition, an appeal to a relevant authority is not sufficient to settle a matter, because opinions amongst experts often vary, and even a consensus should not be exempt from being questioned.

In some situations, an appeal to authority is valid because the person whose authority is cited has the right to make a judgement. For example, if you (and perhaps your friends) think you have written a good essay, but your teacher or the A Level examiners think it is not good, their opinion is the one which counts. Similarly, employees can reasonably be expected to accept the authority of a manager directing them in how to spend their time while at work.

Appeals to **popularity** also do not necessarily constitute a weakness in reasoning. The claim by advertisers, for example, that the product they are promoting is the most popular amongst consumers is relevant information for anyone choosing what to buy, although it does not prove that it is the best product or the best value. Similarly, the appeal to popularity is quite weak in the example: 'There must be some truth in astrology, because most newspapers carry forecasts by an astrologer, and most people read them.' However, it would be reasonable for a newspaper proprietor to argue: 'We should include an astrology column in our paper, because most newspapers carry forecasts by an astrologer, and most people read them.' There are also some situations in which the appeal to popularity is the key point, for example, in an election or when voting on a proposal in a committee: in both of these cases, the most popular choice (that is, the one with the most votes) wins.

To think about

Colin looked on a direct-sales website for a torch to use when taking his dog for a walk on dark evenings. Having rejected torches which appeared to be too heavy or which produced too weak a light, he was left with a choice of six products which seemed to meet his requirements. He did not know any other way of choosing between them and so he bought the one which the website said was the most popular.

Do you think Colin made a wise choice?

It is a matter of common wisdom that people ought to learn from their experience. The proverb 'once bitten, twice shy' highlights one scenario (avoiding a dog that has previously attacked you) in which an appeal to experience (usually referred to in Thinking Skills as an 'appeal to **history**') is a useful tool in reasoning. Previous experience is no guarantee of what will happen in the future, but it can provide a useful warning. Factors which may affect the reliability of an appeal to history include the number of precedents to which the appeal is being made, whether the appeal is being used as the basis for a warning or for optimism, and the degree of risk if things go wrong.

Here are two appeals to history. How strong do you think they are?

1 The security services of Eastland have claimed that their traditional enemy, Westland, interfered in the recent parliamentary election in Eastland; they believe that the actions were personally ordered by the President of Westland. The newly elected Prime Minister of Eastland says he intends to ignore this report, because the security services are unreliable. Thirty years ago, they reported that Northland was preparing to attack Eastland, but after Eastland had taken pre-emptive military action against Northland, it was discovered that the information had been incorrect.

2 Our country is facing grave threats. We are outnumbered by our enemies, and our allies have already been defeated. But we have faced dark days before. We survived then, and we shall survive now. So we must not lose heart, but should fight on.

Another form of appeal to history consists of assuming that the original form of an institution should be definitive. For instance, 'Originally, prison was not a punishment: in ancient times, the normal punishment for criminals was death, and prison was essentially a secure place to keep them as they waited to be executed' gives very weak support for the conclusion, 'We urgently need to find other ways of punishing criminals than sending them to prison.'

Similar considerations apply in relation to appeals to **tradition**. It would be unrealistic and a waste of time to rethink every procedure on every occasion. On most occasions, the fact that 'we have always done it this way' is sufficient justification for continuing to do it in the same way. But if 'we have always done it this way' is taken as an unanswerable objection to every proposal for change, then no improvements will ever be introduced; that is a flawed appeal to tradition.

The opposite of the appeal to tradition is appeal to **novelty**. It is based on the assumption that changes are always improvements. For example, when manufacturers rebrand products as 'new' versions of old favourites, they obviously hope that consumers will infer that the new version is better than the old, although the improvement (if any) is often too small to notice.

Various different **emotions** can be the basis for appeals, including pity, fear, guilt, anger, disgust, pride and envy. Appeals to emotion can be appropriate and proportionate, but they are often used in order to manipulate listeners and readers.

Sample question

A further problem with prison is that it punishes the wrong people. Prisoners probably suffer less than their wives or partners and children. They do not lie awake worrying about how to pay the bills or where the next meal is coming from, but their family probably does.

To what extent is the reasoning in this paragraph weakened by an appeal?

The description of a prisoner's partner lying awake worrying is an appeal to emotion. It does not weaken the reasoning, because it reinforces the point being made, which is that the wrong people are punished by prison.

Practice question

Many scientists believe that the Universe is infinite. They infer that a very large number of planets have the conditions in which life could develop. One estimate is that over a hundred thousand billion potentially life-bearing planets exist. It is very likely that there are many alien species which have both the desire to explore the Universe and the ability to do so.

(Cambridge AS & A Level Thinking Skills 9694, Paper 21 Q3 (a) & (b), June 2016)

How effective is the appeal to authority in this paragraph?

Practice question

There are invariably good reasons for the arrangements which are in place. They have evolved gradually in response to the needs of the situation. Any problems have already been identified and worked out. It is impossible for any change to have such strong support, because it cannot have stood the test of time.

How effective is the appeal to tradition in this paragraph?

> **EXTENSION ACTIVITY**
>
> In groups of two or three students, divide the following appeals between yourselves, taking about three each: authority, popularity, history, tradition, novelty, pity, fear, pride, envy. Devise two examples for each of the appeals assigned to you, one which you consider valid and one which you think is a weakness in reasoning. Share your examples with the others in your small group, and discuss whether they agree with your assessments.

9.4 Weaknesses in reasoning

Inadequate support

It is a weakness if reasoning supports only part of the conclusion which is drawn from it, or if a moderate claim or intermediate conclusion is used to support a conclusion which would follow only from a stronger version.

It does not matter if criminals are harmed by their punishment – indeed, that is the whole aim of punishment – but the harm imposed by prison is enduring and counterproductive. No one would seriously claim that criminals should be punished by being stopped from working for their living ever again, by becoming mentally ill, by their wife or partner leaving them, or by losing touch with their children. Yet there is ample statistical and anecdotal evidence that these are the classic consequences of serving a lengthy term of imprisonment. Rather than inspiring and equipping criminals to become productive and conscientious members of society, prison makes sure that they will never do so.

The argument in this paragraph draws a conclusion about prison in general from evidence about the consequences of 'lengthy' terms of imprisonment. The author ignores the possibility that short prison terms might be effective and might avoid the detrimental effects. Another way of explaining this weakness in the reasoning is that the author is **conflating** 'prison' with 'lengthy term of imprisonment'.

Inconsistency

It is a weakness if one part of an argument's reasoning contradicts, or is inconsistent with, another part. For example, the paragraph discussing the introduction of digital television (on page 268) ended with the Intermediate Conclusion: 'This example demonstrates that improvements are always worse than what they replace.'

This is the first paragraph of an argument about change. The final paragraph of that argument, including the main conclusion, is:

> *Admittedly, some changes do ultimately turn out to have been for the better, but the problem is that we cannot tell beforehand which ones they will be. It is always more likely that any particular proposal will lead to catastrophe than that it will result in an improvement. So the best practice is to be safe, by resisting all change.*

This reasoning is weakened by two inconsistencies.

» The word 'improvement' is used in different senses in the two paragraphs. The point being made in the first paragraph, that changes which are *called* 'improvements' often (or 'always') do not make things better, is weakened by the use of the word in its usual sense in the final paragraph. Since this inconsistency makes the overall argument less clear than if the word had been used consistently, it was probably unintentional.

» The more serious weakness is that the first sentence claims that *all* changes are for the worse, while the final paragraph admits that some changes are for the better. The support which the first paragraph gives to the conclusion is weakened by this concession.

Analogies

Arguments often make use of analogies, in which an unfamiliar concept is illustrated by reference to something more familiar. Politicians frequently use analogies, for example, 'Managing the budget of a country is just like managing the budget of a household: you can't spend more than you earn.' It is not a valid criticism of an analogy to say that the two entities are different, because that is the whole nature of an analogy. Even imperfect analogies can strengthen an argument, but a wild analogy which lacks significant points of similarity or has crucial differences constitutes a weakness in reasoning.

An example of a weak or false analogy is that tobacco is like arsenic, because both of them kill people, and therefore the sale of tobacco should be controlled by the Poisons Act. The weakness of this analogy is that the differences between arsenic and tobacco are crucial to the issue. No one consumes arsenic for pleasure; the harm done by smoking tobacco products is indirect, long term and a matter of risk rather than certainty.

Example

> One of the arguments in favour of space exploration is that it has led to the invention of materials and equipment which have become very important in everyday life. In a similar way, war brings about major progress in science and technology. Radar, computers, satellites and even the internet were originally invented for military purposes, but we would find it difficult to be without them now.

The analogy in this paragraph is a fairly good one. The crucial point (the value of by-products) really is true of both elements of the analogy (space travel and war), and most people are familiar with the fact that equipment and materials developed for space travel have become valued elements of domestic life. The only weakness in the analogy is that space travel is not intrinsically bad, whereas war is.

Sample question

> Recent studies have shown that a large number of prisoners experience mental illness. They should therefore be treated instead of punished. Sending them to prison is as inappropriate and unfair as it would be to punish people for being ill with pneumonia or cancer.

How well does the analogy in this paragraph support the reasoning?

Moderately well (neither well nor badly). The analogy of physical with mental illness does support the claim that people whose criminal acts are caused by mental illness should not be punished for them, but it ignores the crucial difference that pneumonia and cancer do not cause people to break the law or harm other people, whereas those whose mental illnesses cause them to commit crimes have typically done both of these.

> There is also a lot of credible evidence that people have been abducted by extraterrestrials. Although some of the witnesses may be confused, most seem normal, rational and reliable. Since many of those events happened in the daytime, they cannot be discredited as vivid dreams, and the resemblances between the accounts of these experiences cannot be only coincidence. To reject this abundant evidence would be as unreasonable as refusing to believe that many people have visited the White House and met the President of the United States.

How well does the analogy in this paragraph support the reasoning?

Reliance

The fact that you disagree with a claim or a conclusion does *not* constitute a weakness in reasoning. However, *reliance* on an unsupported claim or unstated assumption which many listeners or readers would be likely to reject does constitute a weakness, because it means that anyone who rejects the claim, definition or assumption can reasonably also reject the conclusion. So although identifying unstated assumptions is part of analysing arguments, it can also be a valid way of answering an evaluation question, if the assumption weakens the reasoning.

> It may seem obvious that deploying more police officers in the community would be the best way of improving public safety. However, public safety is a state of mind, which has little relation to the actual prevalence of crime. So police forces should cut back the number of police officers and devote more of their resources to public relations. Sending one extra police officer onto the streets might make a few people feel a little more confident about their own safety, but by spreading the word about low crime and high conviction rates, one additional public relations officer would make a community feel much safer.

To what extent is the reasoning in this paragraph weakened by relying on a stipulative definition?

Although feeling safe is important, most people would say it is more important to be safe. So the claim that 'public safety is a state of mind' is unusual and few people are likely to accept it. Since the IC of this paragraph is derived from this stipulative definition, the reasoning is seriously weakened.

Responding to counter

It is not a weakness for an argument to be one-sided. Someone defending one point of view is under no obligation to show balance. But it can be a weakness if the proponent fails to foresee and respond to an obvious objection to a claim or line of reasoning, because this omission may cause most of the audience or readership to reject the argument.

The use of a counter assertion or counterargument *with a response* can be an effective technique in an argument, but giving the counter *without responding* to it weakens the argument, because it is doing the work of opponents for them.

Many flaws and weaknesses can be alternatively expressed in terms of assumptions, and that approach is just as acceptable as identifying the technical term. For example, the weakness described on page 278, under 'Inadequate support', could be expressed as the assumption that the problems caused by lengthy terms of imprisonment also apply to shorter terms.

Practice question

Explain **two** weaknesses in the following excerpt from an argument supporting the claim, 'The cumulative evidence is overwhelming that members of other species from distant planets have contacted the Earth on many occasions.'

> Since 1984, astronomers from the Search for Extraterrestrial Intelligence (SETI) have been scanning the airwaves looking for radio signals from outer space. They believe they were successful on one occasion. In 2003, they detected signals from an area in space where there are no planets or stars. Since we know of no way in which these signals could have occurred naturally, we can only conclude that someone was deliberately transmitting them from a distant planet in the hope that someone from elsewhere in the universe would reply.

9.5 Applying the skills of evaluating reasoning

AS Level

Within the Critical Thinking paper, questions which focus on the evaluation of reasoning are usually to be found in the fourth question.

Sample question

Read the following passage and then answer the questions below.

1 One of the most widely held convictions in modern Western society is that individuals are all entitled to their own opinions. Many people think they can say anything, however ill-considered, and if they are challenged reply, 'Well, that's my opinion and I'm entitled to it.' But if that opinion is wrong, or if they hold it for no good reason, then they are not entitled to it.

2 The claim to be entitled to one's opinion is a poor excuse for intellectual laziness. It should matter to us that our opinions are not misguided and when someone disagrees with us, we should want to explore the issue and find out who is right.

3 Even worse, the unsupported assertion of an opinion should be recognised as an attack on rationality. The alleged entitlement to one's own opinion apparently applies even if the opinion being expressed is immoral, offensive, contradicted by powerful evidence or nonsensical. Yet humans were defined by the sixth-century philosopher Boethius as 'beings of a rational nature'. So if we voice an opinion without having thought about the issue, weighed the evidence and considered alternative views, we are being less than human.

4 Anyone who thinks that all opinions are equally acceptable is a fool. Some opinions are based on persuasive reasoning, whereas others are merely asserted. Some political opinions create huge social problems, whereas others promote prosperity and national unity. So of course they are not equally acceptable.

5 Admittedly, some judgements do vary between individuals, because of differing personal values or tastes. For example, in a particular situation one person may think it is important to tell the truth, whereas another may prefer to maintain smooth relationships by telling a 'white lie'. Some people like spicy food, whereas others don't. No one has the right to say that any of those preferences is right or wrong.

6 Other opinions, however, are matters of fact rather than tastes or values, and in these cases it is possible for an opinion to be right or wrong. To take an extreme example, anyone who disagrees with the judgement that torturing babies is wrong is a moral imbecile, whose opinion does not deserve to be taken seriously. Anyone can prefer the music of The Beatles to that of J S Bach, if that is their taste, but if they go further and claim that John Lennon was a greater musician than Bach, then they are simply wrong. No one is entitled to hold an opinion which is evidently wrong.

(Cambridge AS & A Level Thinking Skills 9694, Paper 23 Q3 passage only, November 2012)

a How effective is the appeal to authority in paragraph 3?

b To what extent is the reasoning in paragraph 4 weakened by the flaw of a straw man?

c How well does the reasoning in paragraph 5 support the main conclusion?

d How well do the examples in paragraph 6 support the overall reasoning?

a The appeal to authority is not very effective (neither effective nor totally ineffective). The expertise of the philosopher is relevant to the appeal which is being made to his authority, but the sixth century was hundreds of years ago and the author has provided no evidence that Boethius' definition of humans continues to be widely acknowledged.

b It is weakened seriously. It is highly unlikely that imaginary opponents would claim that all opinions are equally well-founded or equally beneficial: they are more likely to be claiming that people who hold those opinions are equally entitled to do so as those whose ideas are better supported or do more good.

c Not at all well. The whole paragraph counters the main conclusion, and the response in the next paragraph is asserted rather than based on reasoning. So paragraph 5 actually weakens the main conclusion instead of supporting it.

d The example of torturing babies supports well the claim that some moral judgements are universally accepted and therefore not matters of opinion. However, the fact that this example is so extreme means it is possible that most issues are not as definite as this. The second example in paragraph 6 is weak because it is not supported by reasoning, but relies on the reader accepting the author's judgement.

Practice question | *Read the following passage and then answer the questions which follow.*

1 Whom would you prefer as your teacher? Someone who just managed to pass a degree examination thirty years ago and has never opened a book since, or someone who is fascinated by his subject and has read widely in it, but left university without taking a degree because the teaching and the course were boring and he wanted to be free to pursue topics that interested him? This shows that possession of a university degree is no guarantee that someone will be a good teacher.

2 The rapid changes in knowledge mean that a university education quickly becomes out of date. Furthermore, most graduates will readily admit that they have forgotten nearly everything they learned at university. The only way a degree could be a reliable indication of competence in a subject would be if degrees had a time limit built into them and needed to be updated every five years in order to remain valid. Under the present system, they mean nothing.

3 In addition, experts are often bad teachers, because they think that their task is to pass on their knowledge to their students. That approach to education belongs firmly in the past. Education is about learning, not

teaching, and the knowledge required to pass an exam is more reliably available from textbooks specially written for the exam and from the internet than from the fallible memory of the teacher.

4 Some people may suggest that teachers need paper qualifications in order to show that they have been taught how to teach, but any teacher knows that is not true. Either you can teach or you cannot. If you can, you do not need anyone to show you how to do it, and if you cannot, then no amount of guidance or instruction will turn you into an effective teacher.

5 The only qualification required to be a teacher should, therefore, be the ability to enable students to pass their exams. Such a change from paper qualifications to a focus on skills would be consistent with current trends, since most employers are now far more interested in the abilities which potential recruits have to offer rather than their academic qualifications.

a To what extent is the reasoning in this passage weakened by the flaw 'restricting the options'?

b 'Possession of a university degree is no guarantee that someone will be a good teacher.' (paragraph 1)
How well does this claim support the main conclusion of the argument?

c 'Under the present system, [degrees] mean nothing.' (paragraph 2)
How well is this claim supported by the reasoning in paragraph 2?

d Explain the **inconsistency** in paragraph 5.

A Level

The second question in the Applied Reasoning paper is likely to ask you to evaluate one of the resource documents supplied, probably the same document used for analysis in the first question.

Sample question

Response by the Student Union of Barchester University to the draft proposals for a new degree of Bachelor of Humanities

1 We are disappointed that, under the draft proposals, degrees will be awarded solely on the basis of written examinations taken at the end of the course. Since the panel which produced the proposals was chaired by the former Dean of Humanities, now retired, it is not surprising that the proposals are so old-fashioned and backward-looking.

2   We recommend that the new degree should be assessed solely by essays and projects written during the course. This will put our university in the forefront of innovation. Instead of remaining in the third rank of universities, implementing our suggestion will make us be seen as trendsetters.

3   Some students perform badly in examinations because they are nervous under stress, have poor memories or find it difficult to think quickly. It is unfair that they should be penalised for these difficulties, because they are not their fault. These problems are especially relevant to this course, because it is aimed at mature students, many of whom are likely to have a history of academic failure.

4   Traditional written examinations assess short-term memory, superficial thinking and the ability to write quickly. These are not the skills which Higher Education should be developing. The purpose of universities is to enable students to explore subjects at depth, to develop their own informed opinions on matters of universal importance, and to ponder unhurriedly on the mysteries of the universe.

5   The former Dean has argued that unseen written examinations produce a wider range of marks than assessment by essays, but that is not a valid reason for relying on them. You could obtain an even greater spread by listing the candidates according to their birthdays, but it would not be measuring anything significant.

6   There is also no merit in the superficial criticism that students might 'cheat' by obtaining their essays from the internet. The ability to answer problems by researching on the internet is, in fact, one of the most valuable skills in the modern workplace.

7   Writing an essay forces students to engage with the material they have been taught or can discover for themselves and to apply it to a specific issue. These are the skills which employers are looking for. Group projects are especially valuable, since they develop and assess teamwork in addition to other skills. So anyone who passes a degree assessed in these ways should be in a very strong position for gaining a job.

Student President

(Adapted from Cambridge AS & A Level Thinking Skills 9694,
Paper 42 Q2 Document 1, June 2015)

a   Identify and explain three weaknesses in reasoning in the Student President's argument.

b   Give an overall evaluation of the Student President's argument by explaining the impact of a key weakness.

You may use a weakness already identified in part (a), but the impact of the weakness on the whole argument must be clearly explained.

a Paragraph 1

The second sentence is to some extent *ad hominem* (a personal attack), although it does make a specific criticism of the draft assessment proposals.

Paragraph 2

Appeal to novelty/assumption – that innovation is a good thing.

Assumption – that other universities will follow in this direction.

Assumption – that 'trendsetting' is sufficient to elevate a university above the third rank.

Paragraph 3

Appeal to pity (but does not invalidate the point being made).

Assumption – that being cool under stress, having a retentive memory and being able to think quickly are not among the qualities which academic courses should develop or assess.

Assumption – that people should not be assessed on the basis of personal qualities (such as natural abilities) which are outside their control.

Paragraph 4

Generalisation – from some of the subjects taught and studied at university (like philosophy and history) to all subjects.

Inconsistency – regarding the purpose of universities with that assumed in paragraph 7.

Assumption – that degrees assessed without exams allow students time to 'ponder unhurriedly'.

Paragraph 5

Assumption – that the range of marks produced by written exams does not measure 'anything significant'.

Paragraph 6

Conflation – of 'obtaining essays from the internet' (which actually refers to buying, or copying, other people's work and passing it off as one's own) with 'researching on the internet'.

Paragraph 7

Assumption – that at least part of the purpose of universities is to prepare students for the world of work.

b The final sentence of paragraph 4 generalises from some of the subjects taught and studied at university (like philosophy and history) to all subjects. This weakens the reasoning to some extent, since the description does not apply to other subjects, such as engineering and physiotherapy. However, the reasoning is not greatly weakened, since the point is being made in the context of a degree in humanities.

Who should vote?

1 Depending on which country you live in, your 16th, 17th, 18th or 21st birthday could be the age at which you can drive, get married, or buy alcohol – at least legally. We have these laws for a reason, but age should not be used as a criterion in deciding who should select the next government.

2 Voting is far too important to be based on such an arbitrary measure as a person's age. Drinking, relationships and driving are personal matters, but voting affects other people. In deciding who should govern us we need to take into account politics, economics, science and human nature. We do not suddenly develop a full understanding of these things when we wake up on our 18th birthday.

3 Many politicians have advocated lowering the voting age in an attempt to show that they are 'in touch with young people', but young people care less about voting and more about fashion and music. In the town of Middlesbrough in the north of England most of the local schools entered a candidate to be Youth Mayor of Middlesbrough. Unsurprisingly, the candidate from the school that cast the most votes won the election. This just shows that teenagers will vote for the candidate they perceive to be on their team, rather than considering the policies on offer.

4 In terms of deciding anything, age is largely meaningless anyway. We might as well separate people based on height. Everyone knows people of the same age with wildly differing abilities, or people of different ages with the same ability. There is no upper age limit for voting: nobody says 'Sorry, granddad, take your opinion elsewhere'. So there should not be a lower age limit.

5 There has to be some way of deciding who votes, and age is at least easy to apply. Alternative systems are practical, though. A basic questionnaire, similar to an IQ test, would be straightforward to administer. People registering to vote could complete the test, which would include questions on general knowledge as well as cognitive ability. Those who got above a certain score would be registered to vote; those who did not could try again next time. That way the people who had the privilege of voting would be those who deserved it.

Trib

(Adapted from Cambridge AS & A Level Thinking Skills 9694, Paper 42 Document 1, November 2016)

a Identify and explain three flaws and/or weaknesses in Trib's argument in '*Who should vote?*'

b Explain an aspect of Trib's reasoning which makes his argument weak overall.

10 Creating arguments

> **By the end of this chapter you will be able to:**
>
> ★ articulate a conclusion and provide reasons to support it
> ★ develop strands of reasoning
> ★ structure reasoning through the use of intermediate conclusions
> ★ strengthen reasoning through the use of appropriate argument elements.

10.1 Supporting a conclusion

It is important to understand the difference between an **essay** and an **argument**. In most of the other subjects you might study at school and university, you will be asked to write essays. If a question asks whether you agree with a particular claim or not, a good essay will discuss the reasons in favour of both sides of the question and then come to a judgement. But you have already seen in Chapter 8 that an argument is different. It consists of a conclusion, supported by reasoning. If an opposing opinion is mentioned at all in an argument, it is only to show why it is wrong. Balance is a virtue in an essay, but not in an argument.

The first step in writing an argument to support a conclusion is to think of some reasons which can be used to support it. It is not likely that you will normally be asked to do this as a separate task. But it is useful to practise this skill in isolation.

Sample question	Give some reasons to **support** and **challenge** the claim 'The punishment for crime should be so harsh that potential criminals will not risk it.'

Support

➤ **Governments have a duty to protect citizens from the risk of being victims of crime.**

➤ **One function of punishment is to educate citizens into not committing crime.**

> ➤ **Reducing the amount of crime is an urgent task.**
> ➤ **There is not much a government can do to make crime less attractive.**
> ➤ **Fear is a very powerful motive in guiding behaviour.**

Challenge

> ➤ **Excessively harsh punishments for crime are unjust.**
> ➤ **Potential criminals are not deterred by harsh penalties if they think they will not be caught.**
> ➤ **Imposing excessively severe punishments on criminals risks encouraging traits of cruelty in other people.**
> ➤ **Excessively harsh punishments are likely to cause resentment and encourage criminals to seek revenge.**
> ➤ **Harsh punishments are unlikely to lead to reform.**
> ➤ **Punishments should never be so harsh that people lose their self-respect or human dignity.**

Practice questions

Suggest three reasons which could be used to **support** and three which could be used to **challenge** each of the following claims:

- The inhabitants of our world should try to contact life in other areas of the Universe.
- Everybody has the right to keep their intimate information private.
- No one should ever advise anyone else that their opinion is incorrect.

10.2 Strands of reasoning

The second step in writing your own argument is to expand your reasons into strands of reasoning. One way of doing this is to provide reasoning to support a reason, which thereby becomes an Intermediate Conclusion (IC). Alternatively, the reason may be the starting point for the reasoning, and the way in which it supports the main conclusion may be expressed in an IC.

Structurally, the arguments given in Section B of the Critical Thinking exam and Document 1 of the Applied Reasoning paper are the kind of arguments you should aim to write yourself. Of course, you should not imitate the deliberate flaws and weaknesses which are introduced into those arguments for the purpose of evaluation.

Your arguments should be divided into paragraphs, each of which consists of a brief strand of reasoning supporting an IC. Follow the rule: a separate paragraph for each strand of reasoning, and a separate strand of reasoning for each paragraph. A simple way of making this structure clear and recognisable is to leave a blank line after each paragraph.

Expand your previous reasons for or against the claim 'The punishment for crime should be so harsh that potential criminals will not risk it' to form complex arguments, each consisting of three stands of reasoning.

Support

Those who contemplate breaking the law weigh up the possible gains against what will happen to them if they are caught. There is not much a government can do to make crime less attractive, so the obvious way of modifying the equation in order to reduce the amount of crime is to make the punishments harsher.

Furthermore, punishment has an educational function, to discourage citizens from committing crime and encourage good habits of behaviour. Trivial penalties would not be significant enough to succeed in achieving this goal. So punishment must be harsh enough to hurt.

Since so many people currently live in fear of crime, reducing it is an urgent task.

Therefore the punishment for crime should be so severe that people will not risk it.

Challenge

The concept of punishment justifies treating people in ways which would normally be forbidden. But the extent of this justification is limited by the severity of the crime: so excessively harsh punishments for crime are unjust.

Such punishments are also ineffective in achieving their purpose, because instead of leading to reform, they are likely to cause resentment and encourage criminals to seek revenge on the society which has treated them so cruelly.

It seems clear that harsher penalties would not actually make much difference to the amount of crime in a country, because people will continue to commit crimes if the motivation is strong enough and if they believe they are unlikely to be caught. Increasing the number and efficiency of police would make criminals more likely to be convicted and therefore be a more effective way of reducing crime.

Therefore the punishment for crime should not be so severe that people will not risk it.

Expand your answers to the practice questions in Section 10.1 to form complex arguments, each consisting of three stands of reasoning.

10.3 Using additional argument elements

The use of other elements, in addition to reasons and intermediate conclusions, may strengthen your argument. These may include examples, evidence, analogies, hypothetical reasoning and consideration of counterpositions.

Examples make an argument easier to understand by relating it to experience. If readers or listeners can relate to the examples, they may be more sympathetic to the point of view being expressed. The first sentence of the argument supporting the claim that the punishment for crime should be so harsh that people will not risk it could be made more persuasive by being illustrated by examples, as follows:

> *Those who consider breaking the law contemplate the possible gains – such as comfortable lifestyle and celebrity status – against what might happen to them if they are caught, for example, forfeiting their wealth and their liberty.*

The only **evidence** likely to be available to you under exam conditions is what is provided in the sources. You should use that evidence when asked to do so. If the topic happens to be one in which you have a particular interest and expertise, you should feel free to use any evidence you may happen to know. You should *not* invent evidence if you do not have any.

For example, the third paragraph of the argument supporting the claim that the punishment for crime should be so harsh that people will not risk it could be strengthened by adding:

> *Recent surveys have shown that people, especially the elderly, consistently overestimate their risk of being victims of crime.*

This is the kind of evidence which a student might possibly remember in an exam.

Analogies can sometimes be used to make the meaning of an unfamiliar or difficult idea clearer by comparing it with something which is familiar. They may also be used in order to persuade people to accept an unfamiliar or superficially objectionable proposal by comparing it with something familiar and unobjectionable. For example, the second paragraph of the argument supporting the claim that the punishment for crime should be so harsh that people will not risk it could be strengthened by adding:

> *Just as loving parents force themselves to punish their children for disobeying them, even though it distresses them to do so, so the judicial system must punish citizens who disobey the law, in order to teach them to behave better in the future.*

Hypothetical reasoning begins with 'if' or a word of similar meaning, such as 'unless'. It supports or opposes a proposal by suggesting what the consequences of various events or courses of action would be. For example, the second paragraph of the argument supporting the claim that the punishment for crime should be so harsh that people will not risk it could be strengthened by adding:

> *If people receive only a light punishment, such as a small fine, for committing a crime, they will conclude that the crime was not important.*

10.4 Considering counterpositions

An argument can be strengthened by considering and rebutting **counterpositions**. For example, the second paragraph of the argument supporting the claim that the punishment for crime should be so harsh that people will not risk it could be strengthened by adding:

> *It is sometimes suggested that punishments do not need to be severe in order to fulfil this educational function, but people do not take seriously punishments which do not hurt them.*

When this process consists of forestalling an objection which *might* occur to a reader or listener, this is a risky strategy, because some people would probably not have thought of this objection if you had not suggested it to them. However, if the objection or counterposition has actually already been put forward, it may be essential to acknowledge and rebut it. Drawing attention to a counterposition without an effective rebuttal weakens the reasoning, instead of strengthening it.

10.5 Applying the skills of creating arguments

Part of the reason why generous time allowances are allocated to both the Critical Thinking and Applied Reasoning papers is so that you have time to **plan** your own arguments before you begin to write them, and you are strongly advised to do so.

AS Level

Two questions in the paper will require you to create a short argument of your own.

In the second question you must use the sources provided in Section A.

You will be expected to make your own judgement on the basis of the sources, and then write an argument to support that judgement, making use of the sources as evidence. Your use of the evidence should include some recognition of how credible or incredible it is.

Draw relevant inferences from the sources. Your argument should have a clear structure, using intermediate conclusions and perhaps other argument elements.

Sample question

'People who want to give their children the best possible start in life should try to arrange for them to be born as close as possible to September.'

To what extent do you agree with this claim? Write a short, reasoned argument to support your conclusion, using and evaluating the information provided in Sources A–D.

> **I agree with this claim to some extent, in relation to countries where the academic year begins in September; in other countries the claim should refer to a different month. In addition, the expression 'close to' must be interpreted as meaning 'after', not 'before', since August is 'close to September', but it is not an advantage to be born in that month.**
>
> **Source A clearly establishes on the basis of diverse research that being born near the beginning of the school year does bring some advantages, and offers a plausible explanation for why this should be so. Source B provides corroborative evidence with specific reference to sport. Source C shows that the benefits of this early advantage affect people for the whole of their lives. Although the evidence refers only to professional footballers, any plausible explanation for that evidence can be applied to many other walks of life.**
>
> **It follows that parents whose children are born in early autumn have given them some advantage.**
>
> **Source D is a weak argument, because it is based on a misunderstanding. The claim that one group of people tends to perform better than another is not falsified by a single exception. However, this comment is a reminder that there are many exceptions to the generalisation, and that there are more important benefits which parents can give their children, such as an encouraging attitude and cultural opportunities.**
>
> **Overall, therefore, parents whose children are born as soon after the beginning of the school year as possible do benefit them, but there are other things parents can do which benefit their children more.**

When addressing the fifth question you should use only your own ideas, and avoid using ideas from the passage provided in Section B, even though the subject of your own argument will have some relationship to the subject of that passage. You will be given a claim, and required to write your own argument either to support or to challenge that claim. You should clearly state your conclusion, which should consist of either the claim you have been given or its opposite.

Support your conclusion with your own ideas. Structure your answer clearly in strands of reasoning, and include Intermediate Conclusions and other argument elements.

'The punishment for crime should be so harsh that potential criminals will not risk it.'

Write your own argument to support or challenge this claim. You must state the conclusion of your argument.

Support

Those who contemplate breaking the law weigh up the possible gains – such as comfortable lifestyle and celebrity status – against what will happen to them if they are caught, for example forfeiting their wealth and their liberty. There is not much a government can do to make crime less attractive: so the obvious way of modifying the equation in order to reduce the amount of crime is to make the punishments harsher.

Furthermore, punishment has an educational function, to discourage citizens from committing crime and encourage good habits of behaviour. It is sometimes suggested that punishments do not need to be severe in order to fulfil this educational function, but people do not take seriously punishments which do not hurt them. So trivial penalties would not be significant enough to succeed in achieving this goal.

Recent surveys have shown that people, especially the elderly, consistently overestimate their risk of being victims of crime. Since so many people currently live in fear of crime, reducing it is an urgent task.

Therefore the punishment for crime should be so severe that people will not risk it.

Challenge

The concept of punishment justifies treating people in ways which would normally be forbidden, such as hurting them, depriving them of their liberty, or taking away some of their money. But the extent of this justification is limited by the severity of the crime, so excessively harsh punishments for crime are unjust.

Such punishments are also ineffective in achieving their purpose, because instead of leading to reform, they are likely to cause resentment and encourage criminals to seek revenge on the society which has treated them so cruelly.

It might be possible to justify severe punishments if they effectively deterred potential criminals from breaking the law. However, it seems clear that harsher penalties would not actually make much difference to the amount of crime in a country, because people will continue to commit crimes if the motivation is strong enough and if they believe they are unlikely to be caught. Increasing the number and efficiency of police would make criminals more likely to be convicted and thereby be a more effective way of reducing crime.

Therefore the punishment for crime should not be so severe that people will not risk it.

Practice questions

Write your own short arguments to support **or** challenge the following claims. The conclusion of your arguments must be stated.

- New technology has enriched the quality of our lives.
- Gaining qualifications is the goal of education.
- All children should study a foreign language at school.
- The most important duty of any government is to maintain peace with other countries.
- The first duty of any government is to safeguard the health of its citizens.
- Selfishness is the best policy for life.

A Level

Roughly half the marks in the Applied Reasoning paper are usually allocated to the fourth question, which is the main focus for the difference in level between the two papers. It is an integrative exercise, which involves evaluating and using the resource documents, producing ideas of your own, and synthesising them into a personal argument to support or challenge a claim.

Your answer should consist mainly of discussion of the sources. Most of your own thinking which you incorporate will probably consist of critiques of the ideas in the sources or responses to them. Use the sources in a rational order, according to the ideas you want to put forward in your argument. Discussing the sources in numerical order would be unlikely to produce a well-structured answer.

You should ensure that your argument has a clear, explicit and rational structure. Use intermediate conclusions to link each strand of reasoning to your main conclusion. Divide your answer into paragraphs – one paragraph per strand of reasoning and one strand per paragraph.

The strongest answers are based on ideas taken from the resource documents, but include some personal thinking and discussion of counterpositions. They have a clear structure and use intermediate conclusions and other argument elements.

You should aim to avoid spending too long on the opening questions, so that you have time to plan and write your answer to the fourth question without rushing it.

'Universities should award degrees on the basis of continuous assessment (CA).'
Construct a reasoned argument to support **or** challenge this claim.

In your answer you should make critical use of the documents provided.

(Brief descriptions of Documents 1–5 are given below to provide context for the 'Support' and 'Challenge' sample answers. Complete versions of these documents are available via your teacher, if required.)

Document 1

Response by the Student Union of Barchester University to draft proposals for a new degree of Bachelor of Humanities, which will be tested by written examination only.

Document 2

A student's argument against CA, due to the pressure of constant deadlines that CA imposes on students.

Document 3

An advertisement from an essay-writing company, explaining, justifying and selling their services.

Document 4

A survey of practice within the European Higher Education Area (EHEA) that focuses on the teaching–learning process. A number of different methods of Continuous Assessment are discovered to be in use.

Document 5

Student feedback

Two graphs recording student satisfaction (at Barchester University) and student results (at Eastway University) on courses assessed by end-of-course exams and CA.

Support

Document 1 argues for an extreme form of CA (eliminating unseen examinations completely), but the benefits of CA are entirely compatible with a varied pattern of modes of assessment, which includes some exercises undertaken under exam conditions and some synoptic assessment at the end of the course. For the purpose of this discussion, I will interpret CA in that way.

Document 1 identifies two important arguments in favour of CA and against the traditional pattern of assessment. It is true that some students underperform in exams (paragraph 3), and that others perform badly on particular occasions, because of illness, bereavement or other unavoidable problems (paragraph 8). CA overcomes both these problems.

Document 4 shows that CA is taking over university courses, and (in paragraph 2) identifies the main reasons why this is so. Now that students are increasingly recognised as 'customers' of universities, it is natural (and right) that student learning should be put at the centre of the whole enterprise and, as this document shows, this implies that courses should be assessed by CA. Table 1 of Document 5 is consistent with the claim that students prefer CA, although there may have been other reasons why the students on courses assessed by CA gave more favourable assessments of their university experience.

Paragraph 8 of Document 1 makes a similar point, that assessment should be used to help students improve, rather than simply label them as having failed. This would be a good reason why marks might have improved on CA by comparison with exams (as indicated in respect of one university in Document 5 Table 2, although this example may have been chosen for that reason, and the improvement in results may be coincidental).

The argument in favour of exams attributed to the former Dean in Document 1, paragraph 5 (which appears to be supported by Table 2 in Document 5) relies on the assumption that there is a wide range of ability and achievement amongst students, which may well not be the case. Perhaps only relatively few students perform significantly better or worse than the majority, in which case the narrow range of marks produced by non-exam assignments may be a more accurate indication of their achievement.

A student in Document 2 explains why – when given the choice – she prefers modules assessed by a single exam rather than: essay + presentation + exam. That is understandable, although it is no bad thing if students are made to work all year instead of for a fortnight in the summer. It is important that assessment should not dominate the learning process. If there is a choice of modules, the burden of assessment should be equal between them, and each module should be assessed by no more than two elements.

The most powerful argument against assessing by essays and projects is that students can easily cheat. The advertisement in Document 3 shows how easy it is to buy assignments, and other students may have friends or relatives who will write the work for them. The attempted rebuttal of this criticism in Document 1, paragraph 7 is fatally flawed. So it is vital that the assessment of university courses should include a significant proportion of exercises in which students are forced to rely on their own knowledge and skills. These may include unseen exams and essays or projects undertaken under exam conditions, with limited or no access to the internet. This is perfectly compatible with CA, and therefore does not constitute an argument against it.

Document 1 is right (in paragraph 6) to point out the benefits of group projects. Although it is admittedly not fair that the marks of able students can be pulled down by a weak member of the group or that an incompetent or lazy student can achieve a pass mark without doing any work, it is not difficult to avoid these disadvantages, for example, by including work diaries in the assessment, identifying each person's contributions and awarding differentiated marks accordingly.

Therefore universities should award degrees on the basis of continuous assessment.

Challenge

There are two major flaws in the arguments in favour of CA, as depicted in the documents provided. Firstly, they confuse learning with assessment. The purpose of assessment is not to show students where their weaknesses lie – important though that is, it is part of the teaching and learning process, not of assessment. The second flaw is they have a 'modularised' understanding of learning; in other words, they think that a three-year degree course consists of separate chunks of knowledge which have to be memorised, at least for a short while. In fact, learning should be incremental, each segment of the curriculum building on the last and preparing for the next. The development of skills is more important than the acquisition of knowledge – especially now that facts are readily available at the click of a mouse. These two errors are fatal to the case for CA, and firmly imply that assessment should come at the end of the course, when it can assess the overall outcome of the learning process.

The student in Document 2 explains why CA is a bad thing from a student perspective. Admittedly, parents and taxpayers may think it no bad thing for students to work hard throughout their course instead of for only a few weeks in their final term; however, feeling 'under constant pressure' is not good for young people in the formative years of their lives, and preparing for assessments is not the only worthwhile kind of learning activity in which conscientious students should engage. Although Table 1 of Document 5 is consistent with the claim that students prefer CA, there may have been other reasons why the students on courses assessed by CA gave more favourable assessments of their university experience; for example, they may have been taken exclusively or mainly by mature students, who were grateful for having been given an opportunity which they thought they had missed. So Document 5, Table 1 does not negate the negative opinions expressed in Document 2.

The most powerful argument against assessing by essays and projects is that students can easily cheat. The advertisement in Document 3 shows how easy it is, and the arguments presented there will probably convince some students that there is nothing wrong in buying coursework from this company. Others may have a friend or relative who will write the work for them. The attempted rebuttal of this criticism in Document 1, paragraph 7 is fatally flawed. So it is vital that the assessment of university courses should consist entirely – or at least mainly – of exercises in which students are forced to rely on their own knowledge and skills. These do not necessarily have to be in the form of a set of essays written in three hours, but they do need to be undertaken under exam conditions.

Although Document 1 is right (in paragraph 6) to point out the benefits of group projects, it is not fair that the marks of able students can be pulled down by a weak member of the group or that an incompetent or lazy student can achieve a pass mark without doing any work. So such projects should not count towards the degree result of an individual student.

The value of timed, unseen examinations is underestimated by some of the documents. Contrary to the claim in Document 1, paragraph 4 that exams test the wrong skills, the ability to remember information and reproduce it accurately and to think quickly are valuable skills, and prospective employers are entitled to expect that university graduates have proved themselves to have them.

Another important problem which can occur with CA is mentioned in the second bullet point of Document 4. Depending on the subject, it may be that the skills and knowledge developed in one module can be forgotten once the assessment for that module has been completed. The necessity of synthesising all the skills and knowledge at the end of a course is the main advantage of the traditional method of assessing courses by unseen exams at the end of three years.

The argument in favour of exams attributed to the former Dean in Document 1, paragraph 5 appears to be supported by Table 2 in Document 5. Although the apparent rise in student performance could be due to a rise in ability or devotion to study, it is more likely that CA exaggerates the ability and performance of students. Since a major purpose of the assessment in a degree course is to differentiate between students in relation to the level of their achievement, this aspect of CA is a serious disadvantage. Any former student whose degree result was based on the traditional method of assessment can reasonably feel quite aggrieved that the next generation appears to be achieving better, just because it is assessed less rigorously.

Therefore universities should not award degrees on the basis of continuous assessment.

Practice question

'The age at which people are allowed to vote in elections should be 21.'

Construct a reasoned argument to support **or** challenge this claim.
In your answer you should make critical use of the documents provided.

Document 1

Who should vote?

1 Depending on which country you live in, your 16th, 17th, 18th or 21st birthday could be the age at which you can drive, get married, or buy alcohol – at least legally. We have these laws for a reason, but age should not be used as a criterion in deciding who should select the next government.

2 Voting is far too important to be based on such an arbitrary measure as a person's age. Drinking, relationships and driving are personal matters, but voting affects other people. In deciding who should govern us we need to take into account politics, economics, science and human nature. We do not suddenly develop a full understanding of these things when we wake up on our 18th birthday.

3 Many politicians have advocated lowering the voting age in an attempt to show that they are 'in touch with young people', but young people care less about voting and more about fashion and music. In the town of Middlesbrough in the north of England most of the local schools entered a candidate to be Youth Mayor of Middlesbrough. Unsurprisingly, the candidate from the school that cast the most votes won the election. This just shows that teenagers will vote for the candidate they perceive to be on their team, rather than considering the policies on offer.

4 In terms of deciding anything, age is largely meaningless anyway. We might as well separate people based on height. Everyone knows people of the same age with wildly differing abilities, or people of different ages with the same ability. There is no upper age limit for voting: nobody says 'Sorry, granddad, take your opinion elsewhere'. So there should not be a lower age limit.

5 There has to be some way of deciding who votes, and age is at least easy to apply. Alternative systems are practical, though. A basic questionnaire, similar to an IQ test, would be straightforward to administer. People registering to vote could complete the test, which would include questions on general knowledge as well as cognitive ability. Those who got above a certain score would be registered to vote; those who did not could try again next time. That way the people who had the privilege of voting would be those who deserved it.

Trib

Document 2

The minimum legal voting age of 25 years and its consequences in Italy

When asked about the minimum legal voting age in the world, your answer would probably be 18 years. You would be right, as this is the average and most common minimum legal voting age across the globe, with only 27 exceptions where it varies between 16 and 21 years. Only one country goes outside this range: the minimum legal voting age for the Senate in Italy is 25.

The political, societal and economic consequences of this unusual constraint in Italy may well affect the whole of Europe. Out of the 50.3 million 18–year-old and older Italian citizens who are entitled to vote for the Chamber of Deputies, 4.3 million (8%) are not allowed to vote for the Senate. Given the substantially different electorates of the two chambers, the political make-up of the Senate and that of the Chamber of Deputies are often

different. This was the case in Italy's elections in February, which have led to the formation of an odd coalition of left, right and middle parties, the 62nd government in just 68 years.

The minimum legal voting age of 25 is both the cause and the consequence of other imbalances in Italy, most often to the disadvantage of the young. In Italy, social spending on the elderly is more than twice as high as in Europe's most successful economies. Italy has the fifth-highest poverty rate among young people. The public debt per young person is €220 000, compared with just €4600 in Estonia. In Italy, the interests of the elderly are well defended by pensioners' lobby groups, but young people do not have a similar voice. Lastly, many Italian senior citizens have greater power than senior citizens living elsewhere. In Italy, most influential positions in politics and business are often occupied by men who could be the fathers or grandfathers of their counterparts in other nations. The President of the Republic, Giorgio Napolitano, is 88 years old. The former (and perhaps returning) prime minister, Silvio Berlusconi, is almost 77 years old.

With one in two adults under 25 unemployed, it is ironic that the group most in need of political change is without full voting rights. The younger generation deserves a stronger role in politics to secure a better future. Despite decades of active debate surrounding this issue, the desperately needed reforms of Italian institutions are unlikely to be realised in the near future. Lowering the voting age from 25 to 18 is a simple measure that could be done immediately and at zero cost. The resulting intergenerational balance would offer more political stability in Italy, which could, in turn, relax Italy's burden on Europe.

Document 3

Comments on a political blog for young people

I can work and pay taxes at 17, why shouldn't I get to decide on the laws that apply to me? No taxation without representation!

JP, USA

Being a teenager doesn't mean you are less intelligent than an older person. Your brain starts to shrink after the age of 18 or something like that. What if an old person has a 'senior moment' as they are casting their vote? Old people got the world in the mess it is today so maybe having younger people decide would get us out of it.

TT, Canada

I'm not interested in politics and I don't know much about it. Maybe if I was allowed to vote I would make an effort to find out.

CG, Spain

We've got all these old people making decisions and laws about the internet, TV and social media. We need some people in there who actually understand these things.

PO, Ireland

You can drive when you are 17 and you could, potentially, kill someone in a car accident. In many countries you can join the army. In Germany we can drink beer and wine from the age of 16. How come you are old enough to drink, operate dangerous machines or weapons but not put a cross on a piece of paper that is never going to hurt anyone?

HH, Germany

We have been studying history at school. There was a time when only rich landowners or taxpayers were allowed to vote. And only then if they were men! Women didn't get to vote in Britain until after the First World War but they had to be 30, when it was 21 for men. It's only been 18 since 1970 but the trend seems to be downwards. I think it is inevitable that the voting age will be reduced to 16 soon.

JM, England

16-year-olds can vote in many countries around the world such as Austria, Brazil, Hungary and Ecuador. They also get to vote in state elections in Germany – seen by many as the richest country in Europe.

AS, Scotland

Document 4

The voting age should be raised, not lowered

To be against lowering the voting age is seen by most progressives as symptomatic of losing one's youth and gaining some grumpiness. So for a relatively young progressive such as myself to be against lowering the voting age – well, I might as well have said, 'Let's abolish the vote altogether', going by the looks I have received from many of my colleagues on the Left.

Reports have recommended lowering the voting age, and some political parties have come out in favour of doing so. This is a mistake, for two reasons. Yes, it is a sad fact that over 40% of those eligible to vote in this country did not exercise their right to do so in the last general election. It is generally agreed that this constitutes some kind of crisis of political engagement. However, by increasing the number of people eligible to vote you merely have the same percentage of a larger number of people not voting, or perhaps an even larger percentage of people not voting.

But the most important reason is that the majority of 16-year-olds are just not responsible enough or mature enough to have the vote. Those who argue against this use the bundling of rights argument: the age of consent is 16; people can get married at 16; people can join the armed forces at 16. Therefore, they think, it follows that 16-year-olds should also have the vote. Well, we know that just because a person has sex does not mean that they are responsible. Animals have sex, yet we do not propose giving our pets the vote.

To get married in England and Wales, people under 18 require parental consent. How many of us really think a 16-year-old is capable of making a life-changing and legally binding decision such as marriage? Financial institutions certainly do not think so. You must be 18 to sign binding contracts or to own land in your own name. Therefore 16-year-olds, married with parental permission or not, cannot apply for a mortgage or own the house in which they live.

Similarly, under-18s need parental consent to join the armed forces, and in normal circumstances are not deployed on operations until they are 18. In fact, the UN supports raising the age of joining the forces to 18.

It is during a person's teenage years that they are most likely to be exposed to new ideas and points of view. This is the age at which people should be able to think through their political ideas and change them at will, debate and try out policies without having to act on them and without having to take responsibility for their ideas.

And it is at this age that teenagers are at their most rebellious and negative, a time when they are more keen on making a statement than acting responsibly. Rebellion against your parents' taste in music and their rules is one thing; let's not make that part of the democratic process by which our government is elected.

Voting is a serious matter. It is what makes a democracy, and must be taken seriously by all voters. I don't think most 16-year-olds are mature enough to vote. So perhaps 'Should we lower the voting age?' is the wrong question. Instead, it should be 'Should we raise it, and if so, to what age?' I am 25. I think this would be a good age.

Document 5

The following graph portrays the results of an exit poll in a general election in a European country. Voters were asked how they had voted as they were leaving polling stations after voting. The polling stations surveyed were typical of the demographic of the whole country.

The proportion of those who did not vote in each age group was established by comparing the electoral register with the number of votes counted.

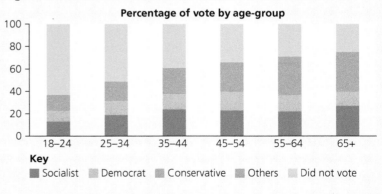

(Adapted from Cambridge AS & A Level Thinking Skills 9694, Paper 42 Documents 1–5, November 2016)

Answers to selected questions

Answers to Activity on page 11

(For the Riddler only!):

The key to this puzzle is to count the number of circles in the four-digit number.

8s are made of two circles (one on top of the other), 6s, 9s and 0s all have just one circle.

Every other digit involves no circles at all.

Therefore 1689 yields 4.

If your group are struggling to uncover this explanation, ask them to give you a number which you will then 'score'. For example, if someone gives the number 8000 then you tell them that scores 5. If they give you 22, then you tell them that scores 0.

When your group has worked out how the puzzle works you should consider what questions were useful in revealing the secret to this problem.

Answers to Deepening Activity on page 13

1   The man is a parachutist, who enters the field from above because his parachute (in the bag) does not open.

2   The woman is in labour and they are trying to get help from a hospital. The man leaves to get help, but when he returns she has given birth (to 'the stranger') and died in the process.

3   The man drew the 'short straw' in a hot air balloon which was travelling over the desert. The balloon was running out of hot air so those aboard decided that one person should jump out, in order to lessen their weight and give them a chance of surviving. The person who chose the broken match from someone's hand had to jump out.

4   Romeo and Juliet are goldfish. Their goldfish bowl has been knocked off the table by the curtain, which blew in the wind (from the open window).

5   The man is walking down Death Row (where prisoners are kept, awaiting execution by the electric chair) with a pardon for one of the prisoners. The lights are dimmed when the electric chair is used. He knows that he is too late to deliver his pardon, so he leaves.

6   The man is a diver swimming into a wreck of an ocean liner.

7   The man has just returned from a trip in which he was shipwrecked on a desert island. He only survived thanks to the 'albatross' that his fellow survivors brought him. He was suspicious that this was in fact the flesh of others who died in the shipwreck and ordered the albatross on his return in order to verify what it tasted of. He concludes that he has eaten his shipmates and decides to kill himself in remorse.

Answers to Practice questions on pages 144–145

1   Correct answer: 3.8 ha
    Distractor 1: 1.4 ha
    Distractor 2: 3.2 ha
    Distractor 3: 1.24 ha
    Distractor 4: 32.6 ha

2   Correct answer: 55
    Distractor 1: 16
    Distractor 2: 28
    Distractor 3: 39
    Distractor 4: 84

3   Correct answer: 98
    Distractor 1: 1
    Distractor 2: 2
    Distractor 3: 50
    Distractor 4: 99

Answers to Practice questions on pages 148–150

1   Suggested answer:

A $750 loan will incur $20 interest per month. There has been an interest repayment day 12 times between June 1st (last year) and May 1st (next year). And there are 12 repayment dates between June 9th (last year) and May 9th (next year). So the amount left is: (750 + (12 × 20) − (12 × 50)) $390.

2   Suggested answer:

The team with the lowest points that is not relegated must have come 'fourth last' in the rankings. It could have been beaten by all the other teams, but it must have beaten those three below it. The minimum points for a team that wins three games is 9 points.

3   Suggested answer:

They must meet halfway between their houses: on the way back, Joe walks at 6 km/hr, which takes 1/2 hour; Harry walks at 2 km/hr which takes 1 1/2 hours. So Joe arrives home 1 hour earlier than Harry.

Glossary of key terms

Ability to see A source's ability to see consists of its access to the evidence about which it is making claims.

Analogy A comparison of an unfamiliar concept or questionable proposal with something more familiar and acceptable. This is done to provide clarification, or for the purpose of persuasion.

Argument An argument is a piece of reasoning, consisting of a persuasive conclusion supported by one or more reasons.

Begging the question Consists of focusing an argument on an uncontroversial aspect of an issue while stipulating or assuming the key point.

Bias Is a motive or tendency to give greater weight or prominence to one point of view rather than another.

Causal flaw An unjustified inference that phenomena which occur together must have a causal relationship.

Circular argument Consists of relying on a claim in order to prove it.

Combinations (noun) A collection or selection of objects where the order of them is not significant.

Conflation Consists of concealing a step in reasoning by treating two words or expressions as if they were interchangeable even though their meanings are different.

Confounding variable A confounding variable is a factor which was not the one being studied but may have influenced the results of an experiment.

Consistency If two claims are consistent, it is possible for them both to be true, whereas if they are inconsistent it is not possible for them both to be true.

Constants and variables (noun) In any problem, one can expect certain values to remain constant (such as the force of gravity on Earth, or the number of people in a family) and certain values to vary (such as the speed of a stone, or the number of people who vote for a candidate). The former are called constants; the latter are called variables. Whether a value is a constant or a variable will depend upon the particular model being analysed.

Continuous variables Continuous variables are things you can measure, rather than things you can count.

Correlation Is a statistical relationship between sets of data, or the tendency for phenomena to occur together.

Corroboration The additional evidence from an independent source which supports a claim.

Counter assertion/argument A counter assertion or counterargument expresses an alternative opinion which an author introduces in order to explain why it

is wrong. If the counter consists of a simple claim, it is a counter assertion, but if the claim is supported by reasoning it is a counterargument.

Counter-attack Consists of rejecting criticisms on the grounds that opponents or other people are guilty of the same or equally objectionable conduct.

Credibility The credibility of evidence consists of the aspects which might make a wise person more or less likely to believe it to be true. Credibility includes the reliability of the source, the plausibility of the content of the evidence and corroboration or consistency with other evidence.

Discrete variables Discrete variables are things you can count, rather than things you can measure.

Equivocation Consists of using ambiguous language to conceal a step in reasoning by shifting (without mentioning it) from one meaning of a word or expression to another.

Evidence Consists of facts or data which support a reason.

Example An example is a specific instance which makes reasoning clearer by illustrating it.

Expertise The expertise of a source is its specialist knowledge or skills related to the subject.

Extrapolation Consists of estimating a value by extending a known sequence of data beyond those currently available.

Heuristic (noun) A process or attitude which enables you to tackle problems/situations you have never encountered before.

Indexical (adjective) Where the meaning or truth of a statement depends on who says it.

Inference An inference is a conclusion which can be drawn from one or more reasons or from evidence.

Limit case (noun) An example that lies at the boundary of possibility according to defined conditions.

Linear A linear relationship exists between two variables if there is a formula involving only multiplying the input by some number and/or adding to it. An example would be taking the input and adding 10 to it; or taking the input and doubling it; or taking the input, halving it and then adding 100. One aspect of linear relationships that allows them to be easily identified is that they always have a 'common difference', that is, the difference between any pair of adjacent terms is always equal. Relationships that are not linear (and which are much harder to identify, and to predict) include those involving squaring the input, and dividing a number by the input.

Necessary condition Something which must happen or be true in order for something else to happen or be true.

Neutrality Is the absence of bias.

Optimisation Finding the value of a variable which leads to an extreme outcome in a mathematical model. For instance, the number of taxi journeys which leads to the maximum profit for a driver in a day.

Permutations (noun) An arrangement of objects where the order of them is significant.

Personal attack Consists of criticising opponents personally instead of responding to their arguments.

Plausibility The plausibility of a claim is the likelihood of it being true, based on the content of the claim in the light of existing knowledge, irrespective of the reliability of its source.

Proxy measurement A proxy measurement or indicator is a statistic which is believed to be closely correlated to a measurement of interest which is not directly accessible.

Quadratic (adjective) Involving squared values, but not higher degrees (like cubes).

Rash generalisation One based on a small quantity of evidence, selected to support the claim.

Reliability The reliability of sources consists of qualities which make them more or less worthy of trust.

Reputation The reputation of a source is the generally held opinion about how reliable it is.

Restriction of options Consists of denying the possibility of certain opinions or actions in order to force or trick someone into accepting an option which they do not choose.

Slippery slope argument Consists of opposing an apparently moderate proposal by alleging that it will inevitably lead to disastrous consequences.

Solution space The range of possible values which satisfies the fixed constraints of the problem.

Straw man argument Consists of misrepresenting opponents' arguments in order to respond to them more easily.

Sufficient condition If a sufficient condition happens or is true, then something else must also happen or be true.

Sweeping generalisation A claim which is generally true but applied in such a way as to exclude exceptions.

Validity Is a quality of the structure of an argument, irrespective of its relation to truth or fact. If the structure of an argument is valid, it means that if the reasons happened to be true, the conclusion would have to be true.

Vested interest The vested interest of a source refers to motives arising from potential personal benefit which might make the evidence more or less reliable.

Index